THE LAST OF THE INCAS

THE LAST

EDWARD HYAMS

AND GEORGE ORDISH

OF THE INCAS

THE RISE AND FALL OF AN AMERICAN EMPIRE

DORSET PRESS
New York

This edition published by Dorset Press,
a division of Marboro Books Corporation,
by arrangement with
Harold Ober Associates
1990 Dorset Press

ISBN 0-88029-595-3

Printed in the United States of America
M 9 8 7 6 5 4 3

CONTENTS

p. 170 route of Atahualpa
in Inca civil war

p. 192 route of Pizarro
1531-1533

FOREWORD

WE HAVE IT on the authority of a distinguished historian, Dr. A. J. P. Taylor, that the object of the historian is not to edify or to instruct, but is to entertain; history should be written because it is fun. And we quite agree. The history of the great empire which the Incas created in the Andes is a grand story; the destruction of that empire by the murder of its chief at the hands of Francisco Pizarro is a tale which has the beauty of tragedy.

When the Sapa Inca Atahualpa, Lord of the World, having been squeezed of his treasure, was throttled to death, his vast and beautifully ordered realm received its death blow. In this book, we have aimed to tell about that empire's creation and nature, and, in more detail, about its sudden and extraordinary end. Our book is not a history of the conquest of Peru; it ends with the first act of that conquest. As for the conduct of the Spaniards thereafter, their internecine brawling, their maltreatment of the Indios and of each other, the reader can find the whole ugly-heroic story in Prescott. Our part of the story, on the other hand, is not widely known and has hitherto existed not in one but only in very many books and manuscripts, some of them not readily accessible.

With due respect to Dr. Taylor, we think it may be useful as well as entertaining to know a little of what happened in the isolated world of the western Andes during the thousand or so years which end with the Sapa Inca Atahualpa's death in 1532. Our reasons for this modest hope are as follows.

7

We believe that the Tahuantinsuyu (the proper name for the Inca empire) was an anachronism of the most interesting kind. Owing to certain accidents of history and technology, it was flourishing in the sixteenth century of our era; but it seems to us to belong to a class of commonwealths which flourished several thousand years before Christ—in its social and political ideas, it was much more like the prehistoric commonwealths of Mesopotamia, Egypt and the Punjab, than like any commonwealth of historical times. If that is so, then its destruction was not only a human tragedy but also an aesthetic and a scientific tragedy. Pizarro and his companions not only were committing one of the first major acts of colonialism, but also were guilty of the sort of crime which is committed when a rare species of animal is exterminated, or an irreplaceable work of art is destroyed. Under certain conditions, which we discuss in the course of the story, the Tahuantinsuyu might have resisted the Spaniards and survived. It could not have been kept as a vast museum piece, it would have had to be "westernized," modernized. But there might have been time to study, in a living fossil, man's most ancient forms of imperial-social organization.

Nor is this all. Economically, the Tahuantinsuyu resembled a socialist state. All the means of production, distribution and exchange were in the state's hands. At the same time, the country was extremely flourishing, and the worst evil of our own world—grinding and degrading poverty—was completely unknown. It seems certain that this social system was a product of the physical conditions under which the Andean nations, ultimately united in the Inca empire, came into being. The geology, the soils, the climates of the whole region were such that large and ordered communities of men, and an urban civilization, could be created only by people working together under strict discipline and to a plan. The theocratic city-states of Mesopotamia must have been socialist states for the same reason. Our system of free enterprise in Western Europe and North America was a product of inexhaustible and readily accessible natural resources; we (in the persons of our ancestors) were in a position to squander natural wealth, and we could therefore afford to limit co-operation and specialization well short of social conscription. But the Andean peoples could not; their communities could grow, their wealth could accumulate, only if they built and operated vast irrigation systems and continually increased their farm lands by mountain terracing on a colossal scale. And the only way to accomplish such works, since these peoples—although they were remarkably fine artists and craftsmen and natural engineers—were technologically in the early Bronze Age, was to combine in a tightly organized society.

Now it happens that the conditions for the future survival of the human race are becoming more and more like those faced by the Andean peoples in the remote past. In Eurasia and later in North America, man was able to increase and multiply and prosper by merely turning the seemingly inexhaustible supply of fertile soil and lush pasture to his own advantage, by farming and stock raising. But in the world of the western Andes, even the very surface area had to be created first, and this, as we have said, predetermined the social and political systems of the Andean peoples. At the present rate of world population growth the ratio of men to resources over the whole world will soon be comparable to that which dominated the lives of the Indians of the western Andes. And if nothing is done to check growth of population, or to increase food production, the ratio will become less and less favorable, so that we shall need all the ingenuity of our technology to survive at all. We have, for our part, no doubt whatever that survival, under these conditions, will entail the end of personal freedom as defined in the Western world and of such wasteful luxuries as "private enterprise."

It may, therefore, be edifying to see how one race of men created social harmony and a workable polity at the expense of that freedom.

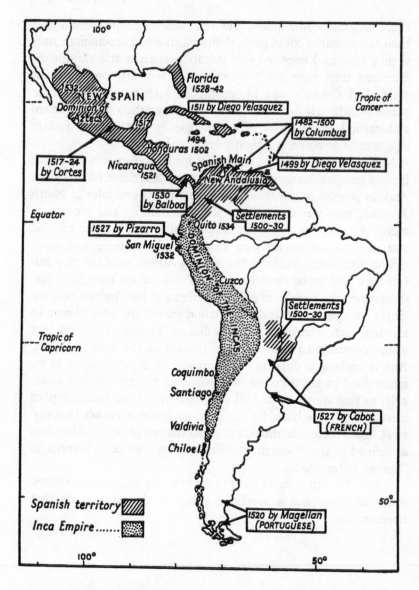

European Penetration of Latin America up to 1532.

1

THE DESTROYER

ON AUGUST 28, 1533, in the main square of Cuzco, the capital of his enormous empire, Atahualpa the Sapa Inca of Peru was received into the Roman Catholic faith. Then, like a common felon, he was strangled to death by the Spanish public executioner.

The Inca, a formidable and successful soldier served by experienced generals, with almost inexhaustible supplies of provisions and something more than 50,000 men under arms, had been defeated by 180 Spanish adventurers led by a brave, illiterate and unscrupulous ruffian known to history as Pizarro. Such an incredible turn of events was made possible by the fact that the Spaniards arrived at a time of great political weakness in the Inca empire. This enabled them to destroy it and to impose instead their own rule, to the lasting misery of the South American Indians. Let us briefly examine the origins of these men who were to be so deadly to the native civilizations of what are now Chile, Peru and Bolivia.

The existence of the American continent was probably known in Europe before Columbus to a few Portuguese, Italians and Scandinavians, and to a few sailors in Japan. But it was the Genoan's "discovery," made at such a propitious moment and under such powerful patronage that it could become generally known and conceded, which gave rise to practical results. Certainly the discovery was followed up with energy; within thirty years of Columbus's landing in Hispaniola, the new-found continent had been coasted from Labrador to Cape Horn by such Spaniards as Pinzón, Ojeda,

Nicuesa, de Lepe, and Bastidas. The Caribbean islands had been colonized; the Portuguese Magellan had found a way through to the Pacific; Mexico had been conquered; Guatemala too had fallen to the Spaniards; and Panama had been established as an important center.

The discoveries were made and the conquests accomplished by adventurers who, if they were sometimes moved by that noble curiosity which makes the explorer, were also driven by greed of gain. They were accompanied by regular clergy, often Dominican friars, whose purpose was to save souls and to spread the power of their Orders and of their Church. Their influence on the men of action was often pernicious, but it was sometimes engaged in softening the brutality with which the American natives were used. Men like the Bishop Las Casas could often by their pacifism persuade the natives to give up their religion and their liberty, when they had refused to yield to force.

The historian Salvador de Madariaga emphasizes that even the most ruffianly Spanish adventurer was always careful to apply for some official sanction before starting out. Although we believe that this desire to possess the moral force of legitimate authority was motivated by a wish to protect whatever gains he might make rather than by any kind of social conscience, it is true that the practice did give the Spanish government a means of asserting its authority when the conduct of the conquistadors became too outrageous. Had the men who went forth from Spain to make their fortunes not insisted upon acting as Crown agents, they might perhaps have set themselves up in independent kingdoms in the lands they conquered, just as the adventurers who poured out of Europe into Moslem Palestine in the Middle Ages made themselves kings of Jerusalem, Cyprus and other countries.

As it was, however, the soldier-adventurers who conquered and destroyed the native American empires handed over their power with remarkable tameness to governors sent out by the Council of the Indies in Madrid. Many of them may have been glad enough to return home with a fortune and a title of nobility in exchange for their conquests. In some cases the Spanish Crown had written contracts with the adventurers—with Columbus, for instance, who was to have 10 per cent of his own takings. Such contracts were not always honored; it was not very difficult to repudiate these agreements on the grounds that the contractor had failed, in some way or other, to carry out his share of the bargain, or, by setting one adventurer against another, to have a troublesome agent arrested and thrown into prison. Columbus, for example, not only was cheated of his 10 per cent, but also was brought home in chains and in disgrace. No doubt his spirit is consoled for these misfortunes by the singular honor of being credited, after his death, with two bodies, one buried at Ciudad Trujillo Cathedral in the Dominican Republic, the other in Seville Cathedral, and both vouched for on unimpeachable authority. Cortes, too, was shabbily treated. For its own purposes, the Spanish Crown supported the idea that the continent of America had been discovered before and was, in any case, nothing much to write home about.

The governments which replaced those set up by the original conquistadors were, as a rule, more liberal in their native policy. It is invariably the case that metropolitan governments are better disposed toward conquered peoples than the colonists on the spot. The mid-twentieth-century reader has only to substitute the names Rhodesia and Algeria for Peru and Mexico, to understand more or less how matters stood as between the conquistadors and the Spanish government. Although a great deal of the verbiage of good will toward the Indios which poured out of Madrid was futile and vain, it is a fact that later, as the new empire was consolidated, the Council of the Indies consistently tried to check the excesses of the colonists. The South American and Central American colonists did not virtually exterminate the Indians as did those of North America; nor did they put down poisonous baits to get rid of the natives, as did the settlers in Australia; nor did they adopt, like the Portuguese government of Angola in 1961, a policy of massacre. They did not, of course, live up to the standard of gentleness set by the Incas themselves as imperialists; but by comparison with other European colonists, the Spaniards did not behave too badly after the first fifty years in the Americas.

It was sometimes expedient for Madrid to give a great conquistador such rank as governor of a province, and to ennoble him, until his failure or death made it possible to replace him with a man born into the ruling class, usually a grandee, supported by trained civil servants. Like the English oligarchy in the nineteenth century, the Spanish aristocracy of the sixteenth realized that the establishment could survive only by admitting climbers to its ranks; the former created the "beerage," the latter a new nobility of colonial adventurers. Such was to be the case of Francisco Pizarro.

Pizarro was born in Trujillo, a town in Estremadura, about the year 1471. He may have been a foundling. Prescott, following Xérez, Zárate and other chroniclers, says that he was a bastard. We find, of course, no reference to this disgraceful condition in such encomia as Pizarro y Orellana's *Varones ilustres del nuevo mundo* (Madrid, 1639), but the author of this effusion was a member of the Pizarro family who contrived, in his account of the hero's antecedents, to ennoble their common ancestors. It would not do to let it be thought that a man of the lower orders and perhaps of ignoble birth could rise to greatness.

Francisco's father was a soldier by trade, and in the records he bears the rank of colonel, but this need mean no more than that he was a soldier of fortune. Of his mother we know nothing but that she was a woman of low origin, Francisca Gonzales, of Trujillo. It is possible that Francisco was born before his parents were married; their marriage, if it ever took place, may have been a consequence of his birth.

Centuries of fame have glamorized the very name Francisco Pizarro; but to his fellow guttersnipes Francisco was little Frank Slate-without-a-father. He is also said to have been neglected and even deserted by his parents: there is a tale to the effect that they, or one of them, left him on a church porch to be brought up as a foundling. Gómara, in his *History of the Indies*, says of him: "*Nacio en Truxillo, i acharonle a la puerta de la Iglesia mamo una puerca ciertos días, no so hallando quien le quisiese dar leche.*" To be abandoned as an infant on a church porch is a hard fate; but to be suckled by a beast, albeit in this case a sow, is a sure sign of future greatness. But there is no real evidence that the child was in fact so treated; and as to neglect, which he is said to have suffered, it may simply have been that he was unmanageable and preferred to play in the streets rather than to submit to house training. Much is made of the fact that Francisco was illiterate whereas his brothers were not; but, given the date, theirs, rather than his, is the exceptional case.

If Francisco was indeed suckled by a sow, he repaid the debt, for when he was old enough he became a swineherd. We are told that as a lad, tending swine, his bold imagination was captivated by tales of the new world discovered in the west; and that in consequence of this he abandoned his pigs and ran away to Seville, one of the ports whence adventurers were setting out to make their fortunes in the new-found lands. This, too, bears the look of legend. The most probable date for Francisco's birth is 1471; it cannot have been later than 1475. He must have been in his twenties before news of the very first discovery reached Trujillo. It was, then, as a young man, not as a boy, that the chance of fortune stirred his imagination. And as to whether he had, throughout his youth, been content with pigs or had, as his kinsman tells us in *Varones ilustres*, fought under his father in the Italian wars and even sailed with Columbus to the New World, we have no means of knowing.

The fact is that nothing really certain is known of Francisco Pizarro until he turns up, almost forty, among the other soldiers of fortune, in Hispaniola (now Haiti and the Dominican Republic). That was in 1510, at which time he appears to have been a man somewhat above the average height, well-formed if not actually handsome; persuasive, insidious and unyielding in manner, and considered by some a man to be feared. He had a good command of words and a cool head, and knowing men well, he could see base motives beneath an appearance of disinterested service. Perhaps, too, he could recognize genuine quality in a man when he encountered it. He is described by diverse contemporaries as false, egoistic, and changeable; a dissembler who was revengeful and whose word was worthless.

He made his start when Alonso de Ojeda was organizing an expedition to colonize Uraba on the mainland. (The Spaniards were still more or less confined to the islands and had not conquered all of them.) Francisco Pizarro volunteered to go.

It is on this occasion that Pizarro's ability to take command first emerges into history. Ojeda being obliged to return to the islands for supplies to save his colony from starvation, Pizarro was left in charge. This may be evidence that between the ages of twenty and forty he had, indeed, had some experience in the New World. He was to wait for another officer, Enciso, to return with stores. When Enciso did not come, Pizarro and his men suffered not only hunger but repeated attacks by the Indians. He soon demonstrated his fitness for this kind of office by keeping control of his men for two months, while enough of them starved to death or were killed by Indians to make it possible for the thirty who remained alive to provision two brigantines with the salted flesh of their horses and return to the islands. A great captain is, among other things, one who can take the responsibility of investing other men's lives to get a dividend of victory, and who can persuade them to let him do it.

One brigantine was lost at sea with all hands. Pizarro's arrived in San Domingo, where he was badly received, but he returned to Uraba under Enciso with a new force, which included Balboa. Enciso's own ship being cast away with valuable stores, and Indian opposition continuing fierce, Balboa proposed what turned out to be the famous march to Darien, so that Pizarro became one of the indomitable handful of men who marched with him across the Isthmus of Panama to view the Pacific. It was in Darien that the first hints of Peru reached the Spaniards. Balboa was engaged in weighing some articles of gold stolen from the natives when—the story is from Prescott, who, for once, fails to quote his authority— "a young barbarian chieftain struck the scales with his fist and, scattering the glittering metal round the apartment, exclaimed, 'If this is what you prize so much that you are willing to leave your distant homes and risk even life itself for it, I can tell you of a land where they eat and drink out of gold vessels and where gold is as cheap as iron with you.'" The anecdote is doubtless apocryphal, but it serves its purpose of revealing what future generations thought of the roles played by, respectively, the natives and the colonists. Later, after Balboa claimed the whole Pacific Ocean for the Castilian Crown, more definite hints of a great civilization to the south were received. The discoverer was shown drawings of a llama, which he mistook, naturally enough, for a camel. Anxious to discover this fabulous land of gold and camels, Balboa did sail south. But he did not get far before he was recalled by his jealous superior officer, Pedro Arias de Ávila (frequently referred to as Pedrarias Dávila), governor of a province with no fixed boundaries called Castillo del Oro. Ávila found it insufferable that any subordinate should be as successful as Balboa. He therefore used Pizarro, who had in the meantime discovered the Isle of Pearls, to arrest Balboa and bring him home to be tried and garroted.

Pizarro's next service was with Espinosa on his campaigns to the north of Panama. By this time the islands had been conquered and were being settled by Spaniards. But although sailors had coasted the southern continent, it was still completely unknown territory. One would have expected even the small-minded Ávila to push his explorations in that direction, but for some reason he did not. All the early expeditions from Panama were sent northwest, in search of a strait through the isthmus and of new lands to conquer in that direction. Veraguas, Costa Rica and Nicaragua were added to the Governor's province; and his all-enduring soldiers, Pizarro among them, fought and starved and suffered and died their way through what is now Honduras, until they met and quarreled with Cortes's men making their way south from Mexico. Not until 1522 was Balboa's initial probe southward followed up, by an expedition under Pascual de Andagoya, who fell ill and brought his ships home again with nothing accomplished, but with confirmation of the tales which Balboa had heard years ago.

The event which probably caused Ávila and his advisers to turn their attention to the south was the conquest of Mexico. The news of this had a particularly stimulating effect upon Francisco Pizarro, who, now fifty, had much experience and little to show for it, a good name as a brave and resourceful officer, but no command. The almost fabulous doings of his remote cousin [1] Hernando Cortes must have served him as an example of what could be done by someone only slightly more distinguished by birth than himself and no more experienced in the new colonial warfare.

When a man to organize a new south-faring expedition was

called for, Pizarro undertook the adventure. He seems to have done so rather reluctantly, and the fact that he did it at all is evidence that his fortune was at a low ebb, for the Governor was sending his really valued men to deal with a mutinous subordinate in the north. Very few people thought anything good would come of a southbound expedition and no man of standing would have undertaken it. It is almost as if Pizarro were driving himself to emulate his reputed kinsman in Mexico, in a spirit of desperation rather than confidence. His lack of enthusiasm may also have been owing to the fact that, unlike Cortes, he was unable to put up any money and would have to seek a capitalist, or several capitalists, to come in with him. They might, as is the way of financiers, take the control out of his hands if he did have any success.

Pizarro found his associates for the expedition in two very different men. Diego de Almagro was a soldier of fortune in his fifties, parents and antecedents unknown, but with a good reputation as a soldier. He was candid and liberal in his manners, and if quick to lose his temper, equally quick to regain it and make amends.

Hernando de Luque was a priest, at one time master of the school attached to Darien cathedral, and now Vicar of Panama. Shrewd and prudent, he was trusted by his parishioners even with the disposal of their money for investment, so that his co-operation was of prime importance to Pizarro. Nevertheless, opinion in the town was divided; by some Luque was thought to be full of crazy schemes and was called "el loco." To Luque fell the work of financing the expedition. Pedrarias Dávila was approached officially, and gave his consent to the venture, in exchange, as usual, for a share of the contingent profits. He may or may not have put up some of the money. Ávila was busy trying to persuade colonists to settle in Nicaragua, a hot, low-lying, very disagreeable country, and he probably took little interest in the unpromising southern expedition. Pizarro became captain of this enterprise; Almagro set about provisioning the ship and recruiting men. The ship, which had been built by Balboa, was purchased from one Pedro Gregario.

Almagro's task was not an easy one, because of the general lack of enthusiasm for an expedition to the south. As a result, his recruits were the idlers and ne'er-do-wells and riffraff who had come out from Spain to mend broken fortunes. They were ready for any undertaking which offered even a chance of profit. The crew of eighty men thus sharked up by Almagro sailed under Pizarro's command in November 1524. Pizarro's subordinate officers were a pilot, Hernando Peñate; a treasurer, Nicolas de Rivera; and an agent of the Crown, Juan Carillo, present to see that the state received its 5 per cent. Almagro was to follow in a second vessel as soon as he could be ready.

The season was ill-chosen, the weather was atrocious, and Pizarro's first landing, from the estuary of the Biru River, placed him in a dismal swamp. The men at once began to lose heart and Pizarro showed his quality by keeping cheerful and inspiring the rest with courage. They re-embarked and sailed south again. But high seas and terrifying storms were met, and food ran short. Returning northward again, and landing, the Spaniards were checked by interminable swamp and dense forest, by continuous heavy rain, by great difficulty in finding even berries and roots to keep them alive as their stores became exhausted, and by the depressing absence of game or any kind of animal life. The consequences were such as we might expect: Pizarro's scratch crew blamed him for their miseries, and called on him to lead them back to Panama before they all died of starvation.

There are two kinds of men who make good leaders in such circumstances—the noble-hearted and high-minded; and the desperate gamblers—and there is no comfort for moralists in the fact that the latter have generally been as successful as the former. If Pizarro was never in his life to achieve nobility of heart or mind, he did respond to challenge with a kind of courage and good judgment. The determination he displayed at this point was that of a man who has nothing to lose—he was over fifty; his credit, in both money and reputation, were all invested in the expedition; return to Panama would mean disgrace, derision, poverty and a wretched old age, the more mortifying by comparison with his reputed kinsman's glittering success in Mexico. The prospect was insupportable. He must go forward. He found the eloquence to persuade his men that a golden future would reward endurance.

Pizarro sent an officer named Montenegro, with the ship and

half her company, back to the Isle of Pearls for provisions. He and the other half of the company then tried to explore inland for a way through forests and swamps to the land of gold and camels. No such route, nor any sign of human life, were found. Pizarro and his men were soon reduced to living on roots, palm-tree buds and shellfish. Some of these were poisonous; men died, others fell sick, and still others preferred to die of starvation rather than die in the agony of food poisoning. Under these conditions Pizarro was át his best: he was cheerful, kind and resourceful; what food was to be found, he found; what nursing of the sick could be done, he did. He persuaded the men, weak and disheartened as they were, to build huts to shelter them from the interminable heavy rain. It seems clear that it was at this time that he won from his men an affection and a loyalty never to be withdrawn.

Time passed and still Montenegro did not return. Twenty men had died, and the remainder were in that state of despondency which makes death welcome, when at last an Indio village was discovered in a forest clearing to which Pizarro had been drawn by a glimpse of light. Pizarro and his gang of famished scarecrows appeared and flung themselves upon the small village store of maize and coconuts. The inhabitants ran away, but as no violence was done or offered them, they returned and, according to the historian Herrera, very reasonably asked the strange thieves why they did not stay at home and grow their own food, instead of coming abroad to rob people who had done them no harm. It was a pertinent question, which, in the following three centuries, all America, Asia and Africa might well have asked all Europe.

The answer, had the villagers but known what their fellow countrymen were soon to learn in horror and agony, hung on their own persons in the shape of some commonplace golden ornaments.

We are not told how the language difficulty was overcome. Pizarro is said to have had native interpreters who knew Castilian but who can hardly have known all the languages of the Inca empire and were unlikely to have known Quechua, a tongue confined to a country still undiscovered. But it was from these poor rustics that Pizarro received the information he wanted. Ten days' journey across the mountains lay the capital of a great king whose country had been invaded by an even greater king, the Child of the Sun in person. The Child of the Sun was the Sapa Inca Huayna Capac, greatest of his great dynasty of emperors. The city was Quito, birthplace of the princess who was Huayna's favorite wife and the mother of his son Atahualpa, last of the Sapa Incas, and eventually Francisco Pizarro's victim.

2

THE SOUTH AMERICAN INDIANS

THE SAPA INCA Huayna Capac was the last of his race to add a province to an empire which united under a single government all the civilized and several barbarous nations of the South American continent. How did these nations come into being, and what were they like?

Man is said to have colonized America from Asia during the long paleolithic phase of his career. It is not possible to date the migration exactly; it may have begun at about the time when the old Stone Age men of the Dordogne Valley were painting their great pictures of animals in the cave at Lascaux, that is, about 25,000 B.C. The route of this migration went by way of a land bridge or an ice bridge now covered by the water of the Bering Strait. In so far as the word "race" has any meaning when applied to human beings, the migrants were Mongoloid. As farming had not yet been invented, they were hunters, and it was doubtless in pursuit of game that they made the journey. There was no single great migration; for century after century small parties of men, women, children and dogs drifted eastward into North America, and some of them then began to move south. Probably by 10,000 B.C. many small communities had reached and spread themselves over those parts of the Andes region which were habitable and offered game and wild vegetable foods. We cannot know what measure of awareness these people had; but if we suppose them as sensitive to their surroundings as the Lascaux and the Magdalena painters, with what awe must they have realized their fewness and feebleness under the mighty loom of the cordillera.

The earliest men whom prehistorians or archaeologists have been able to study in that part of South America which we are concerned with, are called Early Hunters. Communities of these Early Hunters found themselves, let us say about 7000 B.C., living in the Andean region in several diverse sets of geographical and climatic conditions. Some lived on the coastal plain; some in the highlands of the Andean foothills. Man, like other creatures, is shaped and constantly reshaped by his environment; consequently, at least two quite different kinds of human communities developed in prehistoric Peru.

The coastal plain between the Andes and the Pacific was a rainless desert crossed from east to west by a series of roughly parallel rivers. These rivers created fertile valleys along their courses. Such valleys provided a habitat for hunting man, since they were populated by game animals. But South America is not very rich in game; the species are small. The valleys also offered in their flora provision for food gathering, the collecting, probably by women rather than by men, of roots, seeds and fruits to be eaten. In due course it would have occurred to one or to several intelligent matrons that some food plants could be grown at home instead of being sought abroad; seeds dropped on middens or excreted in dung would soon have shown them the way. In short, the coastal valleys of Peru required their human denizens to invent gardening and, thus, agriculture. (The archaeologists' assumption that when hunters give way to farmers the latter are a different and immigrant people, seems to us unjustified.) It should be added that, as each of these valleys was separated from its neighbors by barren desert and in some cases by mountainous spurs of the cordillera, each community developed more or less in isolation.

To the east of the coastal plain lay the foothills of the Andes, and then the high cordillera itself. The foothills contained small plateaus or valley enclaves of fertility, and a few much larger ones: among the latter was the great steppe, at from twelve to fourteen thousand feet of altitude, now called the Bolivian Plateau, with its inland sea of Lake Titicaca. Although there was soil for the growth of plants and particularly of grasses, conditions were hard, and the cold, out of the direct sunshine, bitter. But here, and in similar mountain plateaus and valleys, lived the only large grazing animal of South America, Balboa's "camels," the llama, vicuña and alpaca, which do, indeed, belong to the Camelidae. They constituted game for hunting and, later, flocks for herding and shearing. Thus the mountain people invented stock raising and animal husbandry.

The communities of humans created by the valleys of the coastal plain obviously had to be very different from those which the mountain environment brought into being. In the narrow, tropical valleys, farming would at first have made rapid progress. But there would have been a grave economic crisis when the people became too numerous to be supported by their limited area of fertile soil; in those rainless valleys, survival, not to mention expansion, would have depended on the invention of irrigation. Irrigation, therefore, was invented. Now, any community dependent upon a system of irrigation for its food must be firmly disciplined. The amount of land each man is to cultivate, the amount of water he may use, must be regulated. Even the family's most private business, the breeding of children, becomes everybody's business where growth of population can be allowed only on condition that the community as a whole undertakes further irrigation works in order to bring more land under cultivation.

From all of this it follows that strong, central, socialist-style governments develop naturally in communities dependent on man-made soils.[1] The mountaineers, on the other hand, enjoyed ample rainfall. Once they had either learned farming from the plainsmen or invented it for themselves, they would have been under no necessity to irrigate and therefore under no necessity to develop strong central governments. They therefore probably formed themselves into some sort of primitive, noncollectivist democracies, accepting discipline only from their war leaders.

Americanists say that the Early Hunter period merges into the Early Farmer period between 3000 and 2500 B.C. We must suppose the basic arts of civilization to have been invented during the Early Farmer period. The Peruvian farmers of this time had three agricultural tools: a digging stick, a clodbreaker, or mattock, and a hoe.

With these they practiced, in time, an intensive agriculture not surpassed in success anywhere in the world until our own time. This is not so surprising as it may appear to the urban reader; even today the crop-per-acre yield from gardens intensively cultivated with hand tools is enormously larger than that of farms cultivated by machinery. The Early Farmers of Peru discovered manuring, which of course made their intensive methods possible; the coastal plain valley farmers used guano and fish heads, both of which were to become important to farming in Britain about four thousand years later. The highland farmers used llama dung and human dung. And although we find no reference to this in the authorities, we think it probable that since some of the irrigation schemes carried water through nitrate desert, the coastal farmers of a later epoch may very well have discovered the agricultural use of Chilean nitrate.

Although the highland farmers had no need for that irrigation which the lowland farmers extended constantly during this period, they did run short of arable land. They therefore invented terracing, which not only gave them more room but checked erosion and runoff, and possibly inspired a greater measure of centralization in government. In time every valley was to be a spectacle of tier upon tier of terraces, those at the foot being perhaps a mile wide, those at the top a few feet, and the range of crops varying in kind from the temperate-zone cultigens at the top down to the tropical-zone plants at the lower levels.

The Early Farmers' basic crops were, in the lowlands, maize (but not at first); in the highlands, quinoa and potatoes. The highlanders hunted llamas and small game; they bred guinea pigs and, according to some historians, edible dogs. They preserved their potato crop by exposing it alternately to frost and sun to produce a starchy food called *chuno*. It is probable that the potato was the earliest plant to be cultivated in South America, because root crops seem always to precede grain crops in the history of agriculture. They are easier to cultivate, and they yield a good return for little labor.

The fundamental creative act of man in America was the development of maize. For this grain is an artifact; there is no such thing as "wild" maize unless it be as a farm "escape." And since it was maize that made possible and supported the whole towering and massive pyramid of Peruvian civilization, not to mention the Central American and the Mexican, we shall devote a few words to its history.

Scholars have disagreed as to whether maize originated in Mexico or in South America—in other words, whether Peru owed her advance to the Maya or the Maya owed theirs to the Peruvians. Some, like G. H. S. Bushnell[2] and Nikolai I. Vavilov,[3] take the position that the Mexicans were first in cultivating it, on the ground that maize developed from a grass called *teosinte*. But in their brilliant and closely reasoned study, *The Origin of Indian Corn*, P. C. Mangelsdorf and R. G. Reeves have shown that teosinte is probably historically a younger species than maize and possibly originated as a hybrid of maize with some related species. They have also traced the descent of maize to a mutant of pod corn, the latter to be found growing on the eastern watershed of the Andes, in what is now Bolivia.[4]

Maize is not a teosinte derivative; teosinte may be a maize derivative. Vavilov did not know this; his conclusions would have been different if he had. Our own belief is that maize originated on the eastern slopes of the Andes, among a people of whom we know nothing, and was first cultivated not in Mexico nor in Guatemala, but in Peru. And if this conflicts with the dating of the Peruvian culture phases, then they may perhaps need redating. Indeed, radio-carbon tests, for what they are worth, have shown this to be so.

With regard to the dating of the Early Farmers, no object from their middens has yielded to the radio-carbon test a date earlier than 2500 B.C. or later than 1200 B.C. (We do not know the value of such tests; they may entail large errors.) Such objects reveal that they cultivated gourds and squashes and beans, peppers and esculent roots; that they gathered shellfish; that they hunted marine animals; and that they either cultivated or gathered cotton, which they "spun" by twining, to make nets and coarse cloth. That the Peruvian Early Farmers had cotton has led some prehistorians to deduce an Asiatic discovery of America prior to 2500 B.C. No such deduction seems called for.[5] The evidence, based on chromosome counts, indicates that cotton was introduced into both Asia and America from a common Tertiary habitat in the Siberia-Alaska region and that the two cottons derive from a single protocotton ancestor.

Weaving, at this early stage, was very primitive, being accomplished by a twining-and-darning technique. A few simple pigments were used. Building of dwellings was subterranean—that is, holes were dug in the ground, lined with stones or adobe, and roofed on beams of wood or whalebone. By 1200 B.C. the Early Farmers were making good pots, jet mirrors, earthenware stamps for body decoration, and beads of shell and bone.

We have referred to the fact that archaeologists believe that the Early Farmers, creating their communities on the Peruvian coastal strip between about 2500 and 1000 B.C., were not the Early Hunter people evolved, but of different stock and unknown provenance. The curious refusal of archaeologists to allow a people to invent anything for themselves, and to deduce, therefore, a migrant race from a change in craft styles or economy, seems to us unreasonable. A future archaeologist, digging up London and reaching the 1930–50 "horizon," might by that rule write something like this: "At this time iron, earthenware and enameled cooking-pots give way to a new material, aluminum. It is clear that a migrant people, bringing the new metal and the techniques of working it, overwhelmed the older inhabitants." We see no reason to suppose that the Early Hunters were incapable of turning farmer and devising new crafts and new styles under the pressure of population growth.

As for the progress subsequently made in crafts by the Early Farmers and their descendants, we cannot do better than quote from G. H. S. Bushnell's *Peru*, to which we have already referred:

An important characteristic of all Central Andean peoples was great manual skill associated with very simple apparatus, a feature which they shared with other South and Central American peoples. Their weaving was unsurpassed and is particularly characteristic of the area; they applied most of the known techniques, using both cotton and wool, on a simple back-strap loom. Pottery was skilfully modelled and painted, producing vessels of great artistic merit, but the potter's wheel was unknown. Gold, silver, copper and their alloys were worked by a variety of processes, and the production and working of bronze was finally mastered. Among the useful metals the most obvious absentee was iron, which was unknown anywhere in America except for rare instances derived from meteors. Many other materials such as wood, basketry and stone were skilfully worked, and were used, where appropriate, on a large scale for massive building as well as for the smallest ornaments. As an example it is only necessary to cite the fine masonry of the Incas, with stones between which a knife-blade cannot be inserted. It appears that every-day products, such as domestic pottery and textiles, were made by the members of each family, but that finer ceremonial goods which so far as our evidence goes were generally made to be buried with the dead, were the work of specialists.

The only comment we need add is that because clothes are found in graves, it does not follow that they were made to be buried with the dead.

The so-called "Formative" period which succeeds that of the Early Farmers is dated from 1000 B.C. or earlier to about the birth of Christ. The adoption of maize as the staple crop led to a faster rate of technical and cultural progress. The period is also called "Cultist," since every settlement had a building superior to the ordinary dwellings, a stone or adobe pyramid, which is taken to be the temple of a cult.⁶ The art style of the period is labeled "Chavin," from the name of an important site where Cultist artifacts were found. In this period the loom was further developed, temples built, and a jaguar god worshiped in them. The graphic arts advanced, for the depiction of the jaguar god incised on the Chavin slab illustrated is not only skillful, but highly stylized. Pottery too is more advanced in both design and technique. Gold was worked, but not yet other metals. The Cultist people seem to have eschewed warfare; at all events, no weapons have been found and the single bow dating from this time may just as well have been a hunting bow.

The most important artifact of any people is its language, and in the absence of writing it is the only one of which archaeology can tell us nothing. When Pizarro and his fellow Spaniards arrived in Peru the language spoken all over the Inca empire was Quechua. But this was something relatively new. Quechua was the language of the Inca *ayllus*, or sibs, who composed the imperial tribe. They had three justifications for imposing it upon the whole imperial domain: they were the conquerors, and might makes right; it is expedient to have a single tongue spoken over the whole of any empire of disparate peoples, for it helps to unify the social state and thus match the unity of the political state (Quechua was thus imposed for the same reason as were Latin in the Roman, English in the British, and Russian in the Soviet, empires); finally, Quechua, as a rich and supple language, might be imposed on merit alone.

This language was not called Quechua (Quichua, Q'shewa, Kichua) by its speakers. It was originally spoken by a group of tribes including the Incas and Quechuas, all mountain peoples and neighbors. When it became the general language of the Inca empire it was known as *Runasimi*, "man's mouth," and that is what we should call it; but it has been called Quechua by linguists and philologists for so many centuries that it is convenient to retain the name.[7] That it was imposed on the conquered or allied nations is not surprising; for in the sixteenth century the sixteen to twenty million inhabitants of the American continent spoke at least nine hundred languages belonging to at least one hundred groups or families, an inconvenience of the most tiresome kind, once improved communications had started to open up the enclosed communities to each other.

The language is very rich in consonants, so that special conventions had to be used in order to write it in Latin letters (for example, *cc* for a consonant between *k* and *q*, now written *q*). It has only the five pure vowels but these freely used so that the language is both guttural, sonorous and explosive to listen to. Verbs have what Marcel Cohen[8] calls a prolonged expressive root—for example, *waxaxaxa*, "to roar with laughter"; *pitututu*, "to stink to high heaven." Clearly, a great tongue for dramatic satire, although it does not seem to have been used for that purpose. The root verb was extended by modifying suffixes to the number of at least nineteen, which were used in combinations, to indicate the mode of action and the manner of the subject's involvement in it. Conjugation of the verb was complex: the three persons singular and four plural (an exclusive as well as an inclusive "we") were indicated by suffixes but these varied to accommodate others indicative of time, manner, aspect. Personal pronouns were either independent words or, when serving to complement the object, suffixes. They could likewise be suffixed to nouns to form the possessive. The active verb was turned passive by the suffix *ka*: *munasqua*, "he loved"; *munasquaka*, "he was loved." The *squa* (or *sqa*) makes the past tense. More suffixes were used both with verbs and with nouns to indicate relation, for example, *-ri*, "and"; *-na*, "already." Nouns are suffixed with *-cuna* to form the plural and with other suffixes to form the possessive or to indicate role. Here is a sample sentence:

NOQA MANARASE RIMAYKICHU
I   not yet   to tell-thee [objective] *-not*

MONTE-MAN
mountain-toward [Spanish loan word]

RISKA-YKU-MAN-TA
to go-we [exclusive] *-toward* [syllable for complement to object]

"I have not yet told you that we went to the mountain"

As in all languages developed where relations between members of the family were of religio-social importance (endogamous or exogamous taboos, et cetera), the vocabulary of relationships is excessively rich and is apt to be confusing and hard to master: thus the words used by siblings to and about each other vary not only with the sex of the object, but with the sex of the speaker or subject as well.

In short, we have here a rich and very flexible tongue well suited to become a general language. With the simplification which could be achieved by detaching suffixes and transforming them into independent pronouns, adjectives, et cetera—natural steps in the evolution of the language—Quechua might have evolved into a world language. The great commonwealth of the Tahuantinsuyu, the Inca empire, did not, alas, last long enough for this evolution to take place.

The second half of the Formative, or Cultist, period is called the Experimenter phase, and it extends in time from about 500 B.C. to about the beginning of the Christian Era. Five centuries of experiment and technical progress, during which the cult of the jaguar god, manifest in sculpture and painting, declines yet never quite vanishes. All over the two principal centers of population, the coastal valleys and the highland plateaus, communities grew in number while advancing to a greater understanding and control of their environment. As usual, archaeologists name the resultant cultures by reference to pottery. We will not trouble the reader with tedious details. Very important were, among other things, the development of irrigation—for example, in the Viru Valley—and of terrace building in the highlands. Swiftly increasing populations had to be accommodated. Coca began to be cultivated, the leaf being chewed as a stimulant. Quinoa was added to the highland crop plants. The horticultural technique of propagation by cuttings was invented and applied. This was an enormous step forward, for it enables the cultivator to establish a desirable strain which fails to "come true" from seed; but it also establishes in the cultigen any virus disease the original plant may have.

Housing was poor but improving. In the Viru Valley, during the later Experimenter (Gallinazo) phase, the people dwelt in "agglutinated" villages, which are, to all intents and purposes, villages under a single roof. The buildings were adobe warrens of rooms, each room accommodating one family. Millions of people live in much the same conditions today in London, Glasgow, New York and Moscow. This huddling together of the Peruvian population strengthened the hand of the centralized governments which were to develop.

Each settlement also had a pyramid of adobe or stone, presumably for religious purposes. Irrigation channels grew larger, longer and more elaborate. Fortresses of adobe dwellings and stone pyramids defended by walls were established at high vantage points commanding the valleys—a clear indication that the Andean peoples had taken to warfare. With wealth to invest in the socially stabilizing device of organized religion, and wealth to waste on organized warfare, it is clear that their surplus product was becoming considerable.

Throughout the Formative period, and into the Classic period yet to be mentioned, the cultures of the valleys and the plateaus were differentiating. Thus, in the Classic or Mastercraftsmen phase (approximately 1 to 500 A.D.) there emerged a number of highly organized, centralized and aggressive tribal "states," which are not yet precisely nations, each having its own culture, language, manners and, perhaps, religion. But we should probably think of the distinctions which differentiated one from another as of the same order as those which distinguished the European nations as they emerged from the post-Roman chaos. That is to say, there is one basic culture, but several and diverse expressions of it; one basic religion, but several and diverse cults of it. The principal centers of the Andean peoples' progress in the Classic period were four: North Coast, South Coast, South Highlands, and Central Highlands.

In these, and probably to a lesser extent elsewhere, irrigation and terracing continued to grow and to place more fertile soil at the disposal of increasing populations. By about 250 A.D. all the plants found in cultivation by the Spaniards twelve centuries later were in crop production; the pineapple had arrived from Mexico, the potato from the mountains, the pawpaw and sweet potato from the Caribbean islands. But these introductions, as we have already pointed out, do not by any means imply conscious contact with the peoples of their sources. The only real mystery of Peruvian manners in this and earlier periods is that of the surgical violence done to the people's heads: a large number of skulls dug up by archaeologists show that the owners, when alive, underwent and recovered from trepanning operations, and in other cases suffered deformation of the skull by pressure. No convincing explanation for this practice has been advanced. It can hardly be that prehistoric Peruvian medicine had already discovered that prefrontal lobotomy produces tractable citizens. But, whatever its purpose, it proves an astonishingly high degree of surgical skill with stone scalpels. In his *Studies in Paleopathology*, Dr. Roy L. Moodie tells us:

> I believe it to be correct to state that no primitive or ancient race of people anywhere in the world had developed such a field of surgical knowledge as had the pre-Columbian Peruvians. Their surgical attempts are truly amazing and include amputations, excisions, trephining,[9] bandaging, bone transplants, cauterizations, and other less evident procedures.

In weaving, too, skill advanced to a high level during these and later years: cotton, llama wool and alpaca wool were made into brocades, tapestries, double cloth and gauze. Spinsters and weavers were women; they attained an astonishing excellence in design and workmanship, and by working teams of their looms side by side, they were able to produce cloth in widths up to seventeen feet. Relying on manual skill to the neglect of machinery, they accomplished such tours de force as the stringing of decorative beads on their warps, a process exemplified in certain Nazca tapestries. Much of the weavers' success depended on the spinning of the fibers, so finely accomplished by the spinsters who often took their bowl-and-distaff with them when calling, as ladies of our eighteenth century took their embroidery, that Peruvian tapestry of between 500 and 1000 A.D. sometimes has as many as five hundred 2-ply woolen wefts to the inch. The highest figure attained in Europe before modern times was one hundred.

In metallurgy, delicate smith's work was done with copper for useful, destructive and decorative purposes. Gold and silver were alloyed with each other and with copper. Smelting from ores was practiced, and such processes as casting and cire perdue were invented and perfected. Both welding and soldering were well understood, hammered welds were properly annealed, and some kinds of plating with gold were done.

The gifted Nazca people in the south practiced astronomy, their calculations being made graphically by means of large-scale diagrams on flat ground. In the speculative and abstract sciences, however, the Peruvians were less successful than the Maya of Central America; their diagrams did not enable them to arrive at the degree of accuracy attained by the Maya.

In pottery, technique reached a very high level of perfection. Design, which was highly imaginative, also showed a sophistication that was probably a reflection of contemporary manners. Whereas, for example, sexual behavior depicted on certain earlier, Salinan, pots, bears witness to a no doubt wholesome simplicity of manners, that depicted on some fine pots of the Classic period, from the last stages of the Mochica culture, includes conduct which only the most primitive, or the most sophisticated, societies do not consider perverse. Further pottery evidence of sophistication is to be found in the depicting of refined cruelty, such as the flaying of the face and punitive amputations. Earthenware work also included toys, rattles, whistles and drums. Pottery painting and tapestry design are by no means the only surviving examples of Peruvian graphic art; there is also mural painting. And in one partly preserved mural on a pyramid at Moche, we detect what we believe to be satire, but what may be mere humor, or neither, in the depiction of personified war weapons in revolt against their users. We like to believe that this picture may well mean that in default of a written literature—there was a spoken one—the Athens of classical Peru found its Aristophanes among the painters.

Concerning the difference in art styles which developed in the several centers of culture, our illustrations will tell the tale better than we could do. They will demonstrate the point made above: that, although several protonations of ancient Peru developed their particular geniuses in particular styles, the fundamental style, or, as it were, the *racial* style, is one. Which is to say that all Peru was, artistically, a single "Great Society," in Arnold Toynbee's sense, long before it was politically united. We shall also leave it to the illlustrations to introduce the reader to the Peruvian architecture of the period, which it is beyond our province or competence to discuss.

This Classic period of the Mastercraftsmen is followed by one of change and unrest, during which the cultural, economic and military energy of the several great centers became radiant, with a consequent exporting of styles and techniques. Archaeologists call this period—which came after about 500 A.D.—the Expansionist and believe that this explosion of cultural and economic energy was expressed in warfare. The example had, perhaps, already been given by the Mochica, whom we have ventured to call the Athenians of classical Peru, and who invaded and dominated the lesser peoples of the Viru, Santa, Nepena and Casma valleys. This artistically gifted and warlike people were also leading the way as engineers; they built the large adobe pyramids called Huacca of the Sun and Huacca of the Moon in their home valley. They also built the mighty, earthen aqueduct at Ascope, a work which carries water at a fifty-foot height a mile over the mouth of a dry valley, and which still stands and was, until the exceptionally heavy rainfall of the year 1925, still working well after two thousand years of service. And finally they built the seventy-five miles of canal which still irrigate some fields near the ancient Chimu capital, Chan Chan. All this they did before the Expansionist epoch really began; but the dominant culture of that epoch proper is Tiahuanaco.

The original home of this culture was the Bolivian Plateau and the shores of Lake Titicaca. Thus the Expansionist period perhaps resulted from the descent, probably military, of a mountain people who had created their vigorous culture in the bracing atmosphere of 12,000 feet above sea level, upon plains folk nurtured in a softer climate.

A number of high civilizations have been born of invasions of this kind. A predominantly agrarian and "feminine" community is overwhelmed by a predominantly "pastoral" and "masculine" people of highlanders. We may cautiously compare what happened between the Tiahuanaco folk, whoever they were, and the coastal valley peoples of Peru, to what happened when Doric herdsmen burst upon Pelasgian farmers; or when the Aryan stock-raising people came down upon the peasant India of the Dravidians. Out of such clashes followed by absorption are born nations, entities whose style and will in art receives a political form.

At all events, out of the clash between Peruvian highlanders and lowlanders, between llama herdsmen and tillers of the valley soils, there emerged three states, no longer amorphous congeries of folk, but nations. One of them, Chimu in the north, was, says Mr. Bushnell in his *Peru*, "large and powerful enough to be described as an empire." Perhaps this result was owing to the increased economic efficiency arising from the combination of stock- and crop-raising husbandries. Of, in short, high farming. When one man can, by his work, feed five people instead of three, there is room for the development of civilization.

The significant advance to be noted in the next epoch of Peruvian history is large-scale urbanization. Cities are built. Thus the period which succeeded the Expansionist is known as the City Builder period. But that archaeological-sounding label will not suit our purpose here; it seems to thrust the whole epoch into the very remote past. If we referred to fourteenth-century Europe as the City Builder period, it would make that century seem contemporary with Akkad or Babylon. There is nothing in the least remote or, except technically, "prehistoric" about the City Builder period of Peru. The Peruvian peoples were crystallizing their institutions into nationhood and giving that crystallization expression in great cities, at about the same time as the people of post-Roman, Latinized Teutonic Europe were hardening into nationhood.

Urbanization in Peru seems to have been an expression of the early appearance on the American continent of the Organization Man. Both towns and cities were, from the beginning, planned. In the Old World, as well as in the United States, urban planning has generally been a product of sophistication, not to say decadence; it does not happen until the community has passed its dynamic phase. But planning, of irrigation and terracing, for example, had been imposed upon even very primitive Peruvian communities by the nature of their country; it was in them a habit of mind and not a kind of cleaning-up of the mess produced by youthful exuberance after that exuberance has failed. The conurbation of Chan Chan was a product of the mental habit produced by irrigation and terrace planning and, in that sense, evidence of evolution, not reaction. Similar manifestations were to be found in the small state of Cuismancu south of Chimca, and, to a lesser extent, in the less highly organized state of Chimu in the south.

Chimu towns, large and small, were composed of rectangular blocks of dwellings contained within massive walls. The larger cities included terraced buildings whose walls were decorated with plaster moldings, sometimes very rich and strange. Cities built at the points where the foothill valleys opened into the plain and the irrigation channels began were, it is suggested by the pundits, garrison towns. But they may also have been headquarters of the water-supply authorities; for the management of irrigation water and the immense works associated with it must have required a special administrative department. Urban centers in the middle of the irrigated areas were residential and market towns, for the Peruvian cultivators, like those of Italy and other European lands, lived in towns and went out each day to work in the farm lands; they did not, as in England, live on the farms. There was nothing equivalent to the farmhouse.

The capital city of Chimu would have been a very great city even today. Chan Chan covered eleven square miles. No European or American city was as large as that until the nineteenth century. The ancient cities of the East and the Far East were sometimes as large or perhaps larger; and there, as in Europe and America today, this urban gigantism is always associated with a late and perhaps senile stage in the civilization. But here again Peru must not be judged by Old World standards.

Technologically, Peruvian civilization was now complete, a most striking contrast with European civilization, which was still, so to speak, in its infancy. Yet, as we have suggested, the two civilizations were, politically, at much the same stage. The only advance attributed by archaeologists to this time is the increased but still very limited use of bronze instead of copper. As we should expect, at an epoch when the word "culture" becomes less appropriate to the Peruvian states, and the word "civilization" more so, we find artistic liveliness in decline. Old styles are standardized, stylized, and the mass production of pottery and textiles, to fixed patterns, begins. The country craftsman becomes, as it were, the city hardware manufacturer, with organized labor gangs acting as industrial machinery. At the height of its power, in the middle of the fifteenth century, the Chimu dominion extended from Tumbez almost down to Lima, and the Chimu canal-building operations indicate a very thorough and intense organization of manpower; Chan Chan was drawing water from as far away as the Chicama River, a distance of about fifty miles.

[Although the Peruvian nation-state no doubt was, as Dr. J. H. Rowe has suggested, despotic, this does not imply chattel slavery on the Old World model. There were no rich men owning slaves; and no rich corporations owning wage slaves. There were, on the one hand, officials of various ranks; on the other, the people, the *fellaheen*. But we cannot even compare them with, respectively, the officials and *fellaheen* of the ancient Egyptian state. The difference is of enormous importance and it may be summed up as follows: in the ancient civilizations of Asia and Africa and the somewhat less ancient ones of Europe, men without property or power were expendable as raw material. There was nothing to prevent the Pharaoh from killing tens of thousands of slaves in public works which were of no benefit to the people. But from what we know of Peru there *was* such a barrier between the managers and the managed.]

Where can we find an equivalent social organization? Obviously, in the Communist states of our own time. In them, the state is despotic; but it is, for all its faults, corruptions and abuses—all of them arising out of the fact that men are men, and not out of the nature of the institutions in question—a projection of the people's own will. If a great public work has to be undertaken, Soviet citizens may, and in fact often do, sacrifice their personal interests and even sink their identity altogether, in order to accomplish it. Penal labor camps notwithstanding, the people are not, on the whole, driven to work with whips and forced to do it unfed. Nor are the works simply for the greater glory of the Pharaoh; they are for the public good. This seems to have been the case in Peru; the state was despotic, but it was the expression of the people's will, albeit an unconscious expression; and the works it carried out did not glorify the chiefs or kings or Caesars of this Far Western world; they served the people's welfare.

It is true that Peruvian rulers, as we shall see when we come to the Inca, really could say, "*L'état c'est moi*," so that the greater glory of the state was Caesar's greater glory. But the ruler's ambition was served by the well-being, not the suffering, of the people.

We must, moreover, emphasize once again that in a land where, for geographical, topographical, hydrographical and economic reasons, tight planning of resources has been the very condition of survival, the despot that comes into existence, though incarnate as a man or body of men, is the sum of the people considered as elements of their own organization. We therefore believe that because "despot" is a highly charged word inseparable from its Old World associations, it ought not, in considering the Peruvian states, or even the Peruvian Inca superstate, to be used at all. The pre-Inca Peruvian peoples gave rise to highly organized collectivist states, and finally to the collectivist empire, out of the economic necessity of the land in which they lived.

The production and distribution of food, clothing and services, including road and canal building, were, in Chimu, all functions of the state. Money, being uncalled for, was therefore not invented. Transport was chiefly by porters and by pack-llamas; the Peruvians had no other animals from which to create beasts of draft or burden. What is curious is the failure to invent the wheel; for teams of llamas pulling wheeled vehicles would have been a vast improvement. Yet even this failure is perhaps explicable in terms of Peruvian agrarian prehistory. There can be no doubt that we invent what we need, neither more nor less, just as species invent what *they* need—ducks, for example, needed webbed feet. From the European point of view, or from the Chinese point of view, the pre-Conquest Peruvian needed wheels; he ought, therefore, to have invented the wheel. He didn't. It follows that from his point of view he did *not* need the wheel. And it seems to us that he did not need the wheel because the advanced organization of labor preceded, instead of following upon, technological progress, and by so doing, inhibited that progress. From the earliest times the Peruvian people were so accustomed to accomplishing enormous tasks by organizing themselves into working teams which never overstrained the individual's strength, that there did not exist that drive to invent labor-saving devices which, in a world of every man for himself and the devil take the hindmost, is the great stimulant of invention. It looks very much as if the Peruvians were so satisfied with their collective way of life that they had no need even to think about lightening their labors.⌋

Very little is known about the small Cuismancu nation which occupied the Chancay, Ancon and Rimac valleys. Its capital city, of the same kind as Chan Chan, seems to have been Cajamarquilla, above modern Lima. Archaeologists say that the quality of its pottery indicates "degeneracy." This may simply be evidence of the passage from "culture" to "civilization," a transition which, as Oswald Spengler has shown, entails this kind of falling-off, owing to a loss of exuberance and the triumph of method.

In Chimca (or Chinca), in the south, a nation occupying the Chimca, Pisco, Ica and Nazca valleys, the splendid quality of the adobe bricks used to build the towns is notable. So good are they, that, until the practice was checked, many ancient buildings were torn down to provide bricks for new projects, and these bricks fetched ten times the price of modern ones. The stealing of adobe bricks from Chimca buildings was stopped in time to reveal that the Chimca people built rectangular, planned cities about a terraced center of pyramids and administrative palaces. But the concentration of populations was not nearly as great as in the north; possibly Chimca people, like Saxons, preferred villages to cities. This is speculation. According to the chroniclers, Chimca offered a fierce and prolonged resistance to conquest by the Incas when those mountain warriors assaulted their country. Our own prejudices would lead us to suggest that this is in itself evidence of a greater degree of personal liberty in southern Peru, as compared with that in Chimu. We do not insist upon the point.

As to highland nations, we do not know what they were or, indeed, whether there were any. However, there probably were, since large walled towns have recently been unearthed to the east of the Caxamarca basin. Nothing has yet been published concerning them. Tiahuanacan pottery for this period is dismissed as "decadent" which, again, may mean that the highlanders were becoming "civilized."

We now turn to consider the Incas, of whom nothing has yet been said, but who, in less than a century of consistently successful warfare and diplomacy, were to unite the nations of Peru into that empire which Atahualpa inherited and Pizarro destroyed.

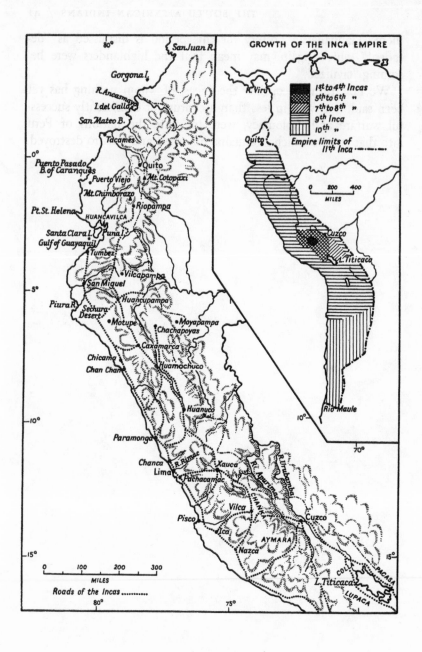

GROWTH OF THE INCA EMPIRE

1st to 4th Incas
5th to 6th "
7th to 8th "
9th Inca
10th "

Empire limits of
11th Inca ....

0   200   400
MILES

San Juan R.
Gorgona I.
R. Ancasmayo
I. del Gallo
San Mateo B.
Tacames
Puento Pasado
B. of Caranques
Puerto Viejo
Mt. Chimborazo
Pt. St. Helena
HUANCAVILCA
Santa Clara I.
Gulf of Guayaquil
Puna I.
Tumbez
Vilcapampa
San Miguel
Piura R.
Sechura
Desert
Motupe
Chicama
Chan Chan
Paramonga
Chanca
Lima
Pisco
Quito
Mt. Cotopaxi
Riopampa
Huancupampa
Moyapampa
Chachapoyas
Caxamarca
Huamachuco
Huanuco
R. Rimac
Xauca
Pachacamac
Vilca
Ica
Nazca
R. Apurimac
CHANCA
R. Urubamba
Cuzco
AYMARA
L. Titicaca
COLL
LUPACA
PACASA

R. Viru
Quito
Cuzco
L. Titicaca
Rio Maule

0   100   200   300
MILES
Roads of the Incas ....

3

THE INCAS

THEIR ORIGINS AND CONQUESTS

At a time before the counting of years began, four brothers and four sisters emerged from a cave twenty miles from Cuzco, followed by the people they ruled. One of their number bore in his hand a golden rod and this, from time to time, he plunged into the ground, sounding the depth of the soil. This was done because the eight siblings were the children of God the Sun and he had sent them to seek a homeland. In other accounts of this beginning, God the Sun brought forth his two children, a boy and a girl, in Lake Titicaca; later he told them to go where they pleased, saying that wherever they halted to sleep or to eat, they were to thrust a scepter of gold into the ground. The scepter was half a yard long and two fingers thick. Garcilaso de la Vega tells us in his *Comentarios reales*: [1]

> He gave them this staff as a sign and token that in the place where by one blow on the earth it should sink and disappear, there it was the will of Our Father the Sun that they should remain and establish their court.

The place where the staff vanished into the ground was Cuzco. The legend is a religious one, but it bears singular witness to Inca science, for the purpose of such an act was, of course, simply to discover a deep and fertile topsoil.

43

It is a fact established by archaeology that the Incas did, indeed, migrate to Cuzco, the site of which had earlier been occupied by a people whose artifacts were strikingly different from the Inca ones found there. And the legend is probably correct in attributing the origin of the Incas as a tribe to Titicaca. Certainly they were a highland people, for no sea-level or low-altitude race would have settled in the rarefied atmosphere of Cuzco. Also, the Inca mummies unearthed by Dr. J. H. Rowe, principal authority on the Inca past, reveal them to have had the short stature and deep chests of mountaineers. (Today, Peruvian pilots of pure Indio blood can fly their aircraft at 15,000 feet without using oxygen masks.) The bodies also reveal that Inca faces were brown, broad and almost hairless, and that they had prominent, sometimes hooked, noses.

In the tale which Garcilaso's uncle told him, by the time the Children of the Sun reached Cuzco—like the Israelites in the desert they took a very long time to cover a small distance—only three sisters and one brother were left. The brother was Manco Capac. It is noteworthy that the first of the Inca rulers to be cleared as historical and not mythical, by scientific historians, is, indeed, Manco Capac.

The rule of the Incas in Cuzco probably began about 1200 A.D. Dr. Rowe calls the period following this, but before they became a great military power, Early Inca. From his findings at Cuzco, it seems clear that the Incas were a backward people by comparison with the civilized nations of the coast: their pottery was rough and of no great merit in design; their tools were of ground slate and bone; they had little metal. They were Stone Age savages at a time when the Chimu people had reached a high level of technical, political and cultural sophistication. But then, the Macedonians, who were to conquer the Hellenic world, were Bronze Age savages at a time when the city-states of Greece had long before produced a Phideas, a Plato and an Aristophanes.

The Incas were only one of several mountain tribes which, as stock-raising mountaineers are always apt to do, preferred raiding their neighbors to working for their living. We should make no very great blunder in thinking of these tribesmen as a sort of South American Afghans, or in comparing them to the Turkish and Mongol horsemen of the Eurasian steppe, with the Andes and the high Bolivian Plateau, instead of the Himalayas or the Pamirs to raise their eyes and stir their hearts. As Professor Louis Baudin has pointed out,

Si le milieu n'a pas determiné la société, il a cependant marqué l'homme de son empreinte. La contemplation des grandioses paysages du plateau a rendu l'Indien grave et pensif.

In saying that the Incas were a mountain *tribe*, we do not use the word in the strict ethnological sense; the body of people we are dealing with was probably a congeries of *ayllus*, endogamous kinship groups, led by the Inca *ayllu* which was to become the royal superfamily, and united by identity of origins, language and interests.

There were other, similar, groups, such as the Lupaca and the Colla tribes of the Titicaca basin, and the Quechua people, allied to and speaking the same tongue as the Incas. And beyond the Quechua lay the territory of the Chanca, the people who were, in due course, to offer the most serious threat to Inca ambitions. Between 1200 and 1400 A.D. all these hardy mountain tribes lived mainly on their herds or by their hunting and on some primitive agriculture, and also by raiding each other with enthusiasm.

Tribes living in these conditions tend to be governed, if at all, rather by elected war chiefs than by hereditary monarchs. But the principle of hereditary monarchy seems to have been early established among the Inca. Manco Capac, founder of the dynasty, and the first Sapa Inca, married his sister Mama Ocllo (or Mama-baco), and their son Sinche Roca succeeded to the throne, which he occupied without distinction as far as we know; he does not seem even to have waged war. Salcamayhua says this was because "being a very proud man and of haughty disposition, he seldom went abroad." In legend, Roca is the great protopatron of agriculture, weaving and mining. His *qoya* (queen) was probably his own sister Mama Cora; their son Lloque Yupanqui, the third Sapa Inca, is supposed to have made laws against fornication and drunkenness. Professor Baudin says that during Lloque's reign the Incas obtained the submission of the Canna and the Colla tribal groups. Other historians do not confirm this. But Lloque's son Mayta Capac was a military character who seems to have started life as a sort of infant Hercules; he talked while still in the womb and was leading armies at ten years of age. Legend aside, it is possible that he extended Inca conquests toward the west and south as far as Tiahuanaco. The more cautious historians give a quite different picture, that of an Inca nation remaining small and insignificant until the last three reigns when, in the space of half a century, they suddenly explode all over their known world. This may well be true, but it seems to us easier to understand the immensity of the later conquests if we suppose that expansion began earlier.

The son of Mayta Capac was Capac Yupanqui. Under this monarch, Inca conquests were—according to Morúa and Garcilaso, followed by Baudin, but not according to Sarmiento or scientific historians—extended toward the west as far as the Nazca territory; to the south toward Potosí; and included victory over the Aymara, who submitted to Inca rule. Again the chroniclers conflict, with some depicting a steadily expanding empire and others, supported by the archaeologists, maintaining the theory of a later imperial explosion.

The sixth ruler in line was Inca Roca. Although we have given the title Sapa Inca to some of his forebears, he was evidently the first to bear it officially. It means "Supreme," or "Unique," Inca. Roca is said to have organized a standing army of twenty thousand men, an unlikely number; some chroniclers attribute all his ancestors' conquests as well as his own to this soldier-Inca, while archaeologists ignore him. He made conquests both north and south; and he was at war, apparently for most of his reign, with the Chanca, a people who were also growing more powerful and more highly organized. This is the version given us by Garcilaso de la Vega. It is rejected by the best modern authorities in favor of the story as told by Bernabé Cobo; according to him, the wars waged by the Sapa Incas from Manco to Viracocha resulted not in permanent conquests or in absorption of the defeated tribes into the Inca empire, but only in destruction of enemy towns or strong places, and in looting.

From Morúa we can deduce that Inca Roca was the first "emperor," in the Roman sense of the word. He declared that certain stones, statues and places were *huaccas* of his and that they were to be venerated, introduced the policy of bread and circuses, and ordered that drinking parties must be public, on the ground that communal drunkenness was less dangerous to the realm than private debauch. He instituted the humble, downcast approach to his imperial person, so remarked upon by the Spaniards on their arrival, years later. The historian Sarmiento says he died in 1088 at the age of 120. Other scholars now consider 1388 a more likely date.

Roca, who supposedly founded the first *Yacha-huasi*, schools in which boys were taught to interpret and to make *quipus* (see below), was succeeded by his son Cusi Hualpa, who became known as Yahuar Huacac upon his accession to the throne. Such a change of name upon accession was not uncommon; there is a suggestion that the name assumed by the Sapa Inca contained an element of the maternal name.[2] If this be true it has a bearing on our discussion, below, of the significance of sister marriage among the royal Incas.

Under Yahuar Huacac the Inca wars were conducted by two generals, Vicaquirau and Apu Maita (*apu* means, roughly, "general"), both members of the royal family. They were not, apparently, very successful, since the Inca state continued to be threatened by the Lupaca, the Colla and above all by the Chanca. The Sapa Inca's son and heir presumptive ("presumptive," only because it seems that the rule, if it was one, of primogeniture could be upset by the old Sapa Inca's will) was called Hatun Tupac. But having been visited by God in a dream, he changed his name to Viracocha, one of the names by which God was known to the pre-Columbian Peruvians. During Viracocha's reign the pressure upon the Inca state by the other warlike highland peoples became greater than ever. Viracocha made an alliance with the Lupaca which entailed helping them against the Colla. The Incas were also busy with their expansion in the direction of Titicaca, where their artifacts have been found and the influence of their improving styles detected. Busy with these undertakings, the Sapa Inca could not even defend his own territory when the Chanca, a powerful tribe engaged in successful raiding, invaded it. Viracocha, old and feeble, fled from Cuzco to a safer place, Caquia-Xaquixahuana, taking with him his favorite son, Urco.

It had been the Sapa Inca's intention to nominate Urco to succeed him, a project strongly opposed by Vicaquirau and Maita. Whether this was merely a question of primogeniture, or whether it was because another son, Cusi Yupanqui, was the legitimate heir not simply because he was the eldest but because his mother was Viracocha's sister, we do not know. What we do know is that this Cusi, whose claim to the *borla* (a fillet and fringe with which Sapa Incas were crowned) was supported by the two old generals, refused to abandon Cuzco, rallied the Inca forces, and drove off the Chanca army. Viracocha abdicated, and Urco either relinquished all claim to succession or abdicated immediately after he succeeded; it is probable that he abdicated and that he was forced to do so by Cusi Yupanqui, who thereafter had Urco's name removed from the *quipu* records, thus causing much annoyance to historians. Cusi, hailed as a great hero, then was crowned Sapa Inca under the name by which the people had acclaimed him, Pachacutic ("Savior").[3]

The Sapa Inca Pachacutic is the romantic hero of Peruvian history. Although he had saved the day when the Chanca were at the gates, his troubles were not over. At home, he had to get rid of Urco, while at the same time following up his victory. The Chanca did not, it seems, consider themselves defeated, for they threatened attack again, and called upon the Inca to surrender unconditionally. Pachacutic dealt with this, or so popular legend tells us, by challenging their chief, Astohuarraca, to personal combat. The challenge was accepted, the Chanca chief was slain in the duel, and his people ceased to trouble the Andean scene. Sober history says that at all events the Inca defeated the Chanca in subsequent battles and eliminated them from the competition for hegemony. The duel tale may not even be good popular history; it has a strongly European flavor.

Pachacuti, as his name is now spelled, was a planner, builder, organizer and administrator of genius. In addition, he was quite ruthless and quite obviously an unfailingly successful soldier. If we forget for a moment our view that some of the conquests attributed by modern historians to Pachacuti and to his son *may* have been accomplished, as certain of the chroniclers tell us, by their ancestors, then [it is to Pachacuti that we must give the credit for pacification of the country around Cuzco. The means adopted, when dealing with near neighbors and old enemies, was massacre; farther from home, the Incas became the gentlest and most liberal imperial conquerors in history. From Urubamba and Vilcapampa, outward in all directions round the capital, the Sapa Inca extended his campaigns until he had a large country at peace and under control. He then set about rebuilding Cuzco on "imperial" lines, initiating new terracing on an enormous scale, setting up an observatory for his astronomers, and devising a suitable organization for administering an empire. He sent his brother, Capac Yupanqui,* to conquer and add to the empire all the land and peoples down to Yanamayo, beyond which place the royal commander in chief was ordered not to venture.

In this order we may perceive that intelligence and that greatness of mind which have earned Pachacuti the enthusiastic admiration of numerous historians, for he treated war as a necessary evil and an instrument of policy, not as a means to personal aggrandizement. The Sapa Inca had seen how continual petty warfare destroyed the works of man and how it thus checked his progress toward some kind of order and a measure of happiness. But he saw also that men must be driven to their own good, since no words or examples will persuade them of it. It is clear that he had no Alexandrine, no Napoleonic paranoid visions. A limited and viable area under proper control was what he aimed at. Unhappily, if history teaches anything at all it is that your *Pax—Romana, Britannica,* or *Incaica*—must be coextensive with the known world or else be no *Pax* but a state of chronic warfare.

The Inca army, as it took form under this Sapa Inca and was perfected under his son Tupac, or Topa, was composed of conscripts from all the provinces under Inca rule. They were simply men under the *mit'a*, the system of annual levy for national

* Not to be confused with the son of Mayta Capac mentioned earlier.

service, not necessarily military—those called up might also be put onto public works. Fighting, in fact, was a form of public works. These conscripts were trained by professionals, and officered by Inca career officers. They were organized on a decimal system, that is, in tens, hundreds, thousands, exactly as they were (we shall come to this below) in their ordinary civil life; thus the lesser officers may properly be called decurions and centurions.⌉

The army's missile weapons consisted of slings and bows. The bow was not an Inca weapon, but it was introduced into their army by conscripts from their easternmost province, men of the forests who normally used the bow for hunting and for war. The small arms for infighting were the mace, with a stone or copper head on a wooden shaft; the hardwood singlestick; the battle-ax, made of stone or copper; and the lance, with a copper, later a bronze, head. Body armor was worn; it was made of wickerwork and padded or quilted cotton. One chronicler says this was reinforced with copper plates on breast and shoulders. And the soldiers carried small round shields usually made of llamahide or some other skin. Defensive works were hill forts large enough to accommodate the whole surounding population, and in that respect reminiscent of early British hill forts.

Thus, apart from the cotton armor, we should not be very far wrong in describing the Inca armament as Neolithic. The curious thing is that the users of this primitive armament developed strategy, administration, mobilization and logistics of a sophistication unsurpassed until our own century in Europe and America, and certainly comparable to that of the Roman practices.[4]

Pachacuti put a stop to war as a sport, a sort of hunting, and made it professional by infusing his troops with a sustained aggressive spirit, by devising proper organization of supply and transport, by efficiently administering conquered territory, and by providing cadres of professional officers. In tactics, either he or his son or one of their generals invented the idea of a reserve to be thrown in when the shock of it could decide the battle.

But wars are not won; they are lost. A great deal of rubbish has been written about the "genius" of successful soldiers. There is, in all history, no evidence whatsoever that the waging of a successful war of conquest, or a whole series of such wars, is proof of genius. Military empires are built by men of great organizing ability, such as may be found at the head of any major enterprise involving large numbers of men and large quantities of material, combined with a strong will, good sense and decided ideas. Put such a man at the head of an army well provided for and well managed, in a world of nations which have lost their nerve, and you have a great conqueror. Twice in our own lifetime Germany has waged war on Europe and Russia with incomparable armies led by professional soldiers of recognized superiority; on both occasions they have been beaten by the people of nations unwilling to be conquered. The nations of the Andean world were, in the last analysis, not unwilling to be conquered. The only really serious resistance which Pachacuti, his generals and his son Topa met with was from savages; and the bravest savages can always be defeated by organized armies, though they may occasionally win a battle.

The Inca's civilized enemies went down like ninepins. They were ripe for a universal "Pax," a Great Society. The spectacle of men behaving so sensibly, instead of manfully and patriotically, is not to be looked for until the exuberance of national youth has been exhausted, just as religious tolerance is to be expected only where religious indifference is well established and all religions are, in Gibbon's great words, "to the people equally true, to the philosopher equally false, and to the magistrate equally useful." Prescott would have us believe that "the Incas, by their wise and temperate policy, gradually won over the neighboring tribes to their dominion as these latter became convinced of the benefits of a wise and well-regulated government." As we know, the Inca's "wise and temperate" policy with their immediate neighbors was massacre. There is some truth, as we shall see, that such a policy did have its effect in the remoter provinces. But we know, too, that even the wisest and best-regulated alien government has never persuaded any nation in the pride of its strength to submit. Nations, like men, learn wisdom too late to make any use of it.

It was, then, the weakness of the South American nations, together with the military *hubris* of his brother who started the real career of foreign conquests, that forced Pachacuti to go beyond his first intention. As commander in chief, Capac Yupanqui not only failed to halt his advance at the Yanamayo, but went on to conquer and loot the rich province of Caxamarca and to boast, in consequence, that he was a greater soldier than his royal brother. Upon Capac Yupanqui's return in triumph with booty and hostages, Pachacuti gave final proof of his fitness for empire by promptly having his brother executed for disobeying orders. Doubtless Capac Yupanqui's boast had something to do with this, but even so, the Sapa Inca demonstrated that he knew exactly how to deal with soldiers who went conquering on their own.

Pachacuti's policy was to use the resources of a shrewd and patient diplomacy before resorting to force; but force, soon widely recognized as irresistible, was always there. By treaty in some cases, and by swift conquest in others, tribe after tribe and nation after nation were gathered in and made part of the imperial domain. These foreigners did not become "subject" peoples—that is, they did not become any more subject than the original Cuzco population. They became citizens of the empire, in which all men were equal, only the Children of the Sun, the royal Incas, being, "more equal" than the others.

If we may, for a moment, compare the Sapa Inca Pachacuti to Philip of Macedon—and there were, in fact, similarities between the careers of these two semicivilized soldier-statesmen—then his son Topa Inca Yupanqui was the Alexander of the Andean world. He possessed a considerable share of his father's genius, all his capacity for work, a bolder vision and less awareness of the limitations of militarism, and, of course, he had his father's foundations to build on. The talents of this prince were certainly equal to those of his near-contemporary Charles V of the Holy Roman Empire. Pachacuti was very fortunate in his son.

This good fortune seems to have been almost a rule in the Inca royal house. There is, indeed, the story of Viracocha's preference for his son Urco over the heir, Cusi, but on the whole a remarkable harmony seems to have distinguished the relations between the Sapa Incas and their heirs. In no case did the heir rebel against his father; in none did the father seek to keep the son down; in several cases the reigning Inca resigned the *borla* in his son's favor during his own lifetime and after the son had long collaborated in empire. Some special explanation is necessary to account for this extraordinary departure from the rule which has been observed in all other royal dynasties. We suggest that it may be found in the strict inbreeding of the royal line, beginning with Manco Capac, an outstandingly able man; he married his sister, and so did other, and possibly all, of the succeeding Sapa Incas.[5]

Supposing their genes to be free from blemish, as it were, the result would have been to "fix" the family genius for government. And, in the light of certain modern experiments which tend to show that acquired characteristics are heritable, it would also have made it easier for each succeeding Sapa Inca to learn the trade of kingship. If there is any other example of royal line-breeding, it is the case of the Egyptian Pharaohs who maintained the longest-lived and most stable empire in history. In short, we suggest, albeit tentatively, that systematic incest in the royal Inca line led to the line-breeding of men for kingship as Jersey cows are line-bred for butterfat.

The chronicler Sarmiento tells us that Topa Inca Yupanqui had two brothers older than himself. They distinguished themselves by putting down revolts of the Colla in the highlands. It was while they were doing this that Topa was born and a mystery is made of the fact that the Sapa Inca at once nominated the infant prince as his heir. The reason may not be so very far to seek; it is at least possible that Topa's brothers were only half brothers, sons of a lesser wife, and that Topa was the first son of the *qoya*, the Sapa Inca's sister. This is speculative, of course. The prince was not presented as their future ruler to the people until he was fifteen years old. Thereafter, as soon as he had reached man's estate, Topa was given responsible work to do.

The prince's first great campaign was in the northern highlands. While Pachacuti remained in Cuzco doing for that city what Augustus did for Rome, attending to his duties as chief of state and as god (like the Roman emperors the Sapa Incas were divine in their own lifetime) and progressively reorganizing the empire as it grew, Topa Inca Yupanqui set out on the task of turning a great power into a universal state, the Tahuantinsuyu, Kingdom of the Four Provinces.]

Beyond the territories of diverse barbarians lay a number of semicivilized nations in what is now Ecuador and southern Colombia. And southwest of these countries was the great civilized nation of Chimu, which could most effectively be attacked from the north, whence no attack was to be expected. There can be little doubt that Inca civilization owed much to Chimu long before Chimu became part of the empire; the radiant energy of a high civilization is extensive; Rome, for example, was Hellenized long before Greece was Romanized. The Macedonian semibarbarians learned from Athens half the arts which enabled them to subdue her; and doubtless the Manchus were half Sinicized before they conquered China. Topa Inca Yupanqui led his troops over great spurs of the cordillera and through dense primeval forests, a march exceeding in difficulty and hardship anything accomplished by Napoleon. He met with a fierce and sustained resistance from the half-civilized Canari; they submitted at last, to be incorporated into the empire, and became a loyal and useful part of it. The Canari people of southern Ecuador still speak Quechua, a language which they had to learn from the *mitmac*, the colonists from the Inca homeland planted in their midst according to a deliberate imperial policy (which we will discuss below). Forts, roads and temples on the Inca pattern were built, the prince recruited a Canari bodyguard for himself, and he showed himself much pleased with the green and fertile Canari country.

Having increased the size of his army and rested his veterans, the prince resumed his northward march, bent on the conquest of the Quitu, a people equal in culture and technology to the Incas, whose capital city, Quito, is now the capital of Ecuador. As Mr. J. Alden Mason puts it, with a touch of humorous bitterness, ". . . the customary conciliatory messages were sent to the chief of Quito inviting him to join the pan-Andean coprosperity sphere, which meant, of course, to yield to Inca arms and domination, or else." The Quitu being accustomed to give orders, not take them, defied the prince. A long and bitterly fought war resulted, the Quitu were beaten, and Quito was transformed from the capital of a proud nation to a provincial outpost of the empire.⟩

It was while he was conducting the Quitu war that Topa Inca heard a tale of certain islands, supposedly rich in gold and people, which lay far out beyond the ocean horizon and with whom the Quitu traded in sailing rafts of balsa wood.[6] Probably with booty and recruits in mind, although Sarmiento says it was because he had "decided to challenge his lucky star and see whether it would favor him at sea also," Topa Inca caused a fleet of rafts to be built and rigged and, with a detachment of the army acting as marines, set sail for what Sarmiento, who was their Spanish discoverer, believes to have been the Galápagos Islands. Until quite recently historians pooh-poohed this story on the grounds that the Galápagos had never been populated by a cultured people. But Thor Heyerdahl, when he visted the islands, discovered potsherds of Chimu type, so that evidently there had once been trade with the islanders; or a colony from the mainland. Cabello de Balboa says that the prince returned (apparently after nine months), with black prisoners, a brass throne, and much gold.

Topa Inca next turned his attention to his final object, the conquest of Chimu. This ancient and civilized people were Maginotminded. They had fortified their obvious frontier with the Inca domain, and it does not seem to have occurred to them that any enemy would be energetic enough to conquer the barbarous and semibarbarous peoples to their north in order to get at them across an unfortified frontier. The Chimu did not yield to the usual threats-and-promises diplomatic offensive, and a situation developed much like that in France in 1940. The aged ruler of Chimu, clearly a patriot of the old school, wanted to fight on, although his army had been severely handled in the first encounters. But he had a fifth column to deal with, advisers who saw no point in having men killed and property destroyed merely for the sake of continuing to call their souls their own, and who realized that in any case further resistance was hopeless. They were probably wise. Professor G. R. Willey has pointed out:

. . . the great valley irrigation systems were highly specialized means of sustaining life, and because of this specialization they were vulnerable to attack and disruption. With the urban type of life of the later periods, the dense population centers imprisoned in narrow valley oases would have appeared as overripe plums to the more mobile highlanders.[7]

In reorganizing the government of Chimu to make it fit into the imperial administrative system, Topa Inca made a minimum of changes. Officeholders, instead of being responsible to the government of Chimu, became responsible to the Inca "viceroy" of the Chinchaysuyu. Presumably, the officials and, later, the people were obliged to learn Quechua; they were speaking it when the Spaniards arrived. We are not told whether Chan Chan, the Chimu capital, became the capital of that province, or whether the north was administered from Quito. We should like to think that prince Topa Inca and his principal officers, military and administrative, felt for Chimu something of what the Romans felt for Athens, and accordingly treated it with respect.

Having settled his business in Chimu, the prince marched his army down the coast, incorporating one after the other all the valley nations as far south as present-day Lima. In these cases, also, the life of the people was disturbed as little as possible. In a later campaign, still more of these small valley nations were joined to the empire, including the ancient Nazca, once famous for its fine textiles and pottery.

THEIR HEADQUARTERS AND GOVERNMENT

Meanwhile the Sapa Inca, in Cuzco, had created an administrative machine capable of dealing with the vast territory now under his government—an area of 350,000 square miles, much of it very densely peopled—and had rebuilt the capital. Cuzco stood in a beautiful valley at an altitude of 10,000 feet and enjoyed an excellent climate despite this altitude, since its latitude was 13 degrees south. The houses of the people, forming geometrically regular streets, were of adobe roofed with straw thatch, so that the color scheme of the city must have been buff and gold. Chimu city-planning was adopted and Cuzco, like other cities, was laid out in geometrically demarcated quarters or wards.

The royal palaces, administrative offices and temples of the city were of fine masonry. For the more massive structures, the builders used perfectly squared blocks of very hard limestone or even harder igneous rock, some of them as much as twenty feet long, which were finely dressed by being ground down with sandstone. These, although so close-fitting that the work has become proverbial, may have been mortared together with bituminous cement. For lighter structures, small, regular, dressed-stone blocks were used, laid with what looks to us like Flemish bond, with sunken joints and bituminous mortar in very thin layers. The stonemasons had two kinds of tools—stone mauls and sandstone blocks. For the rest, skill and lots of time and patience. In a state where waste had been eliminated and population growth planned for, and where equal pay for all workers was the normal rule, there was neither a manpower shortage nor, as far as we know, labor troubles.

Like the Romans, the Incas took their building style with them wherever they went. Just as Europe was dotted with those circus buildings still visible in many South European cities, those monuments to Roman architectural ineptitude and artistic dullness which, like "imperial" building almost everywhere, have nothing to recommend them but size and their unfortunate resistance to the insults of time, so the Tahuantinsuyu was dotted with massive Inca buildings devoid of any distinction but endurance. If one sought a justification for the Spanish conquest it would be possible to find it in the beauty of the South American baroque, which the Spaniards introduced and which is in such startling contrast to Inca megalithic building.

Topa Inca's conquest of Chimu led to a fusion of Inca and Chimu styles in craft objects, so that at this late stage pottery is often Inca-Chimu. Cuzco polychrome pottery of the period is of good quality and design, but standardized in a few shapes, wares and finishes, so that it is evident that the Incas adopted mass production from the Chimu. The colonial pottery, however, is fairly diverse, since, although provincial craftsmen or craftswomen used the Inca models, they introduced modifications in form and color from their own local traditions.

Although copper was still the workaday metal, the Incas introduced bronze into the farthest outposts of their empire. Gold and silver were much mined, but their use was confined to officers of state and to the clergy, both of Inca blood, and to the embellishment of palaces and temples.

The organization of the empire was simple and, like city building and pottery design, geometrical; the Andean Indians seem to have had a passion for mathematical order in all that they did, and it is as apparent in their social as in their physical fabrics. At the top of the social pyramid was the Sapa Inca Intip Cori, Unique Inca Son of the Sun, Chief of State, Benefactor of the Poor, and God. He is referred to by many writers as a "despotic" monarch. We have already advanced the view that such words as *despot*, *emperor* and *aristocracy* ought not to be used when writing of the Inca social system, for they are loaded with misleading Old World associations. If comparisons must be made, then we should say that although the office of Sapa Inca was hereditary, it had more in common with that of a modern Communist Party chairman than with that of a European monarch. And it is this very important fact which explains the relative social benevolence of the Inca, as of the pre-Inca, Andean governments, rather than any exceptional qualities of common sense and good will in the South American Indian. The Inca system combined the advantages of hereditary monarchy with those of a party bureaucracy.

The *qoya* (the word means "star"), the Sapa Inca's first wife and, we believe, usually his full sister, was an important person in the state. But she was so in an unofficial way; her public appearances were greeted by affection expressed with respect and seemliness. It is significant for our argument touching the ancient matriarchy and economic importance of women as the origin of sister-marriage (heiress-marriage) that the *qoya* was known in the vernacular as *Huaccha-cuyas* ("She-who-cares-for-the unfortunate") or simply as *Mamamanchic* ("Our Mother"). It is a pity that we know so little of the characters of these First Ladies of Tahuantinsuyu: the chronicler Morúa was the only one with a sufficiently developed news sense to tell us anything about them. The *qoya* Cora, wife of Sinche Roca, had a taste for beauty in her serving girls, and she liked to have them naked about her; "they had to be very white." Lloque Yupanqui's *qoya*, Mamacura, sometimes called Anac Varqui, was a discreet woman of good understanding. When she went out she was always accompanied by a large escort of chiefs, *curacas* and ordinary people. She did a great deal of official entertaining, made a point of speaking good Quechua and insisted on the court's doing likewise, and was noted for her humor and her use of ridicule in dealing with fools.

Mayta Capac's *qoya*, whose name is given as Chimpu Urma, seems to have been an outstanding woman, a zoologist, naturalist and inventor. She kept a large menagerie and she encouraged angling, but instituted a system of licenses for fishermen. She took an active controlling part in managing the women workers on the royal estates, telling them when and what to sow. She introduced several new plants to horticulture and she was the inventor of chemical warfare, for she studied the poisons to be extracted from snakes, ants and a fruit (probably curare) for use as arrow poisons. She invented, also, the fishbone arrowhead. She was fond of music and invented some new instruments. Finally, she was universally loved.

The *qoya* Chimpu Olla, one of the names attributed to the wife of Capac Yupanqui, was another outstanding queen. She was interested in farming and even worked on the royal farms herself. When her husband went to war, she ruled the kingdom as regent. She was famous for her excessive cleanliness, changing her clothes three or four times a day. She had her meals alone. And she introduced jesters and jugglers to the court.

After so many paragons, it is almost a relief to discover that *qoyas* could be as wicked as Old World empresses, as witness the case of Cusi Chimpu, wife of Inca Roca (not Sinche Roca). She left behind her a legend of cruelty, she was too fond of parties, and she was a drunkard. She poisoned her brother-husband Capac Yupanqui, or so Morúa says, so that she could marry Inca Roca. She had a personal bodyguard of a thousand men and a thousand women, and seems to have been the only Messalina on the list. We do not have a high opinion of Morúa as a chronicler, but there is doubtless some truth in all this.

We have said that the *qoya* was the Sapa Inca's sister and we have mentioned cases in which this is an established fact. It is also an established fact that the mother of Topa Inca was the sister of his father, Pachacuti. Some historians have insisted that sister-marriage was a late and sophisticated practice, possibly designed to distinguish the Sapa Incas from the common people, among whom incest was held in horror. To present the whole case, it must be admitted that descent within an Inca *ayllu* (see below) was in the male line; that an old tradition of female dominion is less likely in a pastoral, highland folk than in a people of peasants; and that the Incas might have absorbed the idea of royal incest from, for example, their contacts with Chimu, where we should on the whole be less surprised to find it in vogue. Moreover, as imperial parvenus, the Incas might, like the Ptolemies in Egypt, have adopted sister-marriage from an ancient but discredited tradition, to give themselves countenance. or the Anunnaki

The Incas had an effective way of securing a loyal civil service. It was provided, at least in the higher ranks, by Incas-by-blood—a sort of formalized and licit nepotism. The many nonroyal sons of each Sapa Inca each became the head of an *ayllu* of descendants. An *ayllu* is an enlarged family group which is ethnologically the antithesis of a clan. Clan kinship is established through the mothers, and exogamy is its rule; in the *ayllu*, endogamy was the rule, and kinship was reckoned in the male line. In the beginning the *ayllu* provided the state with a unit of social organization. But it was denatured by the need to make the unit of mathematically identical size (see below), or nearly so. What in former times had been the real basic unity of a community became in imperial times a mere name.

The *ayllus* of a given community were themselves grouped into two half-provinces, together forming a province. Thus every Andean community had a *hanan* (lower) and a *hurin* (upper) group, to one of which every *ayllu* belonged. And this division was even reflected in the cities, there being, for instance, a Hurin-Cuzco and a Hanan-Cuzco. Although the upper people were given some sort of precedence over the lower, it does not appear that belonging to the lower entailed social or political disadvantages or social disgrace.

An *ayllu* was not only a kinship group but an economic one. The *ayllu* was the smallest individual landholder. But it should be made clear that an *ayllu* did not own its piece of land, it held land from the state. Nobody owned land in ancient Peru, just as nobody owned land in medieval Europe. The idea of land as alienable property, whether of a man or an institution, is a sophisticated and late development in any society, and perhaps an economic evil. In the Inca society it never developed at all.

All the land in the Tahuantinsuyu was divided into three parts: one for the people, one for the Sapa Inca (that is, the state), and one for the Sun (that is, the Church). Contrary to what some writers have maintained, this division was not an equal one; the parts were not mathematical thirds. The partition was accomplished by the following rule: The productive power of an *ayllu's* land was considered in relation to the number of people to be fed, clothed, housed and otherwise provided for at a planned standard of living. This standard insured health to all and gave a reasonable livelihood to every man, woman and child in return for a reasonable stint of work, which did not exceed the worker's capacity and left him adequate leisure.[8] The amount of land required to achieve this standard was set aside for the people; what remained was divided into two parts—we do not know in what proportion—for the state and the Church. In regions where the land was ungrateful and unyielding, the part allotted to state and Church would have been small, in some cases very small; on the other hand, in fertile places it might have been larger than the people's part. But to this we should add that the "welfare" fund—those huge stores accumulated in warehouses all over the country to provide for the sick, the invalid, the military commissariat and the communications apparatus, and to compensate for bad harvests—came out of the Sapa Inca's produce, and thus the people also had their share of the state's part. Furthermore, the civil and military services were supported out of that part. In short, the Inca's third was simply the national revenue.

The Tahuantinsuyu "taxpayer," "head of household," "bread-winner," was called a *puric*. We will define below what this meant, but it is convenient to have the term for use here. Every *puric* had to cultivate his own land and do his share of cultivating the state's land and the church's land. In short, he paid his taxes in time and in labor, not in kind or in money. He probably did none of these things simply as an individual, but rather as a member of the *ayllu*. More probably, he cultivated his own piece (allotted to him by the *ayllu* at the time of his marriage) for himself, but worked as a member of the collective when it came to the state and church lands.

To emphasize the points made above, it is quite wrong to think of the Incas as an aristocracy extorting two-thirds of the national product from an oppressed peasantry in order to live in idle luxury. In return for their fixed and reasonable share of the national product, the Inca upper caste provided sound and reliable administration, justice, welfare services, military services, and religious services. They were heaven-born; but they were more like a bureaucracy, not a European aristocracy, and members of their own caste could be punished for neglect of duty or abuse of power, as we shall see. Some authors have made much of the fact that the Inca caste was "exempt from taxation," that is, unjustly privileged. Of course they were privileged, but the word "exemption" is meaningless in a state where there was no money and where the word "taxation" is misleading. Men paid taxes by working for the state; but the Incas' work was for that same state; therefore, their work was taxpaying work.[9]

As the empire grew in size and complexity, this hereditary bureaucracy was unable to deal with the work to be done. The Incas then found it expedient, as have other imperialists before and since, to throw open the career to talent, or at least to foreigners of consequence. A class of *curacas* was created, a sort of *noblesse de la robe*. It was the Sapa Inca Pachacuti who initiated this reform. *Curacas* were, so to speak, honorary Incas, recruited at first only from Quechua-speaking tribes, but later from everywhere in the empire. They were men who had held rank and office in their own countries. They were distinguished both from the common people and from the Incas by special headbands and by the large earplugs deforming the ear lobes, which caused the Spaniards to call them *orejones* ("big-eared ones"). The first of these *curacas* were the chief men of tribes that had submitted to the Incas without fighting. Rank was attached to their office and it was made hereditary. Like the Incas, *curacas* paid no "taxes"; this need not be looked upon as simply an "aristocratic" or "oligarchic" privilege. Administrators could not work on the land *and* carry out their duties; and land work or its equivalent in the *mit'a* (see below) was the only way of paying taxes in the Tahuantinsuyu.

The four quarters of the Tahuantinsuyu (only three at this point in our narrative) were administrative units. They were: Collasuyu, the old highland homeland of the Incas in the southeast; Chinchaysuyu, whose conquest by Topa Inca Yupanqui we have described; Cuntisuyu in the southwest, also conquered by Topa Inca; and Antisuyu, of which we have yet to write. Each of these great provinces, or *suyus*, was governed by an Inca of the blood royal, but we should not use the word "viceroy," for he was nothing of the sort; he was, rather, a provincial civil administrator with limited powers. He was called *cucuricuc* ("he-who-sees-all") and these "all-seeing" officers were appointed by a council of four, called the Apucama, seated in Cuzco and presided over by the Sapa Inca. It seems that each member of the Apucama was responsible for a particular *suyu*, so that each *cucuricuc* had his opposite number in the capital.

Superimposed upon and penetrating the *ayllu* system was a decimal ordering of the people clearly designed to facilitate administration. We suggest that it derived from the fact that the *quipu*, the instrument of Inca administration discussed below, was a decimal device in its mathematical form. Within the *ayllu*, the population was divided into units of ten *purics* (and therefore ten whole families), over whom was set a nonhereditary headman, the *chunca-camayoc*. He was responsible to his immediate superior, who had "five tens" (fifty *purics*) in his charge. Then came the lowest rank of *curaca*, the *pacha-camayoc*, who was chief of one hundred *purics* and responsible directly to a superior *curaca* who had to answer for five hundred *purics* and their families, two or three thousand people.[10] The officer responsible for one thousand *purics* was called *maranga-camayoc*, he was answerable to an officer with five thousand *purics* in his care, and the latter to the *huno-camayoc* who administered ten thousand *purics* and their families. In the later imperial epochs all these *camayocs* were *curacas*, while the officers above them were invariably Incas. The nearest analogue that we can think of, in modern life, to this system is that of the hierarchy of managers and general managers in the great joint-stock banks of England.

The duties of the *curacas* were to see that land was distributed and redistributed to the *purics*; to see that *purics* did their tax-labor; to oversee cultivation, manuring, irrigation. They had to ensure that every man, woman and child did the work expected of them; and that they were, in return, properly housed, clad, fed and doctored, provided with seed and tools, and perhaps such permitted luxuries as the region afforded and as were not forbidden by the sumptuary laws. They also had to provide the men for the *mit'a*, the national service.

The *curacas* had a juridical as well as administrative function. The *chunca-camayoc* could himself deal with ordinary misdemeanors, but he had to refer serious cases of crime to the *pacha-camayoc* who might deal with the case in his function as a magistrate or pass it to a higher court, according to its gravity. The officials of Inca breeding were the district inspectors, provincial governors, high-court judges, and, in general, the professional managers of the state in all its attributes. There was no class of idle rich, although doubtless a highly placed man was not obliged to work himself into a decline. But even the provincial governors, or *cucuricucs*, each of whom was responsible for a region more than twice the size of New York State and for millions of people, were not "irresponsible." Just as the *chunca-camayoc* had to make a monthly return about his ten charges, so did the provincial governor have to report in full and at regular intervals to the capital. It seems that he could not even dismiss an incompetent officer without getting his decision confirmed by the Apucama. The Incas, with their remarkable, and perhaps unique, "instinct" for good government—an "instinct" bred in them, as we have seen, by the nature of the Peruvian soil and the conditions upon which that soil could be made to support a great community—were aware that their system entailed danger of abuses of power. Consequently, among the duties of a *cucuricuc* was that of receiving complaints of such abuses direct from the victim, investigating, and punishing the official concerned. In minor cases of this order, no appeal to Cuzco was allowed. But in a bad case, the *cucuricuc* could not deal with it summarily; he had to refer it to the Apucama or to the Sapa Inca. It was, in theory, open to any man, however humble, to denounce abuses of power or serious injustice directly to the Sapa Inca. We may compare this right to the feudal *haro*: the humblest Norman peasant was, apparently, entitled to appeal directly to his duke by uttering the *clameur*, "*A moi, mon prince! On me fait tort!*" But it is not clear how, in a great empire, in which a victim of official bungling, stupidity or dishonesty might be fifteen hundred miles from the capital, had no right to leave home and travel to Cuzco, and between whom and the source of justice was a huge hierarchy of doubtless hidebound and obstructive functionaries, was to make use of this theoretical right-in-law.

The *cucuricuc* was not expected or permitted to sit at ease in his provincial capital and wait for business. Carried in a litter, attended by numerous civil servants and by a military guard, ceremonially clad and his manners stylized to a degree which is reminiscent of a Chinese mandarin, he made continual progresses throughout his province, welcomed at each center of population with song and music whose heartiness no doubt varied with the condition of the singer's conscience. Thus he brought his decisions and his justice to the people who could not come to him.

It is fundamental to good government that the executive and the judiciary should be separate, although this may be less important in a land where there is no question of personal liberty, and where, indeed, the idea of personal liberty is inconceivable. Although in Inca Peru everyday legal business was carried out by executive officials, an attempt was made, in both civil and criminal matters, to separate the judiciary from the executive at the highest level. For there existed what we can only call a "Supreme Court," although that suggests a degree of formality and sophistication which may be misleading. It was composed of twelve Incas, six from the *hanan*, and six from the *hurin* half of the royal tribe. In theory, this court seems to have been the highest authority in the land; there was no appeal from its decisions. But in practice the Sapa Inca could, in cases serious enough to touch national policy, reverse their findings. He could do this, not in his capacity as chief of state or head official of the social hierarchy, but, in so far as it was separable from his other manifestations, in his capacity as god.

It is important to realize that the Incas and their allies seem to have accepted the idea of the divinity of the Sapa Inca quite literally. Of course, it is extremely difficult to judge, but it does seem that, whereas any sophisticated Roman of the upper classes knew perfectly well that the Caesar he publicly venerated as god was, in fact, a man and usually a scoundrel, the Inca gentry seem to have believed in the godhead of the Sapa Inca just as simple-mindedly as the common people. That the people should have believed the Sapa Inca to be god is not surprising; the people, in Peru as elsewhere, will believe anything. And when non-Inca peoples resisted the Sapa Inca, it was not because they were prepared to blaspheme the sun-god or ridicule the idea that he was incarnate in the imperial ruler, but rather because they themselves worshiped god in some other, older and, in their eyes, more respectable avatar. But the enormous advantage of having god as your chief of state is self-evident: the would-be rebel must overcome a psychological obstacle of immense difficulty when rebellion is also blasphemy. No man entered the presence of this god without taking off his shoes and bowing his back with a token burden. And the Sapa Incas were remarkable, even among American Indians, for the dignity of their bearing and the impassivity of their countenances.

WORKERS, WOMEN AND CHILDREN

The ordinary Tahuantinsuyuan-in-the-street, the *puric*, was, of course, an agricultural worker or rather a smallholder in his private capacity. But field and bench labor were not the only ways in which he could serve the state and so earn his living. There was also the institution of the *mit'a*, for which men were conscripted to perform military service or labor in public works. The *puric* was properly paid for such service by the community, who saw that his land was cultivated in his absence; and since the time they gave to his land came out of their public, not their private, time, it was the state which paid.

The kind of work a man or woman might do in the Tahuantinsuyu was determined by age and fitness. To this end, the people were divided into twelve age groups, as follows:

GROUP 1. Infants in arms dependent on their parents.

GROUP 2. Children up to one year of age, dependent on their parents.

(Why these were differentiated is not clear.)

GROUP 3. "Playing children," from one to nine. Those from one to five had nothing to do but play. But those between five and nine, of either sex, were required by the state to help their parents by performing such small tasks as were within their capacity; inspectors who paid domiciliary visits could see to it that they did so. No doubt, the children thus acquired a sense of responsibility and of their own importance as citizens at the most impressionable age. The Jesuit pedagogues could teach the Incas nothing about the value of starting young.

GROUP 4. Males, age nine to age sixteen. Various tasks were assigned to these boys, but their chief duty was as *llamamichecs*, shepherds of the llama herds. Incidentally, all llamas and kindred animals were state property. That is, smallholders (*purics*) were never involved in animal husbandry (though they may have owned some domestic animals), but only in agriculture and horticulture.[11]

GROUP 5. Males, sixteen to twenty.

GROUP 6. Males, twenty to twenty-five. Again, it is not clear why these groups were differentiated; it may have been for some administrative reason. The duties assigned to them seem to have been the same. They served as post-runners (the system of posts by relays was very highly organized); as *llama-michecs* set over the younger shepherds; and as pages to officers of rank on active service. The tasks assigned to these groups seem designed to enable them to see the world and get some education by doing so.

GROUP 7. Males, twenty-five to fifty. Backbone of the nation. These men were the *purics* already referred to, with all the duties and obligations and rights of fully adult, male citizens of the Tahuantinsuyu. A *puric* was obliged to be married, within his class. He usually did so between the ages of twenty-five and thirty. At twenty-five, he became head of a household. He had to cultivate his allotted piece of land and pay his taxes by laboring as a member of the collective on the lands of the state and of the church. He must, if conscripted, do national service in the *mit'a*. The younger *purics* might also be called upon to become *mitmac*, that is, members of a group of colonists planted in some remote part of the empire to cultivate and defend his land and to keep a sharp and hostile eye on the natives who were keeping a sharp and hostile eye on him. Although the provincials presumably learned their Inca manners and the Quechua tongue from colonies of other provincials longer subject to the Incas, ill feeling between colonists and natives was discreetly fostered by the government, which knew all about dividing and ruling. The *puric* could not refuse to become a *mitmac*; he was assured only that the land of his exile would be at the same altitude and have the same climate as his own. The Incas understood the importance to health of not sending lowlanders to the highlands, or vice versa.

Also drawn from this group of *puric-cuna* were the men who worked in the national placer workings for gold and the surface mining of copper and silver. But it is probable that this mining was done by men (in this age group) who were sentenced by the courts to this kind of labor as punishment for infraction of the law.

GROUP 8. Males, fifty to sixty. Men in this group were

semiretired. No citizen of the Tahuantinsuyu was ever fully retired, but men over fifty were exempt from civil and military duties and were not even required to cultivate land, their own or the public domain, or to do equivalent artisans' work. They were expected only to assist in cultivation at times when the pressure of work was great—that is, at harvest. They might be required to do work as body servants to a *curaca* or Inca. The *quipu-mayocs* were all from this group; they were clerks, storekeepers and statisticians. At their highest, they were librarians and historians, official poets and auditors, in which case they were called *amautas*.

GROUP 9. Males over sixty. Karsten, basing himself on Huamán Poma de Ayala, says that men between sixty and eighty were "called by a name which seems to indicate that their principal occupation was to eat and sleep." Yet not even these elders were to be quite idle. Those physically able did light work. For example, they twisted the ropes on which Inca bridge building depended. They looked after the poultry (ducks) and small livestock (guinea pigs) and they "guarded the houses of the poor." We do not know what this means; the only "poor" were the invalid, and perhaps the elders helped to look after them. Or they may have acted as watchmen when the men and women were at work in the fields. Of these elders Karsten says, "Their experience of life was valued and their advice was followed." Most important of all, the men (and women) over sixty acted as schoolteachers and they were allowed "to punish and reward children."

To put their case into modern terms, the old in the Inca state were pensioners but the problem of a large class of idle persons made to feel unwanted in their old age was avoided by making proper and suitable use of them while they remained hale. No man who could stand and move was allowed to be idle in Inca Peru; and no man was allowed to suffer want.

GROUPS 10 TO 12. The invalid of various kinds. The blind, dumb, deaf or otherwise "handicapped" persons were, it seems, required to marry within their own group, the blind marrying the blind, and so forth. It would be interesting to know whether this resulted in breeding invalid children. They, like others, were given house and land, and they were expected to work as best they could, so that they probably did not lose their self-respect. Begging was unknown until Spanish times. The state assisted invalid persons either directly, or by directing the neighbors to help them at the state's expense.

Formerly, this sort of social security, as described by Garcilaso and affirmed by that great Americanist Philip Means, was pooh-poohed by nearly all European historians as an idealization of the Inca social system by an Inca anxious to show his ancestors in a good light. But we now have the work of Poma de Ayala [12] to bear out Garcilaso.

> How far the Inca State went in taking care of the welfare of families and of private persons specially appears from the information given us by Garcilaso de la Vega on the authority of the Jesuit father Blas Valera, frequently quoted by him. Garcilaso's statements have sometimes been ascribed to that idealizing tendency which unfortunately in some respects appears in his book when he describes conditions in the Inca empire, but as regards the social legislation now in question they have been fully confirmed by the work of Huamán Poma Ayala and can therefore be regarded as corresponding to reality.[18]

What must have been a very tiresome regulation is reminiscent of a similar state of affairs under the Major Generals during the Commonwealth in England, and in Massachusetts during the rule of the saints in Cotton Mather's day: *purics* were required to have their houses open at all times to an inspector (called *llactacamayoc*) who paid domiciliary visits to see that families were not only working according to the law, but even eating, dressing and washing in the manner prescribed. Thus, dirty housewives were punished by being made to eat the dirt of their unclean houses in public; the husband had to eat some dirt too, "or to drink the dirty water in which face, hands and hair had been washed."

In the later imperial epoch sumptuary laws were strict: the *puric-cuna* might not wear gold, silver or gems, nor eat luxury foods. Topa Yupanqui's government went further: in each region of the empire, the inhabitants of a region were required to wear a distinctive dress and even to cut their hair in a distinctive fashion, so that a man's proper place could be seen at a glance.

Like the males, females were classed in age groups with specific obligations to the community and specific rights. Among the girls of the "playing children" group, the tasks to be performed included helping to mind the babies, helping to carry in water and fodder, weeding, and helping the women to make *chicha*, the maize beer which was the quotidian beverage of pre-Columbian Peru. Instruction in weaving began at five, and it seems also that girls destined for domestic service with the Incas were sent away for training at that tender age. Others went to be trained for service, either as servants or as actual nuns, in the *acclahuasi*—convents, where girls were dedicated to chastity and the service of the sun-god. They were called Virgins of the Sun, much as Christian nuns are called Brides of Christ.

Girls between nine and twelve had one special service highly appropriate to the tastes of most little girls: to them was entrusted the gathering of those flowers and herbs from which were extracted the dyes for textiles and the gathering of culinary, medicinal and ritual herbs. The Tahuantinsuyuan pharmacopoeia was rich and scientifically sound, its most notable items being, of course, coca and quinine. Herbs played and still play an important part in Andean religious rituals. Our authority, Huamán Poma de Ayala, has a rather prim note to the effect that these occupations kept lower-class girls out of that mischief which upper-class girls, apparently the only idle class in the nation, were apt to get into. The gilded youth in this communist state were, of course, the children of the ruling and heaven-born bureaucracy, the Incas, and perhaps those of the *curacas*. It seems that they were apt to be indulged for "they acquired bad habits and vices." As we know, the Soviet Union also has this problem.

Girls from twelve to eighteen worked at home, keeping house and making textiles. Some, too, were shepherdesses, taking care of the state's vast herds of llamas, which by the end of the fourteenth century had become so numerous that pasture was running short, a magnificent tribute to the *michec's* skill in herd management. Some of these girls went out to service in upper-class households;

Virgins of the Sun, as well as those girls who were not to remain virgins for long, were recruited from this group. The latter were the Chosen Women, picked for beauty, who composed what we may call the State Concubinate, that body of girls who made up the households of secondary wives in the royal and noble families and in the highest *curaca* families. It should be made clear that no shame whatever was attached to this service; on the contrary, it was regarded as an honor to be picked for it, especially to be picked for the Sapa Inca or one of the princes. These girls were not idle harem women. It was this class which produced the very finest textile, embroidery and feather work. And, as the greatest importance was attached to increasing the population by breeding from the best stock in the land, their service as mothers was highly honored. Prostitution was not unknown; the prostitutes were women who had lost their *ayllu* status and were consequently unclassed; their customers were minor officials, soldiers, artisans and priests whose duties kept them away from home. Prostitution was quite probably a capital offense even early in the Andean histories; it certainly became one under the empire.

It is notable that whereas a male in Tahuantinsuyu was not adult in law until he reached twenty-five, a woman was adult at eighteen, and she remained in the age group corresponding to that of the *puric* until she was thirty. Of course, the majority married and led the life which their mothers had led. The position of women in the male-dominated, civilized Inca empire (but not in the primitive South American communities) was almost as bad as in Mid-Victorian England. Women were permanent minors, if not chattels. They could not choose their husbands, but were allotted to them. A girl might be as young as fourteen, but more often she was over eighteen when she was married. In this working class, there was no question of romantic love, which is, of course, an aberration of highly sophisticated societies with privileged upper classes having time on their hands. The *puric-cuna* and their women were directed to marry within their group and probably were told which individual to marry, at that;[14] this seems to have worked as well as any other system of arranging for matrimony.

As in all societies which are adequately fed, clothed and housed

—that is, in which health and plenty prevail—more females than males were born every year.[16] We have already seen that surplus girls were provided for in the Inca system, although whether the provision was to their taste we cannot know. It probably was; the idea that there is a "human nature" common to our race all over the world is nonsense; men are conditioned to their fate by mores. The number of young women a great man might draw from the Concubinate for his own use was laid down by a law of Topa Yupanqui: the highest officers in the administrative, executive and judicial services, and the highest military officers, could have fifty women; a *huno-camayoc* could have thirty; and so on, down the scale. The Sapa Inca could have as many as he liked. Some of them were as self-indulgent as Solomon in this respect, and their children were exceedingly numerous.

Spinsters and widows between thirty and fifty comprised the next female age group. They made cloth and pottery, were domestic servants, and sometimes became concubines even at that advanced age. The last female group, that of women between fifty and eighty—there was no provision for people living over eighty—lived much the same kind of lives as the men between sixty and eighty, except that some remained pensioned concubines and trusted old confidential servants, in the upper-class households where they had spent their youth and beauty, and where the care and education of children was often left in their hands. It is pleasant to reflect that many a young Inca gentleman must, like an English gentleman in one of Evelyn Waugh's novels, have had happy memories of his old "nanny" and called on her in her quarters when he returned from a distant campaign or a turn of duty in the provinces. There would, however, have been a slight difference in their relationship, since it was the Peruvian youth's "nanny" who was expected to initiate him, by demonstration, into the facts of life, to be his first mistress, and to be subsequently supported by him when he set up house for himself.

As in the case of men, invalid women were grouped separately. But there was an important service which they could and were obliged to render the state. In suitable cases they were allotted to men of consequence, men from whom it was considered desirable to have as many children as possible and for whom the women might bear children if they could. Inca governments, with their complete control over food-crop expansion and their bursting warehouses, were not afraid of a high birth rate. But they did control the growth of population. The *quipu-mayocs*, with their clear picture of population trends, could advise on how many young women should be drawn into the ranks of the Chosen Women to reduce the number of potential mothers.

To sum up: The whole population of the Tahuantinsuyu worked, save perhaps young girls of Inca blood. The entire burden of taxation was born directly by males of the lower class between twenty-five and fifty, but indirectly by everyone, since the surplus product of the *puric-cuna's* toil depended very definitely upon the organization devised and maintained by the Inca and *curaca* classes, and upon the work done by women, children, the "handicapped," and the old-age pensioners. In the Tahuantinsuyu, we have a "prehistoric" agrarian communist-theocratic empire, of the kind which arose, for example, in Mesopotamia and in Baluchistan some four thousand years earlier; and arising in our own "historical" times in the Andes simply because, as we have seen, the beginning of urban civilization, the first essential step, the invention of farming, occurred just about four thousand years later in the far southwest than in the Near East. Had the Spaniards not wantonly destroyed the Tahuantinsuyu, we should, no doubt, have been able to study, in this bureaucracy produced like those of Akkad and Babylon and Mohenjo-Daro by the need to irrigate land and build terraces, that original collectivism from which mankind declined when the grave corruption of private ownership of land and the right to alienate it crept into the state and destroyed it.

THE QUIPU

It will be apparent that the Incas' social system was simple enough to operate on certain conditions—there must be an efficient civil service, a good system of posts, and a flexible instrument for record keeping. All of these were available. The civil service was

CORE ON·MAIOR·I·MENOR
HATVNCHASQVICHVRV
MVLLO·CHASQVI·CVRACA ~

The *Chasquis*, or relay runner. These runners carried messages and light articles, such as fresh fish for the Inca, at a great speed. The runner blows on his shell horn to warn his relief to be ready. He carries a *quipu*, a basket, and mace of office.

manned, as we have seen, by Incas at the top, by *curacas* under them, and by men past *puric* age. The postal system was excellent. It was operated by relays of runners over roads as well engineered, and sometimes better paved, than the Roman roads of Europe. The stages were about a mile apart over hundreds of miles, so that each runner, of a race so well-endowed with lungs (see page 75), could sprint his stint. All youths were trained as runners, and some writers say that post-runners were provided with a ration of coca to chew (the extract is cocaine), to improve their performance, although in the ordinary way the use of this drug was very strictly controlled. We may surmise that a post-stage would be run in five minutes, which means that official messages traveled at twelve miles an hour. In practice, a speed of six miles per hour from source to destination was maintained.

As there was also a system of visual signaling by smoke, the Inca administration had its telegraph—probably no less efficient than the semaphore system of early-nineteenth-century France which plays so important a part in Stendhal's *Lucien Leuwen*. We come, then, to that instrument of recording, that arithmetical, statistical, communications and records device on which this whole social system was supported, the *quipu*; and its servants, the *quipu-mayocs*.

Among the recorded sayings of the great Sapa Inca Pachacuti, in whose reign we still are in our narrative, we find this:

He who attempts to count the stars, not even knowing how to count the knots and marks of the *quipus*, should be held in derision.

Such counting, was, in short, the equivalent of literacy and it was not confined to specialists but was learned by young men of the upper class in general. It was absolutely essential to the proper working of the state. For, as Professor Baudin tells us,

La statistique est la base de tout système socialiste; elle doit être irréprochable; le calcul de l'homme se substitue au jeu de l'offre et de la demande, l'adaptation de production à la consommation est realisé par voie d'autorité au lieu de s'effectuer naturellement par le délicat mécanisme des prix.

As far as we know, no people of the Tahuantinsuyu ever had an alphabetic or ideographic system of writing. There are some dubious indications that an ideographic system may have begun to develop out of picture writing and out of the device of recording past events of importance by depicting them. There are also one or two obscure and still unexplained references (for instance, at the deathbed of the Sapa Inca Huayna Capac) to what seem to have been "documents"—messages or testaments "written" on wooden battens. Our own explanation of these, however, is that the principle behind the *quipu* and the native "abacus" could equally well be applied by making marks on wood or any other surface. We can dismiss the whole subject of letters in the Inca state with a quotation from J. Alden Mason's *Ancient Civilizations of Peru:*

. . . many Moche pottery vessels picture runners carrying bags, together with kidney-shaped objects, generally identified as beans, that are painted with lines, dots and similar devices. Other scenes depict persons apparently examining these objects. Larco Hoyle claims that these are ideographic symbols, denoting standardised concepts; he also believes that they show close analogies with Maya glyphs. The evidence is purely archeological without historical verification, and conservative Peruvianists, while intrigued at the interesting suggestion, are not yet convinced of its proof.

The *quipu* consisted of a cord to which were tied other lesser cords, of diverse colors and in which were tied knots in significant groups and at significant intervals. To these knots might be tied a third class of still smaller cords or threads, which, in their turn, bore knots. In theory, obviously, there need be no end to this, each lesser thread serving as a subordinate or modifying clause to the one above it in the hierarchy of cords. Some writers have claimed that the *quipu* was a mnemonic device, others that it was a sort of computer, still others that it was a system of numerical notation. To us it seems quite clear that it was all these things and that it may have been more also. The factor left quite out of account by all writers on this subject—perhaps because scholars and desk-

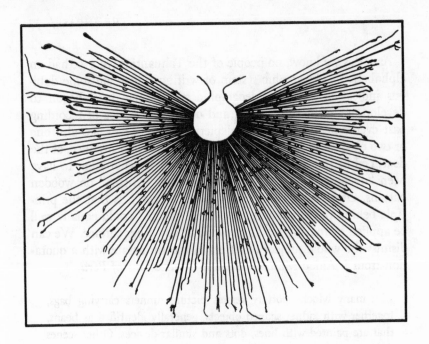

The *quipu*. The smaller illustration (on facing page) shows a *quipu* taken from a grave in which it had been buried. The different colors, thicknesses of string, kinds of knots, placing of knots and tufts, all had significance. This *quipu* can no longer be read, but to demonstrate the possible method of use we have invented the following analysis, reading from right to left.

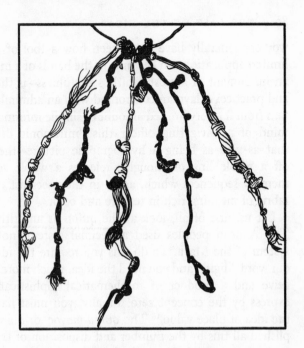

MAIN CORD, yellow-brown. First knot, rank. Six and one knots, age 61. Tufted knot, province.

NO. 1 BRANCH CORD, rose-purple. Of Inca stock (from the color); of the 4th *ayllu* (loop). Two wives and one concubine. One legitimate child and eleven illegitimate.

NO. 2 CORD, green. Probably crops; i.e., his economic consequence in terms of tax value per annum.

NO. 3 CORD, rose-purple and with vicuña tufts. Degree of responsibility for state herds and land.

NO. 4 CORD, red. Red for war. The knots could stand for number of enemies killed, or of wounds received, or both.

NO. 5 CORD. One, one and five knots; 115, say, mourners at his funeral.

workers generally have never seen how a tool of apparently very limited application can become, in the hands of a master craftsman, an instrument of almost limitless usefulness—is the factor of skill and practice. A layman confronted with an admiralty chart can obtain from it a very limited amount of simple information; but in the mind of a navigating officer this "mnemonic device"—for it is that as well as being a hydrographic picture—the chart touches off a whole line of thought, releases a whole second series of memory sequences which, again in the specialist's mind, create a fabric of meaning rich in texture and color.

Let us, first of all, look at the *quipu* as an arithmetical device. The Andean peoples used a decimal system, not the vigesimal system of the Maya. To do this you require the idea expressed by our word "digit"; and you need the idea, much more difficult to conceive and a product of mathematical sophistication, which we express by the concept zero. Finally, you must have thought out the idea of place value.[16] The *quipu-mayoc*, or *quipu* clerk, accomplished all this by the number and disposition of the knots he tied in the main cord, in its pendant cords and in their pendant threads. It will be clear that there is no limit to the size of the figure which can be dealt with in this manner. Thus, quantity was indicated by knots and spaces correctly placed; quality by the color of the cords and threads. The digits 1 to 9 were indicated by knots from a single one to nine tied all together to make a long knot nine loops long. The zero was indicated by a gap.

Most of the *quipu-mayoc*'s work required only simple addition. Consider the task of the clerks whose duty it was to know the maize harvest for the year, say, 1500. Each *ayllu* made a return by means of a simple *quipu* or possibly with the beans which Larco Hoyle believes to have been ideographic. This return went to the officer in charge of a hundred, the "civil centurion," as it were. He compiled *his* return to the officer above him, and so on, until the statistics department at Cuzco received four provincial returns and added them up. (As we shall show below, he did not do this in his head; he had a very ingenious adding machine.) In the *quipu* files for 1500 the main heads would be indicated by the color of the principal cord, say, white for crops, green for population, mauve for births, et cetera. The white cord would have pendant cords for each kind of crop, say, yellow for maize, red for coca, pink for potatoes, et cetera. All the clerk had to do, then, was to tie in the yellow cord the knots requisite to express the total of all four provincial returns for maize.

All that is elementary; but we should like to make a suggestion which, so far as we know, has never yet been discussed. It would be possible and even easy to make a *quipu* which would serve as a logarithmic table of a very simple kind, that is, for multiplying round tens. In view of the fact that no *quipu* has been found with an apparent value in excess of ten thousand recorded, and of the fact that the administration of possibly sixteen million people and of armies numbered in tens of thousands must have entailed working in millions, it is at least possible that the *quipu* was used logarithmically. The logarithmic concept to the base ten is no more sophisticated than the concept zero. And, as we shall see, in default of the Hindu-Arabic numerals or the Latin digits, and of pencil and paper, the *quipu-mayoc* had a counting device enabling him to set down what was passing in his mind and not to rely solely on mental arithmetic.

As to the use of the *quipu* for the recording of history—and we have no doubt whatsoever that it was so used, and very effectively— here is a very much simplified and slightly modified example which we have borrowed from A. de la Calancha's *Corónica moralizada*:

Problem: The *amauta*, a learned man, not a clerk, is required to record that before the time of Manco Capac there were neither king, nor chief, nor cult nor religion, nor administration; that in the fourth year of his reign Manco Capac conquered ten provinces with the loss of five hundred men and inflicting casualties of two thousand on the enemy; that from one province he took booty equal to 1,000 gold ingots, and from another booty of 3,000 silver ingots; and that he celebrated a *Te Deum* to the sun-god.

Method: The *amauta* takes a black cord, black being the color for time. He takes a number of neutral-colored lesser cords and in all of them ties numerous small knots. He ties these cords to the

DEPOCITODELINGA
COLL CA

topa ynga
yupanqui.

asministrador
suyo yoc
apo poma chaua

depocitos del ynga

como

The storerooms of the Inca Topa Yupanqui. The picture shows the administrator giving an account of the stores to the Inca by means of his *quipu*.

"time" cord, from one end to near the middle, let us say the right-hand half. Halfway along the black cord he ties a large knot with a crimson thread passing through it. Crimson stands for "king."

Now we read back to this point: The people [many small colorless knots] before [right of the big knot in "time" cord] the first Inca [crimson thread] and during a very long time [the neutral cords are numerous] had no king [no crimson thread right of the big knot in time] no chief [no violet thread right of the big knot in time] no religion [no blue thread, blue for Heaven, right of the big knot] no administrative subdivisions [none of the threads or cords right of the knot show provincial or subprovincial colors].

So much for the introduction. The amauta now ties four small knots in the crimson thread: we are dealing with events in the Inca's fourth year of power. Left of the big knot in the black main cord he ties a gray thread bearing ten knots: ten provinces conquered. The color for casualties being, say, green, he next ties green threads to each knot in the gray cords, and in each green thread he ties knots for numbers of casualties, these threads indicating the province or origin of the numbers killed. Next, for the Inca army: a red thread tied to the main cord; in it, knots stating number of casualties; tied to them, threads indicating by color the provinces from which the casualties came, that is, their regiment. Next, the booty: a yellow thread (yellow for gold) tied to the knot for the province from which it was taken, bears knots indicating a thousand units (of gold); a white thread (white for silver) records the silver captured, and the knot it is tied to tells us where it was taken. A blue thread (blue for Heaven) tied to the main cord indicates a religious ceremony—in this context, a Te Deum.

Obviously, the amauta or quipu-mayoc reading a quipu had first to know the context or general heading. That was the main clue. Even so, it will be clear that the quipu can only have been effective in the hands of skilled and experienced clerks, and that what it amounted to was a means of making efficient use of that most perfect and compact of all recording devices, the human mind, in which the colored cords and the knots served to touch off the required series of chains of memory. Although there is only a limited number of colors, and although in practice only a limited number of knots could be used or the thing would have become unwieldy, yet since the meaning of the colors, the knot numbers, and the knot places would depend on the context, and that context could be indicated either by some distinguishing mark on the main cord or by the place of the *quipu* in the files, the combinations and permutations of colors and knots were, in practice, infinite. In so far as the *quipu* was used to calculate and to record statistics, its use is obvious. In so far as it was used to record not only numbers but historical events, it can, we think, best be compared to our system of musical notation. For what a musical composer sets down is quantities; it is the executant who, reading the score, supplies the quality, though it is inherent in the quantities, their arrangement, their relationship to each other. Now, one musician may give an interpretation of Bach's *Toccata and Fugue* different from that given by another musician, although the basic values are the same in both cases; so, too, one *amauta* might give, say, a quality to the character of Manco Capac different from that given by another, while both would give the same vital statistics concerning him if both were reading the same *quipu* about his reign.

If we place the score of a concerto before a skilled pianist, we may well be amazed at what he makes of it. Thus, too, the Spanish observers were very often amazed at what a *quipu-mayoc* or an *amauta*, *quipu* in hand, could tell them about the past. The use of social and economic statistics is a commonplace to us, but it has become so only in the last century. The Emperor Charles V would not have had, and could not have discovered from anyone in his realms, the number of his populations, the annual weight and worth of his harvests, or any other elementary social statistics. But the Sapa Inca Huayna Capac could, at a few hours' notice, discover exactly how many people he governed, how many of them were males reaching the age of virility that year, how many surplus females, what volume of all crops had been produced that season and where, what stores he had available in warehouses, how many casualties his armies had suffered in the last campaign and how many of the enemy had been killed. It is no wonder that Inca campaigns were constantly successful. And it is no wonder that the ignorant and superstitious Spanish clergy were amazed at what the native could recall with his *quipu*. But not all the clergy by any means were against the *quipu*. And while the lower ranks came to believe that it was an instrument of magic and the *amautas* were sorcerers, the higher clergy saw the benefits of knowing the population and resources of the country. It must have immediately struck the more intelligent priests that the *quipu* was similar to the rosary and could be used in the same way.

The worthy priest Morúa tells how he met an old *curaca* at Capachica who produced a *quipu* and by its aid repeated to him the whole Christian calendar with all its feasts and vigils; he had made it years before while listening to a friar. The Church encouraged the natives to record their sins on the *quipu* and bring it with them to confession—as they would in any case be inclined to do, since they may have used it for their confessions to the Sun priests and certainly used it for their reports to their decurions or centurions. Morúa also explains why we have so few *quipus* now; he says that even in his day few survived because, as the Spaniards could not read them, no care was taken of the "libraries," and the *quipus* were lost. It is also likely, we believe, that the people of Tahuantinsuyu, being oppressed beyond belief by their conquerors, would destroy many of the *quipus* in the belief that if they fell into Spanish hands they would constitute yet another rod for Indian backs. To destroy essential records in the face of attack is standard practice, after all. Whatever the cause of these losses, the conquered and their conquerors between them destroyed what must have been the most perfect record of a people's statistical history ever kept until modern times. Markham, followed by other Americanists, says:

> There must, however, have been interpreters of the *quipus* [other than the ordinary statistics clerks], those who, with knowledge derived from other sources, could use the knots as reminders and suggesters by which an event could be kept in memory with more accuracy. These were the *amautas* or learned men and councillors.

For them the *quipus* formed a system of reminders giving accuracy to knowledge derived from other methods of recording events and history and traditions.[17]

In addition to the *quipus* there was a kind of abacus which the Inca clerks, accountants and astronomers used not only as a calculating machine but in lieu of paper and pencil, for although they had drawing materials they had no system of numerical notation. This consisted of a box made of wood or stone, with two or three layers divided into numerous compartments, all rectangular but of different dimensions. Beans or pebbles of colors to which various meanings were attached were placed in these compartments; the value to be accorded to a bean or pebble depended on the compartment in which it was placed. Thus, as with the *quipu*, its *place* conveyed its value, its *color* conveyed its quality. Some of these devices seem to have been quite elaborate and it is possible that the Incas borrowed the idea from the Canari of Ecuador. Here is a very simplified example to demonstrate how the thing was used. A box has three compartments whose dimensions are equal to x, $2x$ and $3x$, respectively. A clerk sees that there are three green beans in compartment $3x$; five green beans in compartment $2x$; and two green beans in compartment x. The number of units recorded is 3,520, where $x = 10$, $2x = 100$ and $3x = 1,000$. Units of what? The beans are green which is, say, the color for "potatoes." Answer: 3,520 bushels of potatoes.

These, then, were the physical devices of Inca administration, their ledgers, their computers, their files. And, as we have said, the information calculated and recorded by their means was carried constantly to Cuzco by fast post-runners over a system of good roads. At the time of the Spanish invasion the principal highland road went from north of Quito, south through Caxamarca, Cuzco and other cities, to fork at Titicaca, one branch going northeast round the lake into what is now northwestern Argentina, and the other down to the Chilean coast to link up with the lowland system, an improved and extended version of the old coastal states roads, joined from north to south. Where necessary, tunnels were driven through hills, and bridges, capable of bearing an army on the march or a herd of llamas being driven to new pasture or to shearing, were thrown across rivers and gorges. Stone towers were raised on opposite banks of a river or a gorge; between them were slung five massive cables of maguey fiber, and the three lower cables were then boarded over. The other two served as rails. Some of these bridges, such as the great Apurimac example, were over seventy yards long and lasted, with frequent cable renewal, well into the nineteenth century.

Some of the irrigation canals were remarkable works of engineering. They were lined with stone, carried water as much as five hundred miles, and in important cases, were covered with flat stones provided with inspection man-holes at intervals. A full description of them is to be found in Markham, who inspected many of them personally late in the nineteenth century.

Although they had no writing, the people of the Inca empire had a spoken literature. We shall say nothing of the drama *Ollontay*, which, although for many years accepted as a genuine Quechua play, has been exposed as a Spanish forgery. However, the Inca's people were fond of the drama and had a great aptitude for it, and it is probable that plays, mostly traditional and some religious, meant a good deal in their lives. The Jesuits took advantage of this to make the Indians familiar with the Christian religion, composing comedies for the Indians to act. It is said that the Indian lads as actors repeated the dialogue with so much grace, feeling and correct action that they gave universal satisfaction to their Spanish audiences. These people also had a rich treasury of poetry, and Father Blas Valera goes so far as to say that they had a means of recording it with the *quipus*. Possibly the *quipus* were used to remind the reciter of what he had, in fact, committed to memory.

LAWS AND GODS

Something should now be said about criminal law in imperial Inca times. The sources of our information are the Spanish chroniclers and, more fully, the illustrated manuscript of the Inca historian Huamán Poma Ayala. A trial was conducted as follows: The judge summoned accused and witnesses before him. The witnesses formed a circle round the accused, all being seated on the ground. Each witness told the court what he had seen the accused say or do. Only then, when he knew the strength or weakness of the case against him, was the accused required to plead. If he pleaded guilty, judgment was given and sentence passed without further ado. If he pleaded not guilty and the case made out by the witnesses failed to satisfy the court, then the case was adjourned for the accused's *huno-camayoc* to make further inquiries. Persons of good character who stood accused were not tortured to extract a confession. An accused with a "police record" could be tortured. If neither the evidence nor the torture could make an accused confess, he had to be acquitted, but with this proviso: that if subsequently he was convicted of any crime whatsoever, capital or not, the sentence would be death. In pre-Inca and early Inca times the death penalty was rare; it became much more common in late Inca times. This is quite a normal evolution; thus, the Anglo-Saxons had no death penalty, but the eighteenth-century English imposed hanging as punishment for petty larceny and, in practice, poverty.

Both the accused and the witnesses in court were free to make their statements on oath or not, as they wished. This was because the oath was a religious act involving the divine Sapa Inca and perjury entailed blasphemy. The Tahuantinsuyuan's attitude to the oath was very respectful.[18] "Vain swearing," taking the names of sun, moon, gods or *huaccas* in vain, was not only sinful, but also illegal. To this list Topa Yupanqui was to add taking the names of the Sapa Inca or the *qoya* in vain. This Sapa Inca likewise decreed that women were incompetent to bear witness, on the grounds that they are by nature "deceitful, mendacious and fainthearted." In this, as in other respects, Topa Yupanqui was a good Mid-Victorian, and he proved it by further decreeing that the "poor" could not bear witness in court, on the admirable grounds that the poor man was too easy to bribe.*

* This decree is obscure, for who were the "poor"? It may arise from a Spanish misunderstanding. Conceivably, after this decree only men of Inca blood could bear witness, but it seems very improbable.

Punishment included work in the mines and imprisonment. One prison, the cave Sancay, was full of wild animals and poisonous reptiles and was used for punishing treason. If the convict survived two days in this establishment, however, he was pardoned and released as being obviously under divine protection.

There was no pretense of equality before the law, whereas in Britain and the United States, as we know, justice, like the Ritz, is open to all. We quote, without comment, from Cobo:[19]

Justice was not equal and common to all; for although it was considered important that any offense and crime should be denounced, other kinds of punishment were given to the high-born and rich than those given to the humble and poor. The practice originated in the belief that to an Inca of royal blood a mere public reprimand was by far a greater punishment than death was to a plebeian. The superior position they occupied as Children of the Sun . . . had the effect that they held his laws all the more sacred, so that punishment was dependent upon the social position of the persons who violated these laws. Crimes which, when common people were in question, were punished with death, were, when persons of the noble Inca family were involved, only punished with public reprehension, and this chastisement was regarded as so shameful that it very seldom happened that a man of noble birth was punished.

Murder and robbery with violence were capital crimes. Killing by witchcraft was treated as murder and of the most heinous kind; a condemned witch or wizard was beaten to death and his body was left to be eaten by the condors. Manslaughter, killing in a quarrel, for example, was treated with enlightenment: a killer who could show that he had been provoked and had not sought the quarrel, was punished very mildly; but if the provoked man was killed, his provoker was exiled at the Sapa Inca's pleasure to work in the coca plantations of Antisuyu, where the climate was hot, humid and unwholesome. A civil official who killed a disobedient subordinate was punished by having a heavy stone dropped onto his back from a height of three feet, which might or might not kill him. This punishment was called *hiwaya* and was used in the case of some other serious crimes. A second offense of the same kind was punished by death; Inca law was, in general, stern to abuse of power.

Theft was never a capital offense. The convicted thief was required to compensate the victim, a notion familiar in Anglo-Saxon law but still a novelty to us, and was thereafter exiled to the coca plantations at the Sapa Inca's pleasure; that is, he could appeal for permission to return after some time. Even in the case of robbery with violence, the punishment for a first offense was a severe flogging, and death was the penalty only for a subsequent offense. But as prosperity made both state property and private chattels of increasing social importance, the laws against theft became less liberal, although they were never as savage as they became in Europe. The Sapa Inca Topa Yupanqui also made a number of new crimes capital for a second offense, notably, destroying bridges, removing boundary stones, and perjury. First offenders were flogged.

Killing an adulterous wife was not a capital offense; killing an adulterous husband was. The social values here revealed are identical with the European ones. For rape, first offenders got the *hiwaya,* and death for any subsequent offense. But if the woman was an Inca, then death was the punishment even for a first offense. Adultery was a crime; if the parties were of the same caste, the punishment was flogging for both. If the woman was an Inca and the man a *puric,* then both were put to death. Homosexuality was held in such horror and punished with such ferocity that we suspect crypto-homosexuals to have been as common in the Tahuantinsuyu among the top people as in other places where the dominant social values are masculine. When General Auqui Titu reported to the Sapa Inca Capac Yupanqui on one of his conquests, he mentioned in his report that some of the men of the coastal valley in question were sodomites, ". . . not in all the valleys but one here and one there, nor was it the habit of all the inhabitants but only of certain persons who practiced it in private." The Sapa Inca ordered that the sodomites be sought out with great diligence, and be publicly burned alive; that their houses should be burned, their trees uprooted, and their crops destroyed. That there might be no memory whatsoever of a thing so abominable, a law was issued that "if hereafter anyone should fall into this habit, the whole of his village should be destroyed for one man's crime, and all the inhabitants burned." The histories and chronicles contain no reference to any such holocaust, either because it had been deliberately forgotten or because the punishment was never inflicted, laws of this kind being as futile in Tahuantinsuyu as anywhere else.

Rebellion and treason were capital crimes and the methods of punishment barbarously cruel. After slow and agonizing death, the rebel's or the traitor's bones were made into musical instruments, a curious form of post-mortem mortification.

The law required that a person returning a lost chattel to its owner be rewarded. No debt could be required of a man's heirs after his death. (Debts and legacies consisted of personal chattels —not, of course, either real estate or money, neither of which existed.) Useful plants and animals had long been protected by law; under Topa Yupanqui the laws became stern. A man who wantonly cut down fruit trees or valuable timber trees could be condemned to death, an admirably motivated enactment, although the punishment might now be considered excessive. The wastage of food was illegal except by the Sapa Inca for whom it was obligatory, a ritualization of conspicuous consumption. Moreover, an interesting sidelight on Inca science, the "peeling" of maize was illegal and was sharply punished; the whole grain must be eaten. How had the Tahuantinsuyuan medical faculty discovered that "extracted" flour is less nourishing? We cannot know, but their advances in surgery were equally surprising, especially when we consider that their scalpels were probably of stone and at best of bronze.

The Incas had their game laws; only predatory beasts could be killed by anyone. Hunting of edible game was strictly forbidden except at the great annual festival drives, in which all shared, and in which thousands of llamas, guanacos and small game animals were slaughtered, partly to thin the excessive herds, partly, as it seems to us, to provide a former hunting people with a catharsis. At these festivals the people received their share of the meat.

It is fair to say that on the whole the laws were more liberal and punishments were less savage than those in force in Europe at the same epoch. And, as far as we can judge, serious crime in the empire was rare.

In pre-Inca Peru, and during the imperial Inca period, as in medieval Europe, the law had religious sanction to such a degree that it is not always easy to distinguish crime from sin. Religion in the Tahuantinsuyu was neither more nor less monotheistic than in sixteenth-century Spain. The Hispanicized version of the name of God among the highlanders was Viracocha. Among the principal coastal people His name was Pachacamac, and elsewhere He was called by still other names. God, by whatever name He was known, was remote, unapproachable and almighty. The concept of God under the name Pachacamac was a high and noble one. On the surface, Pachacamac means simply "Creator of the Earth"—*pacha*, "earth"; *camani*, "I create." But upon analysis, this name expresses a much subtler and more imaginative idea and feeling. The verb *cama* means to animate, whence also, in Quechua, *cama*, the soul. Thus, according to Garcilaso, Pachacamac is "He who does to the universe what the soul does to the body." This chronicler— who is far too readily dismissed by every Americanist save the greatest, Philip Means, as unreliable—while loudly and rather comically claiming that he is a good Catholic Indian, has several pages of close and convincing analysis of the Catholic clergy's failure to understand the Indian's notion of God, owing to their failure really to understand Quechua in all its rich subtlety.

According to the same chronicler and also to such respectable authorities as López de Gómara and Agustín de Zárate, the people of Tahuantinsuyu believed in life after death and in the resurrection of the body. They had, as we have seen, their Flood legend. They also had a creation myth, or perhaps several.

. . . in Tiahuanaco the Creator began to raise up the people and nations that are in that region, making one of each nation in clay, and painting the dresses that each one was to wear. Those that were to wear their hair, with hair; and those that were to be shorn, with hair cut. And to each nation was given the language that was to be spoken, and the songs to be sung, and the seeds and the food they were to sow. When the Creator of all things had finished painting and making the said figures of clay, he gave life and soul to each one, as well men as women. . . .[20]

Sun worship, with its ancillary of moon worship, the moon being conceived of as the Sister-Bride of the Sun, was the particular religion of the Incas and perhaps of other Quechua-speaking tribes. When they conquered the whole Andean world, they could not avoid imposing this religion on all the peoples of their empire, if only because their authority was based on their direct descent from the Sun, who was used by the great Creator, or Animator, to breed men, or rather to breed Incas. But the Incas were not bigots, and it is probable that they recognized the moral and spiritual superiority of the conquered religions. Some sort of compromise was contrived, so effective that at least one Spanish cleric claimed that the Indians had a Trinity of God the Father, God the Sun and God the Moon. As far as we have been able to make out, the religion of the Sun stood to the worship of Viracocha-Pachacamac as Shinto stands to Buddhism in Japan, or even as the rather vague "religion of Numa," the official religion of the Roman empire, stood to the Mithras cult and other high spiritual Oriental religions.

More approachable than Pachamacac were the lesser gods, who played the same part as saints in the Roman Catholic religion. These included Earth, Sea, and certain stars, notably Venus. The temples of Tahuantinsuyu housed images of such gods just as the Spanish churches housed images of the saints and the Virgin Mary and of Christ crucified. And these, again as in Christian Europe, were taken out and carried in procession on festival days. Numerous diverse objects were held sacred; these were the *huaccas*. They included rocks, springs, caves, tombs and mummified bodies, notably those of Sapa Incas. These mummies too were paraded on festival days. This veneration of *huaccas* can best be compared to Christian relicolatry and iconolatry.

Temples were cared for by priests. There was a hierarchy, and the pontiff was a close relative of the ruling Sapa Inca. A person who had done evil purged himself by confession of "sins of word and deed" to a priest. Molina says that this confession was public, except in cases of serious crime. The sinner was given a penance to do and was required to purify himself by washing in running water. Divination was practiced, oracles were consulted and animals were sacrificed. On very serious occasions, such as sickness of the Sapa Inca, whose life and health were the life and health of the whole people and the whole empire, there might be a human sacrifice. We say "might be," as this is by no means certain. It is certain that human sacrifice was practiced in pre-Inca times. Garcilaso de la Vega says that the Incas suppressed it very strictly, and he quotes in support of this view that of Cieza de León, whose account of the country and its customs was written from firsthand knowledge in the course of a 3,600-mile journey of investigation, between the years 1541 and 1550. Both of these authorities are supported in their opinion by Blas Valera, the Jesuit historian and translator of Quechua. Finally, we find that another priest, Valverde, Bishop of Cuzco, who was notorious for his anti-Indio, anti-Inca fanaticism, holds that there was no human sacrifice among the Incas' people. Modern historians hold that there was, however, and in their support they have Molina, who says that children were sacrificed on certain festival occasions; and notably during the ceremony called *Capac-cocha* established by Pachacuti, in which case it was a late innovation. They are also supported by Acosta, but since it is never possible to tell when this chronicler is writing of Incaic and when of pre-Incaic times, and since he is contemptuously dismissed as a "credulous Jesuit" by so great a Peruvianist as Markham, it is not clear that his support is worth much. Finally, archaeology supports the view that human sacrifice was practiced occasionally and that the victims were Virgins of the Sun. Young women ceremonially dressed and apparently in perfect health at the time of death, have been disinterred. We are not convinced that sacrifice is the only possible explanation of this. What we do know is that if there was some human sacrifice in the religion of pre-Columbian Peru it pales into insignificance beside the holocausts of victims sacrificed by the Spanish Roman Catholics in their atrocious autos-da-fé.

In order that the quality and sophistication of religious feeling in the Tahuantinsuyu may be judged by the reader, we quote two prayers recorded among others by Molina with the suggestion that they would not be out of place in an Anglican service:

O Creator! O conquering Viracocha! Ever present Viracocha! Thou who art in the ends of the earth without equal! Thou who gavest life and valor to men, saying, Let this be a man! and to women, saying, Let this be a woman! Thou who madest them and gave them being! Watch over them that they may live in health and peace. Thou who art in the high heavens and among the clouds of the tempest, grant this with long life, and accept this sacrifice, O Creator.

Here, for the benefit of those curious to know what sixteenth-century Quechua sounded like, is the same prayer in the original tongue:

Aticsi Uiracochan caylla Uiracochan tocapu acnupu Uiracochan camac churac carica chuyuarmicachun nispallutac rurac camascay quichuras cauqyicasilla quispilla causamus ay maypincanqui ahuapichu ucupichu llantupichu uyarihua ayrihuay ynihuay ymay Pachacamac cansachihuay marcallihuay attollihuay caycoscay tarichacquihuay may picaspapas Uiracochaya.

Note the relative brevity of this richly inflected language. It has the syntactical flexibility and the sonority of Greek.

In concluding this chapter, we should like to say something about the law and customs relating to marriage among the Inca caste. The law touching marriage between kinsfolk was much the same as our own: a man might not marry his aunt, niece or first cousin; nor, of course, his sister. This law was not clearly enacted until the reign of Topa Yupanqui, but it seems to us that this and many other laws alleged to have been made by that Sapa Inca were really only codified by his administration. He seems to have made a codification which gave legal standing to ancient customs with the force of law. Thus, whereas Pachacuti, Topa and Huayna Capac are known to have married their sisters, the law in this matter only became such in Topa Yupanqui's time, but the custom, as we have seen, was much older.

Among the Inca caste a man chose his bride, but he did not get her as a matter of course. Her father being the sun, the suitor went to the temple and prayed for her hand. And he offered his heavenly father-in-law-to-be a trousseau of clothes made of the finest cloth, a simple golden pin or brooch called *tupu*, and other articles of dress which the bride would become mistress of, as of his own person. If the suitor received notice that he was accepted, he went to the bride's parents' house for a banquet and drinking session. Acceptance of the young man was decided not by the girl (who may, however, have been consulted), nor by her father (who doubtless, however, knew how to make his wishes known), but by the girl's mother; Father Martin de Morúa is emphatic on this point. The marriage ceremony consisted in feasting, including heavy drinking and some dancing, for several weeks, and in the young people publicly joining hands. But first both bride and groom had to go to confession so as to be in a state of grace; and one or several *pillcu llama*, red llamas, were sacrificed by a priest.

Marriage, as a rule, was monogamous, and even among the highest in the land there was only one legal wife with full rights as such. But concubinage was general and the Sapa Inca would present desirable girls from among the annual collection of Chosen Women from the provinces to favored men of consequence. Men of all classes went into one year's official mourning (black cloak) for a deceased wife and could not remarry during that term. Bernabé Cobo tells us that the priests were accustomed to represent the loss of a wife as punishment for a man's sins, from which we may deduce that wives were valued and perhaps loved. It seems that widows were not allowed to remarry; however, they inherited their deceased husband's holding and civil rights, so that in the Tahuantinsuyu (as in Britain until fifty years ago) a woman could become a citizen and a real adult person in the eyes of the law only by being widowed.

At least from Topa Yupanqui's time, wives and concubines received some protection from the law against ill-treatment at a husband's hands. Moreover, before the birth of a child, the husband as well as the wife had to fast, abstaining from meat. The mother-to-be went to confession and she prayed for an easy delivery.

The institutions of ancient Inca Peru were remote from our own. The people of the Tahuantinsuyu may, therefore, seem very strange in their manners and customs. Yet were they so very different from ourselves? Here, from their own spoken literature, is a short story:

A young *puric* was called up to do his *mit'a* service and having been assigned to military duties went to fight in the wars. His young wife, left with her son, was very sad. As if to console her a white butterfly entered the house every day, so consistently that her little son asked her, "Mother, what is this butterfly?" His mother answered him idly, "It is my lover." The day came when the young farmer, having completed his term of service, returned to the house. His wife was at work in the fields but the boy was there and his father asked him if they had missed him and been sad. The child told his father how they had spent their time and he added, "And every day mother's lover came to see her." The young husband was passionately angry so that when his wife returned and entered the house, having his weapons still about him, he killed her. Later in the day as father and son sat sadly together, the white butterfly paid its daily visit to the house. "Look, father," cried the child, "here is mother's lover come to see her!"

4

ATAHUALPA'S FATHER

BY THE TIME that prince Topa Yupanqui had conquered the coastal states and incorporated them into the empire, his father the Sapa Inca Pachacuti had been reigning for thirty-three years and was, according to Sarmiento de Gamboa, one hundred and twenty-five years of age. He was probably in his eighties. At all events, he evidently felt that the time had come to retire; when his son returned to Cuzco in triumph in the year 1471, the old Sapa Inca abdicated in Topa's favor to spend his few remaining years in contemplation. Thus Topa Yupanqui was crowned with the *borla* during his father's lifetime. And when, a few years later, the old man knew that his time to die had come, he called his councilors of state and his sons about him and addressed them. (The English is Sir Clements Markham's.) Turning to Topa, he said, "My son, you know how many great nations I leave to you, and you know what labor they have cost me. Mind that you are the man to keep and augment them."

He made his other sons dig furrows with the *taclla*, and he gave them weapons, in token that they were to serve and fight for their sovereign. He turned again to Topa and said, "Care for them, and they will serve you."

The dying man gave instructions relative to his obsequies and ordered that his mummy was to live in the palace called Pata-llacta. And when this necessary business had been dispatched and the

98

people were silent about him, the tired old man sang a brief song in a low and sorrowful voice:

> I was born as a flower of the field
> As a flower I was cherished in my youth.
> I came to my full age, I grew old.
> Now I am withered and die.

So singing, Pachacuti died. Of this Sapa Inca the two men for whom the study of ancient Peru was a work of love, Clements Markham and Philip Means, say that he was the greatest man the American race has ever produced. Perhaps he was; yet, in the light of the history which has come to our knowledge since the lifetimes of those great Peruvianists, it is possible that the epithet should be applied, rather, to his son and successor.

When a Sapa Inca died, that was by no means the end of him. We have already observed that mummies, especially those of royal persons, were among the *huaccas*, cult objects of the people's religion. The mummies of former Sapa Incas lived in palaces reserved for them, had a large and frequently renewed wardrobe and, exacting in their tastes, kept a rich table and a harem of the prettiest Chosen Women. They were cared for by a large body of priestly servants who thus acquired a vested interest in a socially damaging form of what we may call conspicuous waste. The mummies, moreover, often wanted to pay a round of visits, and when they traveled, they did so in great and expensive state. Although this cult of the dead did not, in the Tahuantinsuyu, become quite the economic burden it became in Egypt, it was excessive; and during the last reigns of the imperial epoch it became a serious drain on the state's share of the national product. As we shall see, Huáscar Inca's military effort against his half brother Atahualpa in the coming civil war was, according to his own complaint, crippled by the expense of maintaining the dead in state. But it does not appear that the people, the *puric-cuna*, suffered from it; they were not, as in Egypt, oppressed for the greater glory of dead kings. In time they might have been, but the resources and organizations of the Tahuantinsuyu were capable of supporting a good deal of waste.

The cult of the dead was not the only form of conspicuous waste in the later phase of the imperial epoch. When Topa Yupanqui became Sapa Inca his manner of life changed accordingly. He never wore the same clothes two days running, and the clothes he discarded were burned since they must not be defiled by contact with the skin of any lesser man. Nor could he live in his father's palaces; new ones had to be built for the new Sapa Inca. The food served to him and not eaten, and the dishes in which they were served, were likewise destroyed after use. All this entailed a waste of wealth in terms of materials and man-hours, but the waste did not spread to the population as a whole, nor even, on a serious scale, to the Incas below royal rank. It was left to a later American nation to devise built-in obsolescence on a mass scale.

Accession to the supreme office did not put an end to Topa Yupanqui's military career. The savages of the tropical forests on the eastern watershed of the cordillera were making a nuisance of themselves by raiding the imperial domain. These barbarians were not very numerous, and the damage they did was probably slight; historians and such travelers as Mr. Sacheverell Sitwell have wondered at the great effort made by the Incas in putting down so trifling a nuisance, and at the equally great economic effort of building vast fortresses to keep the frontier covered thereafter. But the region threatened contained the state coca plantations, and as these were worked by convicts who may often have been disaffected persons, the government in Cuzco may have envisaged the alarming possibility of a rising supported by a barbarian invasion. There could have been another reason for putting forth an apparently excessive amount of force in crushing these savages: they were reputed to be cannibals, and the people of the Tahuantinsuyu, with their religious belief in bodily resurrection, had a particular horror of being eaten.

Whatever his reason, Topa Yupanqui led a great army into the forest, embarked it aboard a huge fleet of canoes, and put the fear of the sun-god into the barbarians, while he rounded off and consolidated the province of Antisuyu.

While he was so engaged, news reached him that a revolt had broken out in the region of Titicaca. The revolting provincials were Colla and Lupaca tribesmen—the highland nations were always much more troublesome than the lowlanders—who had been told by a deserter from the Inca army that Topa's punitive force had been defeated and the Sapa Inca himself killed. The Colla and Lupaca were joined in their revolt by two other Aymara-speaking nations, Pacasa and Omasuyu.[1]

Only the most perfect military and civil organization could have enabled the veteran army of the Inca to accomplish the feat which this revolt made necessary. In a time far too short for the enemy's comfort and calculations, Topa Yupanqui moved his entire force from a tropical rain-forest not much above sea level to mountain plateaus at twelve thousand feet and there used it against the rebels with complete success. The training and discipline of his men must have been of the highest order and their powers of endurance remarkable. It is also possible that, the greater part of the army being born to high altitudes, the officers and men involved left the forest with relief and regained the mountains with such joy that they fought exceptionally well. The four revolting nations were crushed in a series of battles composing a short, sharp campaign.

By this time it had been brought home to the Sapa Inca that, as we have suggested above, a *Pax Incaica* would have to be co-extensive with the known world whether he liked the idea or not. Probably he did; he may have developed that lust for world dominion which is the most serious occupational disease of royal soldiers. Having crushed the Aymara-speaking alliance, he marched eastward into the highlands of what is today Bolivia and added them to the Antisuyu province. He then crossed the country from east to southwest to deal with that part of the coast which had not been subjugated during Pachacuti's lifetime. Northern Chile was conquered and the army led south into barbarous lands. But here the Incas encountered the most ferocious resistance in their career of conquest; it came from the Araucanians, a people of uncivilized warriors fanatically attached to their freedom. Their resistance was so implacable and their country so little worth having, that when Topa Yupanqui had incorporated the best of it into the Tahuantinsuyu and cleared it of the natives, he decreed that the river Maule was to be the southernmost frontier of the Inca state. He fortified and manned it, revisited the east for a brief final campaign of consolidation, and then returned to Cuzco to spend the rest of his life in peace and administration.

When the Sapa Inca felt himself growing old he built a palace to die in on the plain of Clinta. There he became seriously ill. His one remaining duty was to name his successor, and his choice fell upon the legitimate heir, Tito Cusi Hualpa, whose mother— the qoya—was Topa Yupanqui's sister Mama Oclla. In 1493, in the twenty-second year of his reign and the eighty-fifth of his lifetime, Topa Yupanqui died.

Soldier, statesman and builder, an administrator of genius and an organizer of exceptional capacity, Topa Yupanqui was remarkable also for having introduced into the rigid social organization of the state a new element which, in due course, would probably have steadied it, liberalized it, and given it a new power of endurance. This was the new class, standing outside the ordinary social system, called *yanacuna*. The origin of this slave class is almost as curious as its subsequent development. In Topa's youth, one of his brothers, doubtless resenting the boy's nomination as heir over the heads of his elders and military betters, is said to have organized a conspiracy against him. It was exposed, and six thousand men accused of manufacturing weapons for the conspirators were assembled for punishment in the town of Yanayacu. They had, under the law, earned death. Topa, however, spared their lives. But he condemned them, and their descendants thereafter, to serve the Incas as slaves forever. These *yanacuna* were outsiders; they were not counted in Topa's great census of the nation, nor in any census made later. They had no rights and they paid no taxes in work, since all their work was for the Incas. They became what Cieza de León calls *criados perpetuos*, hereditary servants. Thus, in the beginning it was a disgrace to be one of the *yanacuna* and the word itself was a pejorative.

But the *yanacuna* came very soon to provide the domestic staff of the Sapa Inca himself and of other royal persons and high officers of state. Now, this was very honorable work. Provincials who sent their sons to be, as it were, pages in the royal and noble households, were in fact sending them to perform the same duties as those of the *yanacuna*. Soon the whole class of upper domestics became known, whatever the individual's origin, as *yanacuna*.

It seems always to be the case that men in intimate attendance upon princes, or at least those of them who are intelligent or attractive or both, earn their masters' friendly regard and favor. This is what happened, and certain men who began as slaves ended as provincial governors, filling their high offices as to the manner born. Had it not been for the Spanish invasion and conquest, the destiny of this class, which had thus broken the strong bonds which tied every man to the condition he was born to, might well have been brilliant; one recalls the slave class in the Ottoman Empire, which, as the Mamelukes, became rulers of Egypt. And it is the existence of the *yanacuna* class which makes us doubt the soundness of Dr. Arnold Toynbee's judgment when he says that the Tahuantinsuyu may well have been ripe for death as a great society, so that its collapse was merely hastened rather than brought about by the Spaniards. For the first time in many generations, high position was open to talent; and the men who began as slaves and ended as viceroys might have given the whole system a new lease on life.

If Topa Yupanqui was really eighty-five when he died, then his heir was the son of his old age, for the new Sapa Inca was a minor upon his accession. It is possible that Topa was younger when he died than the chroniclers make out, for they seem to have exaggerated the ages of the Sapa Incas; it seems probable that he was not more than seventy at the time of his death. Although some historians give him a reign of fifty years, it was probably not half of that. However, we cannot be certain that these Peruvians did not, indeed, live longer than we do. In the second place, minority, among the Incas, was probably longer than it is with us; as we explain below, a boy assumed the equivalent of the *toga virilis* at fourteen; but a *puric* was not an adult citizen until twenty-five.

The new Sapa Inca's debut is obscured by the fact that some of the chroniclers, including Garcilaso, seem to have confused his career with his father's, and thus they have him leading armies and winning wars during Topa's lifetime. But it seems clear that when the old Sapa Inca died, the young heir to empire was at Quispicancha with his tutors. It does not follow that he was a schoolboy; but he was certainly very young. When he was brought to Cuzco to be crowned with the *borla* and was presented to the people in Rimacpampa, the great public place before the Sun temple, the Cuzcans greeted him delightedly with cries of *Huayna! Huayna!* which can be translated freely *"The boy-king!"*

At all events, his name and title upon accession became Huayna Capac, the correct meaning of which is "young chief full of virtues."

The accession of a minor to an imperial throne is invariably a cause of trouble. The youthful Sapa Inca had numerous half brothers, the sons of Topa Yupanqui's concubines. One of them laid claim to the unique office on the grounds that it had been promised to him. His name was Capac Huari, and he had a fairly strong party at court but no following in the country. It seems that his claim was contrived by his mother rather than by himself. Support in the country and among the principal officers of state was all for the legitimate heir, Huayna Capac, and after Capac Huari's mother had been arrested and executed for treason, no more is heard of her son. But it is at least possible that the business of his claim to the throne may have had some influence, a generation later, on Atahualpa.

A serious weakness of the Inca imperial system is to be found at this point of succession: there were too many factors, in addition to that of natal legitimacy, affecting the issue. As we have said, the heir had to be of pure Inca royal blood—that is, his mother had to be his father's sister—but there might be several sons of that marriage and there was no law of primogeniture, a convenient if inequitable device. The choice among possible heirs was therefore made by the old Sapa Inca, either long before his death by associating a prince in the work of empire as the later Roman emperors appointed an heir to play Augustus to their Caesar, or on his deathbed. But even that was not the end of the matter, for there were two other powerful bodies with interests vested in the person of the monarch: the church and the army.

The army, naturally, wanted a soldier leader. The influence of the *Apu-cuna*, the generals, could make itself felt either by pressure on the Sapa Inca during his lifetime, or, on his death, by making it clear to the clergy that there would be trouble if their man was not chosen by the gods when it came to consulting the augurs. For— and this is how the church wielded power—it was necessary that the old Sapa Inca's will and the heir's legitimacy be confirmed by heaven. Heaven's will was determined in the Roman manner, by consulting the entrails of a sacrificed beast. A llama was sacrificed by the high priest, and divination was practiced according to ancient rules by examining its organs. Whether or not we believe that this oracle was ever "fixed" must depend on the degree of sophistication we accord to the Inca clergy. Presumably, the people had to take the high priest's word for it that the auguries were good or bad. (If the lungs of the victim were still breathing upon extraction, the augury was excellent.) Presumably, too, the high priest and the principal *Apu* (the commander in chief under the Sapa Inca) and close kinsmen, could and did get together to make sure that heaven, their own interests and the national interest were in accord. Moreover, as we have seen in the case of Capac Huari, court parties led by the ambitious mother of a possible heir could and did make trouble.

Huayna Capac's minority entailed the appointment of a regent. The first appointed, presumably by the Apucama, abused his trust by conspiring to seize the throne. There could be no clearer evidence of the advanced state of sophistication reached by the Tahuantinsuyu; whatever the people may have believed about the divinity of the Sapa Inca, it is obvious that members of the upper class were no longer held in awe by the notion that their king was god. The regent's plot was exposed and the empire was faced by one of those situations which call for a strong man without personal ambition and loyal to the state and its institutions. The part is usually played by a veteran soldier who is apt to discover that he was ambitious after all. Happily for the Tahuantinsuyu the man of destiny in this case was a civil officer, the *cucuricuc* of Chinchaysuyu who acted with rare decision and integrity. He arrested the regent and executed him without delay; he appointed himself regent; and he filled the regency with honor and discretion until Huayna's majority.

At this stage in our narrative we are chiefly concerned to make clear, both to ourselves and to the reader, the nature of the claims to the throne which were to be made by Huayna's sons Huáscar and Atahualpa. The question is best considered here, because the claims arose in part from Huayna's marriages and love affairs, which were involved. Moreover, the truth is obscured by a pretty legend with a strongly European-romantic taint, which was long accepted by historians. This, briefly, is as follows: Huayna's first-born son was Huáscar, begotten of his sister and *qoya*, Rahua Ocllo. But after Huayna had reconquered Quito, which had revolted from the Tahuantinsuyu under a native prince, he fell in love with that prince's daughter, married her, and became so attached to her person and to her beautiful country—it will be recalled that his father had loved the northern province—that he settled there for the rest of his life. By the princess of Quito, Huayna had a son who, because of the love which the Sapa Inca bore this lad's mother, became a favorite child. The boy's name was Atahualpa, and Huayna, displaying at the end a weakness which not even Marcus Aurelius was free from, desired to raise him to greatness. He therefore divided the empire, leaving the three southern provinces to Huáscar, the legitimate heir, and Quito, or perhaps the whole of the Chinchaysuyu, to Atahualpa. The disastrous outcome was what, had he not been blinded by love, the Sapa Inca should have foreseen.

Now the spirit of this tale is true, but in detail it is false. A good, well-rounded story is worth the sacrifice of some mere facts; but not when it completely falsifies the values of the people in question. And since these doings led to a civil war which greatly weakened the country when it came to dealings with the Spaniards, Atahualpa's claim to the *borla*, or what he must have believed was a good claim, should be reported as clearly as possible. After weighing and comparing the conflicting and confusing accounts, we believe the truth to have been more or less as follows:

It will be recalled that Topa Yupanqui, before his accession, had conquered Quito and incorporated it into the Chinchaysuyu. Among the booty which he brought back to Cuzco was a girl, either the daughter of the deposed Quitu chief or, in any case, a woman of high caste, Tocto Palla[2] by name. How Huayna came to know her and whether they were of an age, we cannot say; it is possible that she was given to the prince by his father, to serve in his household. It seems most likely that they were both in their teens. Either as his "white slave" or as his boyhood sweetheart, Tocto Palla bore a son to Huayna; and this son, the prince's firstborn, was Atahualpa.

But when Huayna Capac became Sapa Inca he was obliged to marry his sister. His first *qoya* was his eldest sister; here is Salcamayhua's description of the wedding, which was also the coronation:

> . . . and they assigned as the wife of Huayna Capac his own sister Coya Mama Cusimiray, according to the custom of his ancestors. They were married on the day of the coronation, when all the walls and roofs of the city were covered with rich plumes of feathers, and the streets were paved with golden cobbles. The people were gorgeously dressed in *cumpis* and plumes. The Ynca came forth from the house of his grandfather Pachacuti Ynca Yupanqui followed by the Apu Curacas of Colla-suyu and councillors; while Mama Cusimiray came out of the palace of Tupac Ynca Yupanqui attended upon by the Apu Curacas of Chinchaysuyu, Cunti-suyu, and Anti-suyu, with all their Auqui-cuna according to rank. They were in litters and Huayna Capac did not hold the *tupac-yauri* but only the *champi*. Many attendants of less note surounded him, all dressed in shining shells and mother-of-pearl and well-armed with their *purupuras* and with bracelets of silver. They say that fifty thousand men guarded the city and the fortress of Sacsahuaman, and that the festival was a wonderful sight.

Auqui-cuna means unmarried princes (*auqui*, "prince"; *cuna*, plural). The *tupac-yauri* was the scepter of unique office, made of gold. We cannot find the meaning of *purupuras*. The *champi* was a club, probably a ceremonial club.

The *qoya* Mama Cusimiray proved to be barren.[3] She was, therefore, replaced as *qoya* by her younger sister Rahua Ocllo, who bore
a son, Tupac Cusi Hualpa, known to history as Huáscar. Now, there
is a very curious and macabre story which is not generally accorded
any importance, which suggests that this replacement of one sister
by another may not have been quite in order; that, in short, Huayna
and Rahua Ocllo were not properly "married." The passage from
Salcamayhua's *Antiquities*, quoted above, goes on to describe the
religious part of the wedding ceremony, consisting principally of a
ritual shoeing of the bridal pair with golden *llanques* (sandals).
Possibly Huayna did not go through this again with his younger
sister, but just took her to his bed.

[All we need to remember, however, is that there may have been
something irregular in the union between the young Sapa Inca and
his second wife; that Huáscar was born five years *after* Atahualpa
and not, as the legend has it, before him; and that whereas in Inca
law Huáscar was at least heir presumptive, Atahualpa, as a bastard
—bastardy was perfectly respectable, of course, but an insuperable
obstacle to the unique office—was not really a possible heir.]

The first years of Huayna Capac's reign were peaceful; they were
spent, as had become customary, in going on progresses through
the vast Inca dominions. He was a popular Sapa Inca. Doubtless
his youth endeared him to the people. He was received everywhere
with singing and dancing, his road was strewn with flowers, and his
litter was greeted with joyful shouts of his own name (which was
itself a term of high praise) and with such ejaculatory praises as the
title *Huaccha-cuyac*, which we may render "Friend of the poor."[4]

It was while he was on a progress that the Sapa Inca received
news from Cuzco of Huáscar's birth, and he hurried back to the
capital to celebrate it. But the principal ceremony, in the royal as
in all other families, was not until the weaning and hair-cutting of
the boy child. Then the festivities included dancing. Dancing,
among the Incas, was confined to men. Each province, and probably each tribe, had its own dance and did not borrow figures or
steps from other tribes. The Inca dance is described by Garcilaso
as "stately" rather than lively, and "without hops or jumps." "They
held hands, each man giving his hand not to his neighbor but to

the next man but one, giving first one hand and then the other, until they came to the last, as it were in a chain."

On the occasion of Huáscar's weaning-and-shearing ceremony, his father decreed that a gold chain be cast for the dancers to carry as they went through the dance. This chain later disappeared; the Spaniards never got their grasping hands on it, and for all we know it may still exist, guarded somewhere in the mountains by men who wait in sullen silence for the day when their race can reassert itself. It is described as having been twice the width and length of the square called Huacaypata. This, it seems, means that the chain was seven hundred feet long. The Accountant General Agustín de Zárate says that according to Indios who had seen it, the two hundred dancers, all of them *orejones*, that is, *curacas* and Incas, were scarcely able to raise it. The same chronicler says that in Quechua a "chain" is *huasca*, and that consequently the baby Tupac Cusi Hualpa became known as Huasca Inca. Inca, tacked to a prince's name, has approximately the significance of "Augustus" in the late Roman Empire. But as "Chain" was not a suitable name for a prince and possible future Sapa Inca, they added the sound we render by the letter *r*, making Huáscar, a word which has no meaning but is still reminiscent of the golden chain of the weaning dance.

We cannot tell whether, had peace continued in the Tahuantin-suyu, Huayna Capac would have been content to govern without trying to expand. He may possibly have had as much spirit and as much ability as his father and his grandfather, especially if our theory of line-breeding is viable. Had he decided to push the northern frontier as far as his armies could go, instead of stopping as he was to do in the event, then the Inca armies would have pushed on up the coast and conquered the small kingdoms of Chibcha and Cochle. They then would have clashed with the Spaniards in Panama, where they would have wiped out the invaders, and/or come into violent contact with Aztec Mexico. A very few years would have made a colossal difference. Mexico was in an unsettled condition, and Moctezuma was debilitated by his own Hamlet-like nature. It is at least possible that the Tahuantin-suyu might have become coextensive with all Central as well as

Andean America; and, under rulers line-bred for the work, they might have presented too powerful a front for any European conquest. As it is, we do not even know for sure whether the existence of the great federation of states to their north was known to the Incas.

Huayna Capac was provoked to his first campaign by the rising of a barbarous people, the Chachapoyas, on the northeastern frontier of the empire. From that time almost until his death, the Sapa Inca was engaged in dealing with similar outbreaks. But the theory that, because of resistance by the Araucanians south of the Maule and revolts and raids on other frontiers, the Tahuantinsuyu was cracking up will not bear examination. After all, it required four centuries of similar but far more numerous and sustained assaults to make any serious impression on the Roman Empire, whose social stability was no more massive than that of the Tahuantinsuyu.

The Inca state was very rich, magnificently organized and administered; and if it be held that such an empire must either expand or fall and cannot simply stand still, there is the example of the several Chinese and Egyptian Great Society empires to refute this opinion; and there is the fact that in any case there was nothing to check the continued expansion of the Tahuantinsuyu until it came into contact with the Mexican federation. There were, it is true, certain weaknesses appearing in the internal structure of the great state: we have already referred to the drain on resources entailed by the cult of dead Sapa Incas. When Huáscar came to power, he was determined to put a stop to that—and doubtless Atahualpa would have followed the example. And, as we have suggested, the rise of the *yanacuna* might well have led to a refreshing liberalization of the social and political systems. Finally, it must be pointed out in this connection that the Tahuantinsuyu had shown itself as well able to survive the civil war which was to be fought between Huáscar and Atahualpa, as the Roman Empire to survive the strife between Pompey and Caesar. A great and powerful machine capable of running indefinitely can be smashed by a trifling accident, a monkey wrench in the works: Pizarro and Almagro were the monkey wrench in the works of the Inca social and political machine. Its real weakness was, as will appear, its rigidity, its machinelike quality.]

Huayna Capac showed his ability as a soldier by "pacifying" the Chachapoyas and passing beyond them to add two more small provinces to the Tahuantinsuyu. The frontier was pushed back beyond Moyapampa in present northeastern Peru and into the tropical forest. The Sapa Inca then returned to Cuzco for rest and refreshment and to celebrate his successes. Thereafter he set out upon another progress, visiting the extreme eastern and southern limits of the Inca domain.

It was either during the course of this progress or upon his return to the capital that Huayna received very disturbing news: Quito and other extreme northern provinces were in revolt. The Sapa Inca was again obliged to set out on a campaign of pacification. Was this a case of Marcus Aurelius, desirous of living a peaceful and studious life, but forced to spend his time keeping the frontiers? Or did Huayna, in the manner of Trajan, eagerly welcome an opportunity to crush the troublesome northerners once and for all, and perhaps to push beyond the Quitu toward the old Maya kingdoms in Honduras, of which the Incas may have had some inkling? The Incas had a particular horror of popular revolts. Huayna Capac had often heard his father repeat a saying attributed to the proto-Sapa Inca, Roca, that it is enough for the base-born to learn the occupation of their fathers, for to order and govern is not the work of the common people, "and to entrust such work to them would be to endanger and injure the republic."[5] And as to the kind of revolt which is the product of one man's ambition rather than the people's discontents, the Sapa Inca Topa Yupanqui had taught his son that ambition and avarice prevent a man from knowing how to moderate either his own actions or those of others, diverting the mind from the public good and lessening the understanding so that the ambitious follow their own opinions rather than the advice of the wise and virtuous. In short, the Sapa Incas had, like ourselves until recently, ready-made formulae for convincing themselves that aspirations to liberty, in colonials, were tantamount to crime.]

Huayna set out for the north at the head of his armies. With him went Atahualpa, already his favorite son; the boy was twelve years old, and this early initiation into the duties of his rank must have interfered with his education.

As a member of the royal caste, Atahualpa received a more formal education than the children of the *puric* class. His tutors were all uncles or cousins; from the *amautas* of Cuzco's *Yacha-huasi* he received religious instruction. By this time, although sun worship was firmly maintained as the state religion for social and political reasons, men of education had probably outgrown it and were to be satisfied only with the richer and more subtly flavored spiritual nourishment to be found in the worship of Pachacamac-Viracocha. Atahualpa's grandfather, Topa Yupanqui, had very advanced religious views and had not hesitated to express them. Father Blas Valera reports him thus:

> Many say that the Sun lives and that He is the maker of all things. Surely, he who makes a thing assists at its creation, but many things are made when the Sun is absent. Therefore, He is not the maker of all things. And it may be concluded that He does not live, because He makes so many revolutions, and yet is never tired. If He was a living thing, He would become tired as we do, and if He was free He would visit other parts of Heaven which He never reaches. He is like a tethered beast that always makes the same round, or like a dart which goes where it is sent, and not where it wishes.

It is important to realize that skepticism of this order may have been in the atmosphere of Atahualpa's environment, since some of his incomprehensible mistakes have been attributed to a superstition almost as gross as that which, according to Suetonius, governed the lives of Roman patricians.

It is possible that since he was taken by his father on the northern campaign at the age of twelve Atahualpa did not complete the four-year course at what we feel entitled to call Cuzco University. The education of boys of rank was attended to by the *Yacha-huasi* in Cuzco. This school, reputedly founded by the (Sapa) Inca Roca, was enlarged, improved and given new importance by Pachacuti. The word "university" is not altogether out of place, for the professors, *amauta-cuna* and *haravec-cuna* lived in the college—*Yacha-huasi* means "house of teaching"—and gave a set course of lectures. It might, however, be nearer the mark to compare this institution to the house of a teaching order of monks. The house of teaching was an important national institution with great influence in government circles. The *amautas* were responsible for teaching theology and philosophy; the *haravecs* for literature and probably history. We would remind the reader that *amauta* can be rendered in English by something conveying the idea philosopher-scholar-savant-theologian, with the emphasis on the last word, so that we might compare the *amautas* to the Oxford divines of the nineteenth century. *Haravec* means "poet," but probably with a connotation that we can express by the words "ritual" and "bard." The *haravec-cuna* composed the literary faculty of the college.

All these learned men were Incas, and at least some of them were of the royal *ayllus*. They were greatly respected and many of them had disciples living with them, so that in one sense they were more like Hindu *gurus* than like Occidental scholars and pedagogues. Philip Means says, "It is not too much to say that the *Yacha-huasi* was the brains of the State." If it is true that the importance of Cuzco University was as great as that, then it is less wonder that the Tahuantinsuyu was well governed; it was almost Plato's republic.

Morúa says that the boys spent four years at the college. Those who came from the provinces speaking Aymara, Arawk, or some other language than Quechua, spent the first year learning Quechua. Second-year students studied theology, ritual, and religion in general. Third-year men devoted their whole time to the study of the *quipu*, learning how to make full use of it. In their fourth year, the students made use of the *quipus*, under guidance of tutors, to "read" history and "many other things." Among the other things, geography may have been included, since relief-map making was one of the Inca skills; and probably some measure of accountancy, some mathematics (arithmetic), and some astronomy. The tutor was either an *amauta* or a *haravec*, according to the subject; but our knowledge of how this school was run is very small and we can only arrive at the nature of the course of teaching by inductive reasoning from the kind of knowledge a man of rank seems to have had in adult life.

[Means says that Pachacuti's policy of encouraging youths of *curaca* rank from the conquered provinces to attend the *Yachahuasi* in Cuzco was valuable in that these foreign students could "be deeply imbued with the Incaic idea and so come to be important agents for the dissemination of Incaic propaganda." Possibly.] But history does not always bear this out; Indians and Africans of the former British Empire, educated in England, returned to their own lands to lead the rebellious nationalist movements which created the present Indian and African republics, although it is true, especially in the case of India (but not of Pakistan), that the British political system of parliamentary and cabinet government has remained the model and ideal.[It would be interesting to know how many alumni of the Cuzcan House of Teaching were to lead their peoples into either passive or active alliance with the Spaniards against the Inca imperialists.]

At all events, Atahualpa, like all the boys of his rank and below it, probably received the kind of formal education which Pachacuti had insisted on, laying it down that a man of rank should have a knowledge of the "sciences" as firmly as Atahualpa's grandfather Topa Yupanqui had decreed that the *puric-cuna* should not. In addition to his academic education, the young prince was trained in arms. This kind of education was as important among the boys and young men of the Inca as among high-born youths in medieval Europe; so much so that nineteenth-century historians, uninhibited by that terror of analogue which afflicts historians in our own times, did not hesitate to write of the Inca youth's preparations for "knighthood" or to employ, in this connection, the word "chivalry." We are here, however, on the side of the moderns; both terms mislead, falsifying the very different spirit of Inca feeling and tradition.

The first ceremony in Atahualpa's life had been that weaning and shearing which have already been described. Then, and until the puberty ceremony, called *guarachicui*, he was known by some temporary name, a mere expedient for calling and addressing him and without that power of spiritual and almost mystical *identification* which his man-name, yet to be given him, would have. This final and decisive name, Atahualpa, which probably means "Fortunate Warrior," was given to the lad at his *guarachicui*. This ceremony was normally performed at the same age as confirmation among Anglicans, a year later than the *bar mitzvah* among the Jews; that is, in the boy's fourteenth year. But it is possible that by special favor of the Sapa Inca, Atahualpa may have been allowed to have his *guarachicui* at the age of twelve, before setting out for Quito with his father and the army. We suggest this because, for strong religious and traditional reasons, the ceremony had to be performed, among the royal and noble Incas, in Cuzco, and Huayna Capac must have realized that his expedition to crush the rebellious Quitu might take longer than the two years required to bring his son to the proper age of manhood (not the same thing as legal majority).

The *guara* was a garment, and *guarachicui* means "the putting on of the *guara*." The ceremony can, therefore, be closely compared with the Roman lad's assumption of the *toga virilis*, at seventeen. And just as the toga was worn by all adult Roman citizens, so the *guara* was worn by all adult Incas. Atahualpa's first *guara* was made for him by Tocto Palla, for it was customary for a boy's mother to weave the cloth for it with her own hands, with loving care and certain religious observances. And although Tocto Palla was a Quitu lady, she would surely have adopted the customs proper to her royal lover. The assumption of the *guara* and of the definitive name were one ceremony. Among the *puric-cuna* the name given was a family one, borne by the lad's grandfather or great-uncle; it was, also, always a plant or animal name, this being, no doubt, a vestige of totemism, although there seems to be no evidence of taboo associated with one's name. Among the Incas, however, the choice of name was influenced by different considerations. The same names, in diverse combinations, do recur, and in some cases the name included elements from the distaff side.

Having taken the *guarachicui* and the name Atahualpa, the young prince put on the *usutas*, sandals made for the occasion by members of his family of fine gold reed and llama sinews. Next, he had to endure the piercing of his ear lobes for subsequent distension by jeweled ornaments. This part of the ceremonies was confined to youths of Inca and *curaca* classes.[6]

Before Atahualpa underwent these ceremonies, however, he had first to undergo a physical ordeal and an examination in soldierly and athletic prowess. The examination was as follows: All the boys of Inca rank who on the day of the ceremonies had attained the required age within the year in question were assembled in the great square outside the Collacampata palace, which lay between Cuzco proper and the great hill fortress of Sacsahuaman. There they were "instructed in the use of weapons . . . and in certain handicrafts . . . by some older members of the Inca family." As the trial of prowess followed at once, we suppose this to mean that the boys' mentors went formally and in public through the motions of an instruction which had been going on in private for some time. The boys then showed what they had learned. This being concluded, there followed a six-day fast during which candidates received nothing but raw maize and water sufficient to keep them alive. This, too, may have been a kind of military endurance test; just as Roman soldiers received raw wheat as their ration, Inca soldiers received raw maize. The fast was broken by a feast. All this must have tried the strength of a fourteen-year-old child, and Atahualpa was perhaps only twelve. But he was a forward lad, strong, bold, handsome and cunning and no doubt well able to compete with boys two years his senior, and perhaps to earn the envious admiration of the seven-year-old Huáscar among the spectators.

When Huayna Capac, accompanied by Atahualpa, set out for the north at the head of a large conscript army he cannot have foreseen that he would never return to Cuzco alive.

The first battle of the campaign, fought against the Pasto of the extreme north, was a shocking reverse for the Sapa Inca. The Pasto commander, leaving women, children and old men to tempt the enemy with hope of easy victory, withdrew until the Inca advance guard had occupied the territory, and then attacked in force, driving the imperial troops back onto the main body of the army and inflicting very heavy casualties. Their victory, however, did the Pasto no good: it served only to irritate the Sapa Inca, whose counterattack, and subsequent systematic conquest of the Pasto country, was carried out not with the usual Inca moderation but with punitive ferocity.

But among all the peoples of the loose northern confederacy or alliance of civilized, semi-civilized and barbarous nations which were in revolt, those who gave the Incas most trouble were the Cayambi. They were a people of Cara stock living in what is now northern Ecuador; Cieza de León and Garcilaso call them Caranques, while other chroniclers refer to them by different names. All the people who had revolted with the Quitu proper fought very bravely for their liberty; but only the Cayambi came near to succeeding in their resistance. Not only did they fight in the open; they had strongholds and fortresses which they defended with an obstinacy only once before met with in the whole imperial history, and that was in the extreme south when the Sapa Inca's grandfather Topa Yupanqui came up against the Araucanians.

Garcilaso, following Cieza de León, says that the origin of the northern revolt was the Inca law which forbade the eating of human flesh. By his account, the Caranques, or Cayambi, were cannibals. Prizing their nasty diet above life itself, they plotted in secrecy against the Inca governor, rose in mass on a prearranged day, and massacred the *cucuricuc*, his officers, and all the garrison troops. Certainly, the Quitu were not cannibals, but it is possible that some of their savage allies were.

For this indulgence was the thing they most prized in their bestial lives. . . . When the appointed day arrived they killed the officers of the Inca with much cruelty, and offered their heads, hearts and blood to their gods, in recognition of their having freed them from the dominion of the Incas, and restored their ancient customs. They ate the flesh of the murdered people with much pleasure and voracity, swallowing it without chewing, in revenge for having been deprived of this enjoyment for so long a time. They did this with all possible insolence; which caused Huayna Capac much sorrow and anger when he received the news. He ordered troops and officers to be assembled, to punish the crimes of these savages, and followed the army that he might be present at what might happen. The captains came to the country of the Caranques and, before they began the war, they sent messengers in the Inca's name, offering pardon to those who might submit and ask for pardon. The rebels, like barbarians, not only would not surrender, but sent very insolent answers back, so that nothing remained but to kill them. When Huayna Capac learned the new insolence of these brutes, he joined his army, to carry on the war in person.

The Cayambi war seems actually to have broken out while the Sapa Inca, having dealt with the Pasto rebellion, was governing the Tahuantinsuyu from Quito. Huayna was kept in that provincial capital not only by the heavy work to be done in the north but, like his grandfather Topa Yupanqui, by inclination. He experienced a growing attachment to the country with its high rainfall, lush vegetation and beautiful landscapes. There is also a hint of evidence that the Sapa Inca's health, not always good in the south, was better in the warmer, wetter northern climate.

Huayna Capac did not at once leave Quito to deal with the Cayambi insurrection. His kinsman, Colla Topa, an experienced officer, was placed in command of a large punitive force and moved north with a personal guard of two thousand men of *curaca* rank, a sort of *corps d'élite*, and an auxiliary force of Colla led by their own officers, formerly their own hereditary chiefs.

This first campaign was inconclusive; there was much fighting, with heavy casualties on both sides, but the Cayambi remained in possession of their strongholds. A second campaign became necessary—the total duration of this war is uncertain, but it should probably be counted in years—and this time it was led by the Sapa Inca in person.[7] The Cayambi were pinned in their strongholds, and at last in a single stronghold, but this held out. When the Incas assaulted it, the defenders made desperately fought sorties to drive them off. One of the Sapa Inca's brothers was killed leading a frontal attack of this kind, and Huayna Capac himself was knocked down and barely rescued by his bodyguard. In taking the stronghold at last, the Sapa Inca used the kind of stratagem which is popularly, but perhaps mistakenly, supposed to have been used at Senlac by William of Normandy, and which, simple and obvious though it be, seems often to work and earns the captain who employs it a reputation as a man of military genius. He detached a strong force under an *apucuraca* to march round and behind the stronghold undiscovered, and, having given his subordinate time to get into position, himself withdrew in feigned retreat. The Cayambi poured out of the stronghold to finish off the retreating enemy, the secret detachment moved in and took possession of the place, the apparently retreating main body of the army turned and fought and the Cayambi, trapped between two forces and in the open at last, were destroyed.

What followed was uncharacteristic of Inca policy and is good evidence for the bitter feeling roused by this long struggle, by the high casualty figures—it is said that they amounted in all to twenty thousand killed—and by the Sapa Inca's exasperation with the Cayambi and their allies for wasting his time and resources in ultimately useless resistance. A large body of prisoners, estimated at between two and twenty thousand, but perhaps about five thousand, were slaughtered, and their bodies were flung into a lake which thereafter became and is still known as Yahuarcocha, the Lake of Blood. This unusual, and in the Tahuantinsuyu perhaps unprecedented, atrocity seems to have cowed the barbarous allies of the Quitu, for they gave no more trouble to the Sapa Inca and his army. But it reveals in Huayna Capac a taint of cruelty, which was to become more apparent in Atahualpa.

It was probably in 1513, the twentieth year of his reign, that Huayna Capac set out on his northern campaigns. He must have been between thirty-seven and forty years of age. At the conclusion of the Cayambi war either his health or his inclination, or policy, caused him to decide that the Tahuantinsuyu had now reached its northern limit of expansion. He was approaching fifty, which, by the standards set by his ancestors, was far from old, and there is no apparent reason for his failure to push on through Colombia and up the isthmus. He decreed that the river

Ancasmayu was to be the northern frontier, in token whereof he caused boundary stones to be raised. The line he chose is now the Colombian-Ecuadorian frontier.

The Sapa Inca's work in the north was not finished, however. Without returning to Quito he set himself to pacify and reorganize the reconquered and newly conquered territories, to fit these provinces into the social and economic system of the Tahuantinsuyu in general. They presumably came under the government of the Chinchaysuyu, but in practice the whole system was modified by the fact that the Sapa Inca himself remained in the north and in personal control of that province. He associated Atahualpa, still his favorite and now in his late teens, in the work. For, being still under the influence of his first love, Tocto Palla, and of his inclination for the country and people of Quito and its provinces, he had probably already made up his mind that this land was to be the young man's heritage. It is true that, in his account of the Cayambi war and resettlement, Sir Clements Markham says that "the prowess of Atahualpa was not such as to satisfy his father." Whether or not this was so, and the young prince did in fact show a certain indolence, a want of decision and perhaps even of ambition, yet it must have been clear to the Sapa Inca that there were strong reasons of state for giving the Quitu and their half-barbarous or quite-savage allies and neighbors a prince who was both an Inca and one of themselves. He had reason to know that these northeners were a proud and turbulent race; they were rich in natural resources; the plentiful rainfall and tropical climate made them independent of that social discipline which the soil and rainfall (or want of them) had imposed on the more southerly provinces; they were a long way and a difficult way from Cuzco. It would always be difficult to control them. It must have seemed to Huayna Capac that the problem could be solved by giving the Quitu Atahualpa for their prince, whose mother was of their blood and chiefly house. It would be possible to give them, under him and his heirs, at least the appearance of independence although Atahualpa would in practice be subservient to the unique authority in Cuzco, and little more than a *cucuricuc* bearing the vain symbols of royalty. And if, as Markham suggests, Atahualpa lacked those qualities of leadership and ambition expected of a Sapa Inca or his viceroy, did not that make him all the more suitable for the role which Huayna Capac was designing for him? The Quitu were not accustomed to the unquestioning obedience of the southern provincials; an easygoing prince would be less likely to provoke them to revolt. Atahualpa, on the other hand, would be less likely to resent or revolt against his unique brother's authority and that of the Apucama, in Cuzco.

Some such reasons as these must have been used by the Sapa Inca to convince himself that the course he wanted to take, for emotional reasons, was politically sound.

Huayna Capac's military career was not yet at an end. There were, to the west of his new conquests, some small coastal nations whose lands were famous for their wealth in gem stones. The army was employed to subjugate them, which it did with little difficulty, and a valuable booty—valuable, that is, for its aesthetic quality and its splendor, in emeralds, turquoises and mother-of-pearl—was taken. Thus, by about 1522, the Tahuantinsuyu had reached its greatest extent, an area not much less than that of the combined Common Market countries in Europe, or that of the eastern seaboard states of the United States. It was a domain that contained three hundred and eighty thousand square miles of mountain, forest and savanna, of farm land and pasture land, of lakes and rivers and seacoast, of cities and townships, of irrigation canals and roads, temples and palaces; it included land at every altitude from sea level to fifteen thousand feet, and climates from the equatorial at Quito and the new provinces (Esmeraldas) to the temperate of the southernmost province which lay between 30 and 50 degrees south.

The Sapa Inca had no wish to return to Cuzco and decided to spend the rest of his life in Quito. The Tahuantinsuyu ran like clockwork; he could govern as effectively from there as from the capital, given the excellent system of roads and posts already described. It should perhaps he emphasized in this connection that the Sapa Incas were not like the rulers of nations which had not yet invented physical geography as a science and thus were compelled to rule without knowing exactly the position and extent of their dominions in space, and the relation of the several parts to each other. The Inca *amautas* made and used relief maps constructed correctly to scale and it is probable that the Sapa Incas were as well able to visualize the geography and even topography of their empire as any modern government. In Cuzco, Huayna had an uncle and a brother as regents presiding over the Apucama and perfectly capable of transacting such business as must still be done in the capital. And if, despite these facts, it still seems strange that he did not wish to return, or at least did not return, to Cuzco, it is possible that he may have been influenced not only by inclination but by the fact that the northern frontier was the least secure of all the limits. Also, disturbing rumors of aggressive and probably dangerous foreigners were reaching the court.

The only son of historical importance whom the Sapa Inca had with him in Quito was Atahualpa. In Cuzco were Huáscar, now in his teens and involved in a love affair which was to be tragic; two much younger sons of the blood royal, Manco and Paullu, whose mother was probably the Sapa Inca's cousin, and yet another son who may have been royal, may have been as old as Atahualpa, whose existence is well attested, but yet questionable since his mother is said to have been that Mama Cusimiray, Huayna's eldest sister, who was superseded for barrenness. This prince, Ninan Cuyuche, was a possible heir. Yet it was Huáscar who was regarded as heir apparent and who had been looked upon as *the* heir from the day of his birth. There is one obvious explanation of these confusing circumstances: that after Huayna Capac had taken Mama Rahua Ocllo as his second *qoya*, but not put an end to all intercourse with the first, Mama Cusimiray conceived and bore a son, Ninan Cuyuche, who although, in that case, *younger* than Huáscar had a good claim to the *borla* as being the son of the Sapa Inca's *eldest* sister.

In the year 1523 a barbarous but well-organized people, the Chiriguana of Paraguay, made one of their quite massive, periodical raids across the Inca frontier. This raid was of singular import, for the raiders were accompanied by Spaniards and perhaps led by a Spaniard. Alejo Garcia and his companions were survivors from a ship which had been wrecked on the Brazilian coast in about

1520. They turned up in Paraguay, we know not how, and either took service with, or took charge of, the Chiriguana invasion, marching with these barbarians to the Andean foothills in present-day Bolivia. We have no account of Garcia's adventures, since he was killed by the natives on his return to Paraguay. The Chiriguana, who had seized the country within the Inca frontier from its primitive inhabitants, raided for loot, not for conquest. But they succeeded in capturing an Inca frontier fortress. They constituted no serious threat to the Tahuantinsuyu, but they were a destructive nuisance and had to be dealt with. Huayna Capac sent the *apucuraca* Yasca, an able veteran, to throw the barbarians back across the frontier. That general brought the Chiriguana to battle and defeated them; he also got a sight of the Spaniards and reported what he had seen to the capital and to the Sapa Inca in Quito.

It is perfectly possible that Garcia and his friends were not the only Spaniards to get into the Tahuantinsuyu before the arrival of Pizarro and Almagro. It may very likely have been such unsung free-lance adventurers who left, in the Inca domain, a very terrible ally to prepare the way for the two Spanish captains: the virus of smallpox, a disease unknown to pre-Columbian America and therefore devastating to its natives. This most lethal of the invaders of the New World from the Old must have started making its hideous way through the Four Provinces at about this time, as if sent in advance by the Europeans to get rid of the one man, Huayna Capac, who would certainly have made conquest of the empire, with the means at Pizarro's disposal, quite impossible.

By 1523 smallpox had become epidemic, raging in many cities of the empire. Huayna Capac, still in his early fifties and perfectly capable of governing for another twenty years at least, was one of its first victims. Here follows the tale which some nameless and unprinted poet of the Quechua tongue made of the tragedy:

. . . The Inca returned to Quito where he solemnized the Capac-Raymi. At the hour for eating, a messenger arrived in a black mantle, who reverently kissed the Inca and gave him a *puti* [a box or parcel] which was covered up. The Inca bade the messenger open it, but he excused himself saying the Creator's command was that the Inca himself should do so. Thereupon the Inca opened it and there came flying out a quantity of things like butterflies or bits of paper which spread abroad until they disappeared. This was the pestilence *Sarampion,* and in a few days the general Michaca Mayta died, with many other captains, their faces being covered with scabs. When the Inca saw this he ordered a house to be built of stone, in which he hid himself, and there died. After eight days they took out the body quite dried up and embalmed it and took it to Cuzco on a litter, richly dressed and armed as if it had been alive.[8]

Among the butterflies which flew from this Andean Pandora's box, one was missing: Hope.

In the last years of his long reign, not only did Huayna Capac receive direct intelligence of the Spaniards accompanying the raid on his eastern frontier, but he was kept informed of the activities of these foreigners in their exploring expeditions down the Pacific coast, and possibly of their doings in the far north. He knew of Balboa's arrival off his coast, and the news seems to have caused him grave anxiety. It is possible that he was disturbed, as some chroniclers say, by the feeling that the arrival of these mysterious, and by all accounts terrible, strangers was in fulfillment of an ancient prophecy made by a member of his own family. Like all oracular utterances, this prophecy was so obscurely and ambiguously worded that it could be made to fit almost any untoward event; it was attributed, by popular tradition, to the Sapa Inca Viracocha. It was interpreted—probably after the event, however—as declaring that after a certain number of Sapa Incas had run their course, there would be no more, since there would come to the land a people never seen before, to destroy the religion and polity of the Tahuantinsuyu.

It is at least possible that if Huayna Capac was disturbed by the arrival of the strangers it was because he was superstitious;

it is equally possible that it was because he was wise, and better informed than we know. He had been reigning over a vast empire for thirty or more years; and he might very well have had intelligence of Spanish doings in the islands. We just do not know, but we suggest that Arawk-speaking natives of the islands may have fled from the Spaniards and some of them may have got as far as the Inca frontier with news of the disaster which had come upon their nation. But if there really was such a prophecy concerning the Inca royal line, it is not the only one in history.

⌐Great and terrible events are—or perhaps we should say, used to be—preceded by portents. The sheeted dead did not shriek and gibber in the Cuzcan streets, but there were great earthquakes in the mountain provinces and tidal waves on the coast. The moon was observed to have three great rings about it, the first being the color of blood, and the *amautas* interpreted this as a portent of plague and of war, notably of civil war. A green comet, among several ordinary comets, was observed by the astronomers with consternation; a thunderbolt struck one of the royal palaces. But far more terrible even than these was the portent of the sick eagle:

> . . . a portentous and evil omen fell out in Cuzco which astonished Huayna Capac and terrified the whole kingdom. While the solemn festival of the Sun was being celebrated, they saw an eagle, which they call *anca*, flying through the air, and pursued by five or six kestrels and as many small hawks of the kind that is so beautiful that many have been brought to Spain. In Peru, they are called *huaman* and in Spain *aleto*. They attacked the eagle alternately and felled him by their blows. The eagle, unable to defend himself, fell into the middle of the great square in that city, among the Incas, that they might help him. They took him up and saw that he was sick, covered with scurf as if he had the itch, and almost bald of his lesser feathers. They fed him and treated him kindly but nothing availed, and in a few days he died without having been able to raise himself from the ground. The Inca and his people considered this to be a bad omen, and the

soothsayers said many things touching its interpretation, according to their rules, but all were menacing and foretold the loss of the empire, and the destruction of their polity and idolatry.

The bird was obviously suffering from a severe increase of feather lice; nearly all wild birds have these to a greater or lesser degree, and this condition must have been common enough and known to the Peruvians, who kept aviaries. One suspects the priesthood may have used the incident to influence the succession in a manner pleasing both to the gods and their own interests. Huáscar had given evidence of a desire to curtail the cult of the dead Incas and to reduce the expense of the train of servants dedicated to the service of each one which would not endear him to the hierarchy. A fortuitous incident of this nature could be most advantageous.

Either just before his illness or immediately after he fell ill, the Sapa Inca did his best to settle the succession. Accounts of what happened are conflicting, but it seems clear that Huayna Capac named Ninan Cuyuche as his heir, and not Huáscar, but that this was a formality as Ninan Cuyuche was already sick of the smallpox; conveniently, the augury for his succession was bad. Huáscar was named as next in line. It is said that the augury for Huáscar's succession was also unpropitious; yet the fact is that he did succeed, and it is at least possible, indeed very likely, that the priesthood, after Huáscar's brief and disastrous reign, spread it about that they had forecast disaster.

Meanwhile, some time before, Huayna Capac had made provision for Atahualpa's future. He summoned Huáscar (not Ninan Cuyuche, which is significant), to Quito and, having admitted at once that Quito was part of the empire and should have fallen to the heir with the rest, frankly told the prince that he loved Atahualpa and would grieve to see him ill-provided for. He asked Huáscar to break the entail—that is, to allow Atahualpa to inherit the principality of Quito "which belonged to his maternal ancestors." The old ruler pointed out that Atahualpa would be of more service to the Sapa Inca as a prince ruling a kingdom, than as a poor relation. He may also have pointed out that at least two of the *apucuracas*, including the ablest soldier in the empire, were strongly supporting Atahualpa's cause. Finally, it was made clear that Quito was to be permanently allied with and tributary to the Tahuantinsuyu.

To all this Huáscar is said to have agreed very readily, and even to have offered more. He then returned to Cuzco, where he had long been leading a life of luxury and self-indulgence, fawned upon by those with an eye to the main chance as if he were already Sapa Inca.]

To the reasons which we have already given for Huayna Capac's division of the Tahuantinsuyu, another should perhaps be added. As a very experienced statesman, the Sapa Inca may well have begun to realize that the empire was becoming too big to be administered as one unit; it was becoming unwieldy, and this presaged a threat of internal trouble. A measure of decentralization probably seemed advisable, especially since the Sapa Inca's opinion of his sons' ability was not high. There is, perhaps, a parallel to be drawn with Bonaparte's division of his European empire into semi-autonomous kingdoms governed by members of his family or staff disguised as monarchs.

[There is an extremely peculiar story to be found only in Salcamayhua's *Antiquities*, touching the succession. This Inca writer says that after Huayna's body had been conveyed to Cuzco and there placed with the mummies of his ancestors,[9] and after general mourning had been decreed,

> ... then Yuti Tupac Cusi Huallpa Huáscar Inca made his mother Rava Ocllo marry the dead body in order that he might become legitimate, and the ministers of the temple performed the ceremony out of fear. ...

Whatever arguments and intrigues, recriminations and macabre ceremonies may have preceded the event, the event itself is not in doubt.\While Atahualpa remained behind in Quito, assuming the princeship of that country and strongly backed by the Apucuraca Quizquiz, himself a Quitu, and by the Inca veteran general Chalcuchima, Huáscar was crowned Sapa Inca by the high priest in Cuzco; and he named Atahualpa the Incap Ranti (Viceroy) of Quito, in an official dispatch. Meanwhile, the *qoya* Rahua Ocllo set out to escort Huayna Capac's body back accompanied by Huayna Capac's old friend, councilor and fellow soldier, Auqui Tupac Yupanqui, who went as Atahualpa's representative.

Of Atahualpa at this time we know that he was a strikingly handsome young man of about twenty-five, brave, reasonably intelligent, endowed with common sense, but more remarkable for a fine presence and charm than for the rarer qualities which distinguished his father and his great-grandfather, or for the genius which made Topa Yupanqui a great man. But he also had the immensely valuable distinction of having been much loved and brought forward by his father, Huayna Capac, who had added to his other virtues as a sovereign the supreme one of a very long reign (about thirty-seven years) and had thus become not merely a well-liked monarch, but an institution. It is improbable that Atahualpa insisted, at this time, on the elaborate state and excessive respect for his person which, as we shall see, he insisted upon after he became Sapa Inca. The atmosphere generated by the independent spirit of the Quitu, that spirit which had been fostered by a fertile soil and an adequate rainfall, was simpler and more bracing than that of Cuzco, where manners, etiquette and protocol had become rigidly stylized.

The youthful Sapa Inca Huáscar did not resemble his half brother. While Atahualpa had, albeit with only fair aptitude, been away campaigning in the north and learning the trade of government, Huáscar had remained in the luxurious capital, indulged and deferred to, yet barred, by his youth, from taking any but a formal part in the work of administration, which was directed from faraway Quito, where the political, if not the social, status of capital had necessarily been transferred with the person of the Sapa Inca.

The greatest event of Huáscar's life, until he was crowned Sapa Inca by the high priest, was his passionate love affair with Chumpilaya, a girl of *curaca* rank whose parents had brought her from Ica on the coast to the capital, and whose radiant beauty earned her the sobriquet of Curi Coyllur (the "Golden Star"). Both the prince and his sweetheart were in their early teens. It is written that Golden Star fell as deeply in love with Huáscar as he with her. And when she bore the prince a daughter, the girl was given her young mother's court name, becoming a second Golden Star. It was a bad day for the Tahuantinsuyu when these two met; for the prince was not of a temper to bear with stoicism the tragedy which his love was to entail. And although the love affair of a prince is a very trifling matter it may, by affecting his conduct at some political crisis, have far from trifling consequences. Golden Star was poisoned by a jealous rival among the *pallas*, or "ladies of the court," and she died. This blow fell upon the young lover some time after he had been crowned, when the war with Atahualpa was threatening the state; it cannot have steadied his never very firm hand, though alone it cannot account for his collapse.

When the dowager *qoya* arrived near Cuzco with Huayna's body, Huáscar was informed that Atahualpa had remained behind in Quito, and he became furiously angry. He had, after his coronation, at once recognized his half brother as Incap Ranti of Quito; but this recognition was clearly conditional upon Atahualpa's showing proper respect for his Sapa Inca. Huáscar was driven by rage to commit an act which showed his own want of assurance—showed, too, that the quality of the long line of able men whose heir he was, had failed at last. He caused Auqui Tupac Yupanqui, his brother's envoy, his father's friend, the empire's valued old councilor, and of princely rank, to be arrested with his whole suite, questioned concerning Atahualpa's bearing and intentions, and, the answers failing to satisfy the Sapa Inca, to be put to death. It was an atrocious act: and the dowager *qoya*, deeply grieved and extremely angry at this wanton judicial murder, never forgave her son for this crime. She withdrew from the court at once, establishing her own household at a village near Cuzco.

It was now necessary for Huáscar to marry his sister, Mama Rahua Ocllo's daughter, Chuqui Urpay. The mother's consent was necessary. The dowager refused it, partly because she did not want to see her daughter married to a monster of injustice who was, perhaps, showing signs of a cruel nature, and partly to thwart the son who had wounded and angered her. It was a long time before she gave way to the persuasions of councilors and clergy and allowed policy more weight than resentment. Her consent to the marriage was given at last, but very halfheartedly.

Upon learning of the way his envoy and old mentor had been treated, Atahualpa showed no open resentment. We do not know what his feelings were; but he was always culpably ready to see his friends ill-treated provided his comfort and his immediate policy were not disturbed. There was in his character a strain of indolence, of weakness—already remarked upon, even by his doting father—which led him to come to terms when he could, even when he should not have done so. He seems to have been ready, at least for several years, to submit to Huáscar and to behave with as much humility, short of appearing to do homage in person at the court in Cuzco, as his generals and mentors, Quizquiz and Chalcuchima, would stomach. It is impossible to admire the way he swallowed the murder of Auqui Tupac Yupanqui; but it is important to remember that by wearing the *borla*, Huáscar became god; that Huayna Capac had expressly ordered the brothers to agree together and Atahualpa to acknowledge his junior's paramountcy and submit to him and serve him. We must also remember that these men and women of the Andean world were in some ways different from ourselves, different in their manners and therefore in some of their feelings, for otherwise we shall be astonished and baffled when we learn, for example, that the next envoy sent by the Incap Ranti to his imperial brother was none other than the son of Auqui Tupac Yupanqui, and that the young man expressed no distaste for the mission.

This youth, Quilacu Yupanqui, is described as handsome and dashing, a great favorite with the dowager *qoya* and foster brother to her daughter, the new *qoya*, Chuqui Urpay. He was sent to Cuzco with a suitable suite and instructions to pay homage to the Sapa Inca and confirm the submission of Quito and her prince to the Inca State. It is possible that, under the influence of Quizquiz, Atahualpa was showing cunning and policy rather than a loyalty which amounted to want of spirit; his submission may have been put on to gain time, and he may already have foreseen, or had pointed out to him, the possibility of usurping the *borla*.

Indeed, subsequent events tend to show that this was the case, for when an army was rather suddenly required for action against the Tahuantinsuyu, it was ready.

When Quilacu arrived at Suriti he received a warm message of welcome from the dowager *qoya* and an invitation to stay with her until he heard that the Sapa Inca would receive him. He accepted, and the old lady sent out a party of pretty girls to meet him, and among them according to one chronicler was the Golden Star, daughter of the Sapa Inca and his murdered sweetheart.[10] Sarmiento tells us that the Golden Star, "fairest of the fair maidens of Cuzco," and the Quitu ambassador fell madly in love with each other.

Sir Clements Markham, with his charming gift for making the Incas behave like English ladies and gentlemen in an idealized setting, tells us:

> There was a brief but delightful time under the shade of the molle trees, on lawns carpetted with *cantut* and *amancay*, where the noise of bubbling fountains mingled with the songs of many birds. Lofty mountains surrounded the little valley, and here all but love was forgotten.

We may perhaps here interpolate one point not yet mentioned: If the scene evoked by Markham suggests a formal garden as the setting for his lovers, it is at least a fact that the Inca royal gardens were remarkable, especially for their golden and silver ornaments in the forms of fruit trees, singing birds and other objects of virtu, and for their fountains, the Cuzcans having, it seems, almost an Arab love of running water.

At all events, from his idyl the young envoy was summoned with his embassy to Calca, in the valley called Vilcamayu, where the Sapa Inca was in residence. Quilacu, entering the presence bare of foot and his back stooped under a token burden, as was required of even the greatest officers of state, placed Atahualpa's precious gifts to his brother at Huáscar's feet and delivered his message of submission and loyalty. The Sapa Inca was not appeased; either he had information from his intelligence service that this submission was bogus, or his temper, brooding and implacable, at times even hysterical, would not allow him to behave like a man of sense, much less like a gentleman. He scowled at the ambassador, spurned the presents, and accused Quilacu of being nothing but a spy. Quilacu's friendship with the dowager *qoya* may have had something to do with this. Certainly, a more experienced *chef de mission* would have known better than to stay with the Sapa Inca's formidable old mother, in whose house he must be supposed to have heard a good deal of complaining about the Sapa Inca's unfilial conduct. Perhaps, too, the chronicle is correct about the love affair, and Huáscar had heard of that too, though there could be no objection to Quilacu on grounds of rank or breeding. The ambassador's four elderly colleagues were arrested and put to death and Quilacu himself was sent to Cuzco under escort and imprisoned.

He contrived to send an old servant to Mama Rahua Ocllo to give an account of his reception by her son. Whether the old lady was able to help him we do not know. She probably was, for there is no obvious reason why he, like his father and his colleagues in the embassy, should not have been murdered. In the event, he was spared: he received the Sapa Inca's order to return to Quito and there to tell his master that he, Atahualpa, would soon have to give an account of his viceroyalty to the Sapa Inca.

5

THE MASTER GAMBLER

WE LEFT Captain Francisco Pizarro and his disheartened companions in a remote village of semisavages in a province of dismal swamp and primeval forest on the northern outskirts of the Tahuantinsuyu, an empire of which they knew nothing except what they had just been told of Quito's riches. Had they not been desperate men, they would probably not have believed these tales, but they were obliged to do so or give up all hope. A brief account of what happened before the effective attempt on Peru was made, is now necessary.

While Pizarro was robbing the doubtless simple savages of their few crude gold ornaments and waiting for the ship he had detached to return, Diego de Almagro, his partner, had set sail from Panama in a second ship and, following a trail of blazed trees left by Pizarro along the coast, tried to rejoin the captain. In this search he got as far south as 4 degrees north, there landed at the mouth of the River San Juan, fought a skirmish with some natives in which he lost an eye and won some gold and, failing to find Pizarro, returned to Panama. There, his ship having at last reappeared with provisions, Pizarro was able to join him. The failure of their venture made it much harder to get money to finance a second attempt. But the *alcalde* (mayor) was impressed by the prospects and invested some capital through the priest Luque, one of Pizarro's partners; and a second expedition sailed in 1526. There were two ships, one commanded by Pizarro, the other by

Almagro, and both piloted by Bartolomé Ruiz who turned out to be as brave and enterprising as he was skillful. The ships carried a total of 180 men. They sailed straight to the San Juan, where Pizarro landed with the soldiers, while Almagro went back to Panama for more men and stores, and Ruiz, in the other ship, set out to explore the coast farther south.

Ruiz crossed the equator and went as far as 1 degree south. He fell in with a raft under sail out of Tumbez and from it he obtained two or three native prisoners, some specimens of Inca workmanship, and a good deal of valuable information. Meanwhile, back in Panama, Almagro found a new governor who gave him permission to recruit reinforcements, so that the old soldier was able to sail back to the San Juan camp with eighty new men as well as fresh stores. At San Juan, Pizarro and his men had been making difficult forest marches in search of a way inland, and they had again suffered seriously from starvation, disease and the weather. Thus, up to this point, only Ruiz had made any contact at all with the Tahuantinsuyu, and the Spaniards, driven by appetizing hints and their greed of gain, seem to us like a small swarm of flies hovering and darting round some great resting beast whom they can exasperate but never harm.

The whole expedition having embarked in the ships, Ruiz set a southerly course and sailed on until they decided to make the land at Atacames in the province of Quito. Here, for the first time, the Spaniards found themselves in what was clearly civilized country. Not for nothing had the Sapa Incas Topa Yupanqui and Huayna Capac worked for years to build up their favorite dominion; Pizarro and his followers saw land under intensive cultivation, numerous towns, some of them large, but also bodies of disciplined troops ready to deal with them if they started looting or attacking the inhabitants. One gets a curious impression of both sides keeping at arm's length, making little if any contact, both wary and nervous. Nor is it at all clear why official action was not taken to call the foreigners to some account of themselves. Pizarro, far from being encouraged by what he saw, seems at this point to have lost his nerve for the first and last time. He was, it seems, eager to return to Panama, presumably to report the discovery and get more help; the potential opposition of the natives was more than he had bargained for, and of a superior kind. Almagro was for trying to do more with the force at their disposal. There was a violent row, but at last both men came to their senses and it was agreed that while Pizarro waited with a party of soldiers on Gallo Island, which had been discovered by Ruiz in latitude 1°57' north, Almagro should again return for recruits so that their force might be sufficient to march into the well-policed country they had found.

The arrangement pleased nobody. The men left on Gallo were frightened and discontented, and presumably it was because only he could keep them in hand and encourage them by his own gallant bearing that Pizarro was chosen to remain with them. Some of his men, however, sent letters by members of Almagro's crew, asking to be rescued. Almagro learned of this, and the letters were seized and destroyed—all, that is, but one; this, enclosed in a large ball of cotton sent as a present to the governor's wife in Panama, reached its destination. It was written in doggerel and it is well worth quoting, for it gives us a very good idea of the state of mind of the men who had been marooned on Gallo:

> *Pues Señor Gobernador*
> *Mirelo bien por entero*
> *Que alla va el recocedor*
> *Y acá queda el carnicero.*

> *Keep a sharp watch, Lord Governor,*
> *For the drover while he's near,*
> *Since he goes home to get the sheep*
> *For the butcher, who stays here.*

Pizarro had kept one of the ships with him at Gallo, but so mutinous did the men become that he was at last obliged to let the more troublesome of them take the vessel and follow Almagro. The Governor of Panama, convinced by Almagro's return followed by that of the second ship, and perhaps by the doggerel letter, decided that the captains of the expedition were incompetent, refused to allow any more recruiting, and sent two small ships to Gallo to take off and bring home every Spaniard left on the island. They were commanded by Don Pedro Tafur, and their arrival was greeted by Pizarro's men, worn out and utterly cast down by hunger, sickness and incessant rain, with shouts of joy and relief. But Almagro and Luque had sent Pizarro a letter urging him not to give up hope, to refuse to return, and to hang on just a little longer to give them time to bring the Governor round. The letter was not needed; Pizarro, always at his best in adversity, had fully recovered his nerve and had no intention of giving up. He had had ample time on Gallo to review his state; he was over fifty, his small capital was all gone, his credit was pledged to the last farthing, his reputation was lost, and he faced the fact that he might as well die where he was as return to Panama to be laughed at, perhaps punished, and anyway to rot slowly into a miserable old age. He was, in short, in the strongest position possible for an adventurer: he had absolutely nothing but the fag end of his life to lose.

It was at this point in his career that he showed himself capable of rising magnificently to an occasion. When his men were drawn up on the beach ready to embark aboard Tafur's ships and eager to sail for home and comfort, Pizarro drew his sword and with its point marked a line in the sand. He then turned to his men and made them a short speech which must surely have inspired Garibaldi's famous "blood, sweat and tears" call, so effectively quoted to the English by Winston Churchill in 1940.

Gentlemen, this line signifies toil, hunger, thirst, fatigue, sickness and every other kind of danger that must be met with in this conquest until life be ended. Let those who have the courage to meet and overcome the dangers of this heroic enterprise cross the line in token of their resolution and as testimony that they will be my faithful companions. And let those who feel unworthy return to Panama. For I will not put force upon any man. I trust in God that, for His greater honor and glory, His Eternal Majesty will help those who remain with me, though they be few; and that we shall not miss those who forsake us.

We who have read history, and whose lifetime has been punctuated by calls to arms by a score of soldier politicians and political soldiers representing as many conflicting causes, know that no man can hope to lead others in action unless he is prepared to invoke the gods. Even the Communist chiefs have their god, Historical Necessity. The difference between our own times and Pizarro's, however, is clear: Pizarro almost certainly believed that there was a god who would help him because He preferred Spanish Christians to Peruvian heathens. But the majority of his men were not convinced of it. Sixteen only, with more faith in their god and the future or with less to hope for from the present, crossed the line. The reader will decide for himself whether they were the noblest, moved by heroism, loyalty and religion, or the basest, as desperate as Pizarro himself and moved only by cupidity or the hope of repairing their fortunes. Doubtless, there were among them men of both kinds, some faithful hounds and some ravening wolves; and the thoughtful will be struck by the fact that either would serve the leader's purpose equally well.

Pizarro and his loyal sixteen transferred themselves from Gallo to the neighboring and smaller island of Gorgona, where the water and game were better, while Don Pedro carried the less adventurous majority back to Panama. There, the Governor shrugged off Pizarro's heroism as an act of madness and refused all further aid. But he was a less obstinate, more imaginative official than his predecessor Pedro Arias, and at last he yielded to Luque and Almagro; he would allow one small ship to return to Gorgona and to spend six months, no more, in further exploration. This vessel, piloted by Ruiz who carried with him the Peruvians he had taken from the raft, reached Gorgona after Pizarro and the sixteen had been there seven months and had almost given up hope. But hope revived as they went aboard. Ruiz, who was at last able to use the information he had obtained from the raftsmen of Tumbez and who, we suspect, would have managed the whole affair much better in the first place had it been left to him, steered directly for the Gulf of Guayaquil.

The luck had changed, as it does when all the men of an expedition are resolute and, for whatever diverse reasons good and bad, of one mind. Ruiz sailed his ship to the gulf in twenty days. Sails were lowered and the anchor dropped off Tumbez late in the year

1527, when the uneasy peace between the Sapa Inca Huáscar and his half brother Atahualpa, Incap Ranti of Quito, had lasted two years. And the Spaniards could now confirm the impression already gained that they would have to deal not with tribes of savages but with a civilized nation or at least with barbarians upon whom a social and political order had been imposed. They still, at this stage, had no idea of the extent and power of that civilization, or perhaps not even Pizarro would have dared envisage its conquest.

The scene of Pizarro's landfall is probably one of the most impressive in the world. Beyond the strip of littoral the mountains tower to an immense altitude, domed by Chimborazo and pointed by the snowy peak of Cotopaxi's cone. But it is probable that Pizarro and his men had no eyes for these natural grandeurs; their attention was absorbed by the spectacle of houses built in orderly streets, of cultivated and elaborately irrigated farm lands, and of the flotilla of balsa rafts which, making out from Tumbez, was now steering for the ship as it headed in toward a suitable anchorage. These rafts were transports carrying troops on an expedition against the savages of Puna Island. Ruiz ran his ship alongside the flotilla and Pizarro invited the chiefs on board. The invitation was accepted, the men of Tumbez being assured by their fellow citizens already aboard the Spaniard that the strangers were "a wonderful race of beings who had come hither for no harm but solely to be made acquainted with the country and its inhabitants." Thus Prescott; and whether this misinformation was a manifestation of innocence or of treachery induced by fear, we do not know. Probably of innocence, for in nearly all of the first contacts between Europeans and the other races of mankind, the latter have at first shown themselves trusting and affectionate and ready to be impressed, only later showing resentment and offering violence when the ferocity of the white men became manifest.

Pizarro asked the Peruvians—the Spaniards had decided that Peru (from *Biru*, the name of a river discovered in the course of the first expedition to the coast) was to be the name of this country—for fresh provisions. The *curaca* of Tumbez, who is said to have thought the visitors a race of superior beings but whose generosity may well be attributed to the ordinary courtesy of men accustomed to a regime of plenty, sent out rafts with pineapples and other fruits, corn, coconuts, game, fish and several llamas on the hoof, which Pizarro now beheld and admired for the first time, and could compare with the crude drawings he had seen in Balboa's possession.

The provision balsas, however, carried a passenger more interesting than llamas. An Inca of high rank, probably an official on a tour of inspection, happened to be in Tumbez at the time and he decided that he had better investigate the strange vessel. He and Pizarro were able to converse after a fashion, for the captives taken by Ruiz had learned a little Castilian. The Inca officer asked why the Spaniards had come to the Tahuantinsuyu. Pizarro, with what seems to us now mere brass effrontery—he had about two-score men with him!—but which probably was a manifestation of that confidence now so hard to understand, replied that he was come to assert the supremacy of his master, the greatest and most powerful prince on earth, over this land, and to save its inhabitants from that darkness of the mind in which, worshiping an evil spirit, they doomed their souls to perdition. He had, he said, come to give them knowledge of the true and only God, Jesus Christ, and of eternal salvation through belief in Him. What the interpreters—appropriately enough they were simple fishermen—made of this is not recorded. It is hardly surprising that the Inca made no reply whatsoever.

On the following day pigs and poultry were presented to the *curaca* by Alonso de Molina, who called in person as Pizarro's envoy. His report of the state in which the *curaca* lived, of his gold and silver plate service, of the gold and silver which lavishly decorated the temple to that evil spirit which Pizarro had come to cast out, was disbelieved. A Greek officer, Pedro de Candia, Pizarro's most faithful and most useful lieutenant, was sent ashore in his turn, for he was trusted as a man who always kept his head. Candia, after impressing the Peruvians with the power of his harquebus and the flashing steel of his armor and his sword, brought back a report which surpassed Molina's. He had seen all the sights and they had made his eyes pop; he had seen, among other things, the garden of a House of Chosen Women, and he was able to describe not only its living plants, but its ornamental fruit trees of solid gold and silver.

The Spaniards now had the knowledge they had come for. They sailed on, coasting down to latitude 9 degrees south. With them they took a native of Tumbez who was christened Felipillo, and who was to be Pizarro's interpreter, spoiled favorite, and perhaps *âme damnée,* for several adventurous years. The southerly voyage enabled Pizarro and Ruiz to confirm the impressions of their discovery. They could return to Panama now, for Pizarro was triumphantly vindicated. The voyage north was prosperous. In Panama, Pizarro reported to the Governor and to his own delighted associates. With them it was agreed that he should go to Spain and seek a commission from the Crown to undertake the conquest of Peru. Pizarro had to beg and borrow money for the journey, and in the spring of 1528 he and de Candia sailed for Spain.

The Emperor Charles V was in Toledo, where he received this latest of the Spanish adventurers whose American gold and silver was to ruin the commerce and impoverish the people of half his empire.[1] Charles was about to set out for Italy and had not much time to give Pizarro, but he was impressed, and he left orders that a contract should be made with him. Negotiations were carried on between Pizarro and the Queen Mother's government and the contract was not signed until July 1529, for Spanish cabinets were always slow in transacting business and rather distrustful, as well they might be, of ruffianly adventurers. While he was waiting, Pizarro met and talked with Hernando Cortes. By the terms of the contract Pizarro was appointed Captain General of Peru and its *adelantado.* He was ennobled with the Order of Santiago and granted a coat of arms. For a bastard swineherd to be ennobled— made an *hidalgo,* a "son of someone" (*hijo de algo*)—we may be sure was a great triumph for Pizarro. Thirteen of the sixteen who had crossed the line on the sands were ennobled by name. Almagro was appointed Governor of Tumbez, and his promotion to the rank of marshal was envisaged. Luque was made Bishop of Tumbez and "protector of the Indians." Ruiz was created Grand Pilot of the South Seas, an appointment which carried no emolument. Candia was made commander of the artillery.

From the court Pizarro went home to Estremadura, where he had no difficulty in recruiting his four brothers; presumably they had not made a success of life at home. The eldest, described as his father's only legitimate son, was Hernando. Markham, following Prescott, says that he was "a big tall man with thick lips and a very red nose, brave and proud, with an uncompromising temper and ruthlessly cruel." Perhaps the red nose was evidence of a bad digestion, which would account for the evil temper too. Juan and Gonzalo were Francisco's father's bastards and illiterate.

Another half brother was Francisco's mother's bastard, Martin de Alcantara. With these four, as tough a gang as ever set out to make their fortunes, Pizarro sailed from Sanlúcar de Barrameda in January 1530, accompanied also by his young cousin Pedro Pizarro acting as his page and to become his historian, and by an acidulous, fanatical, inquisitorial Dominican, Friar Vicente de Valverde, likewise a kinsman of Pizarro.

It is hardly necessary to say that Almagro, on hearing the results of his partner's embassy, was furious: Pizarro had grabbed all for himself and fobbed off his associate with a worthless trifle. Almagro was no Ruiz, to be satisfied with a high-sounding and empty title. True, he had come off better than Ruiz, the real discoverer of Tumbez; there would be pickings from the citizens for the governor of Tumbez, none from the fishes of the South Seas for its Grand Pilot. Pizarro did his best to keep the peace with the old soldier, but Almagro never trusted him again. Almagro also conceived a particular dislike for Hernando Pizarro, who in turn often treated him with contemptuous hostility. Despite the stormy atmosphere created by this disharmony, preparations went forward, doubtless under the quiet guidance of Luque, the Bishop of Tumbez. As before, Pizarro was to go on ahead, Almagro to follow after an interval of time with fresh men and provisions. Pizarro, with 183 men and 37 horses, set sail in three small ships on December 28, 1531. Two weeks later he landed in San Mateo Bay, and while men and horses marched south along the shore, the ships returned to Panama for reinforcements and supplies which were being sharked up in that colony and in Nicaragua. They returned with 30 men and 27 horses: the venture, clearly, was still not very popular. With 213 men and 64 horses, then, Pizarro continued his march along the shore, through populated country, until he reached the Gulf of Guayaquil, and there he ferried his men and beasts across to the island of Puna. It is not clear why; he may have thought of it as a base, or he may have wanted to clear his rear. At all events, he massacred the population which, though he did not yet know it, had been sacking Tumbez. Then he re-embarked his army, and sailed over to Tumbez, where he found everything greatly changed for the worse. During his long absence, the civil war which had long threatened between the Sapa Inca Huáscar and the Incap Ranti of Quito, Atahualpa, had been fought and won and lost.

The events which led to the ruin which Pizarro found in Tumbez will be described in the next chapter, but it will be convenient to say here that Huáscar had been defeated and was held prisoner by his half brother's generals; and that Atahualpa, now Sapa Inca, lay at Caxamarca across the cordillera from Tumbez, on his way from Quito to Cuzco.

Pizarro certainly thought he saw his opportunity in the reduced state of the whole country, which was the aftermath of the civil war; but, as we shall see, the ruinous condition of Tumbez was misleading. The struggle between Huáscar and Atahualpa had done little to disturb the massive stability of the Tahuantinsuyu, its inhabitants had continued in their peaceful and laborious ways like the peasants of medieval England ignoring the battles of the gentry engaged in their Wars of the Roses. It is true that, like those peasants, like peasants and farmers everywhere and in all history, it was the *puric* who bore on his broad back the whole cost of the war. But the patience of the peasantry is almost inexhaustible and the farmer's way of life teaches him resignation. This, and this alone, accounts for the fact that he so rarely rises and hangs his oppressors or leaders, kings and commissars, presidents, prelates and prime ministers.

The state in which Pizarro found Tumbez, then, must have

encouraged him although it depressed his men. The captain, while in Spain seeking his commission, had met his reputed kinsman Cortes and no doubt had heard the details of his conquest. And like everyone else he must have been particularly impressed by the desperate trick which had enabled Cortes to paralyze the whole Mexican civil and military force for months. This tale of treacherous audacity is well known, but its influence on Pizarro's conduct was so great that it must be briefly retold.

After Cortes had been a week inside Mexico, both his European force and his Tlascalan allies were paralyzed by the kindness, friendliness and gentleness of the Mexican "emperor" Moctezuma. Cortes had great cause for anxiety. His soldiers, described by Prescott as rude and licentious, might at any moment provoke the Aztec natives to a brawl; the Tlascalan allies might get out of hand; the Mexican people were becoming angry and impatient about the Spaniards' presence and Moctezuma's failure to act; worst of all, his superiors might send a stronger force into Mexico and someone better-born and more influential at court would snatch the vice royalty and the riches of Mexico from him. He knew that he must act to break the peace with Moctezuma.

The great difficulty was to pick a quarrel with so accommodating and mild a man as Moctezuma. A suitable bone of contention was found in the treacherous murder of two Spanish soldiers by a Mexican cacique, for which Moctezuma was in no way responsible and of which he knew nothing, facts perfectly well known to Cortes. Plans were carefully made, an audience was sought, and a mass was celebrated in order to involve God in the piece of dirty work ahead. As usual, the Spaniards were graciously received and showered with presents of gold and silver; the emperor was held in lighthearted talk until Cortes saw that the requisite number of his men had slipped into the room or to their posts outside. The Spaniard then raised the question of the murder. It was obvious to all that this was news to Moctezuma, who, nevertheless, with that tiresome mildness which made him so hard to provoke, at once agreed to send for the chief responsible, and without further delay he sent away a messenger bearing the royal signet by way of warrant, to summon the man for trial and punishment.[2] The Aztec emperor's sweet reason forced Cortes to improvise another scene for his sinister comedy; he declared himself satisfied that Moctezuma was innocent but said that it was important also to convince his own monarch, that great emperor whom Moctezuma had already, though not yet formally, acknowledged as his divine overlord. To this end, let Moctezuma transfer his residence to the palace occupied by the Spaniards. Here, in Prescott's words, is what happened:

> Montezuma listened to this proposal, and the flimsy reasoning with which it was covered, with looks of profound amazement. He became pale as death; but in a moment his fase flushed with resentment as, with the pride of offended dignity, he exclaimed, "When was it ever heard that a great prince like myself voluntarily left his own palace to become a prisoner in the hands of strangers!" Cortes assured him he would not go as a prisoner. He would experience nothing but respectful treatment from the Spaniards, would be surrounded by his own household and hold intercourse with his people as usual. In short, it would be but a change of residence from one of his palaces to another, a circumstance of frequent occurrence with him. It was in vain. "If I should consent to such degradation," he answered, "my subjects never would!" When further pressed, he offered to give up one of his sons and two of his daughters to remain as hostages with the Spaniards, so that he might be spared this disgrace.[8]

After two hours of argument one of Cortes's officers lost patience. "Why do we waste words on this barbarian? We have gone too far to recede now. Let us seize him and, if he resists, plunge our swords into his body." Moctezuma did not understand the words but he understood the tone and gestures and he asked the girl who was called Marina, who was Cortes's mistress and who spoke Aztec, Maya and Castilian, what the angry Spaniard was saying. The girl explained as gently as she could and then besought her king to go with the white men to their quarters where he would be treated respectfully and kindly, whereas if he refused they would use violence and probably kill him.

It was in vain that the unhappy prince looked round for sympathy or support. As his eyes wandered over the stern visages and iron forms of the Spaniards, he felt that his hour was indeed come; and in a voice scarcely audible with emotion, he consented to accompany the strangers, to quit the palace whither he was never more to return. Had he possessed the spirit of the first Montezuma, he would have called his guards around him and left his lifeblood on the threshold, sooner than have been dragged a dishonored captive across it. But his courage sank under the circumstances. He felt he was the instrument of an irresistible Fate!

The comedy was sustained: Moctezuma was treated in appearance as a guest freely residing with friends to honor them and please himself. The irony of the Spaniards' bowings and courtesies must have been very bitter to so sensitive and intelligent a man. For he was, of course, closely guarded and guard duty was so strict and onerous that at least one officer, later punished for his want of expedient hypocrisy, was heard to exclaim in the emperor's hearing, "Better this dog of a king should die than that we should wear out our lives in this fashion!" In the end, of course, this outspoken character had his way: having first obliged Moctezuma to swear allegiance to the Spanish Crown; having next forced the Aztec to call in the whole national treasure in gold and silver plate and having thus wrung every penny they could get out of him; having held the captive person of the king as a shield between themselves and the growing anger and impatience of the Mexican people; having nevertheless so provoked the Mexicans by robbery and by blasphemy of the Aztec gods that they did revolt and try to expel the pestilential aliens, Cortes and his companions foully murdered the man who had trusted, protected, submitted to and enriched them. The single satisfaction denied them was the saving of Moctezuma's soul as they destroyed his body. For when at the end he was called on to ensure his salvation by confessing Christ, this man, who has been called pusillanimous by the historians, proudly replied to the priest Olmedo, whose distress and concern were genuine, "I have but a few moments to live, and will not at this hour desert the faith of my fathers." [4]

Such, then, was the example recalled to Francisco Pizarro's mind when he heard, in war-shattered Tumbez, that Atahualpa, the Moctezuma of this more southerly empire, lay not far away at Caxamarca. Pizarro had his problems: the natives of Tumbez were scattered and out of hand; the Spaniards' baggage was looted and stolen; there was brawling and killing between Spaniards and Peruvians. Still, Pizarro was encouraged; the empire was apparently ravaged by civil war, and he saw an opportunity in this state of affairs. La Fontaine, in later years, was to point the way in verse:

> Pour un âne enlevé
> Deux voleurs se battaient
> L'un voulait le garder,
> L'autre voulait le vendre.
> Pendant que nos deux champions se battaient
> Et que les coups de poings s'échangaient,
> Arrive un troisième larron
> Qui saisit maître Aliboron.

The Captain General sent out a body of horse to take any Peruvians they could catch. They returned with prisoners and among them, by luck, was the *curaca* of Tumbez, who explained the state of his city and the lawlessness of its citizens by saying that the men of Puna, taking advantage of the civil war, had raided Tumbez, driven its inhabitants into the woods, and sacked the town. Nor could the *curaca* yet look to the government in Cuzco for help, as the war was barely over. Pizarro, by his devastation of Puna, had unwittingly been avenging Tumbez and leading a punitive expedition for the Cuzcan government. Knowing that the excesses committed by his own men had been responsible for the Peruvians' robberies and raids on his baggage, Pizarro accepted this explanation and agreed to overlook the whole business if the *curaca* would promise obedience, which that officer hastened to do.

The Spaniard's politic mildness was dictated by the fact that he had his hands full of trouble already; his men were losing faith in him and had nearly lost their stomach for the enterprise. The former expedition had left two white men in Tumbez, and they had vanished. It transpired that they had been killed, probably in a brawl rather than legally, because one of them had violated a girl. For some reason, this had a depressing effect on morale. When Pizarro tried to encourage the men by reading aloud a short note supposed to have been left with a Peruvian by one of the dead Spaniards, "Know, whoever you may be who may chance to set foot in this land, that it contains more gold and silver than there is iron in Biscay," this was dismissed with derision as the Captain General's propaganda and a clumsy forgery at that; and probably it was.

It was now that Pizarro began to show his mettle as a leader. He saw that nothing was to be gained by waiting; his object must be to seek, find and secure the person of this Inca Atahualpa who seemed to be master of the country. Yet he was far from easy in his mind; he would have preferred to wait until he had some clear idea of the extent of the Inca empire, of its resources in men under arms, of its wealth and social organization. He did not like acting in the dark. But the example of Cortes had taught him that there was only one attitude to strike when leading a small force of desperadoes against unknown but certainly overwhelming odds: he must be bold, resolute and, in due course, bloody.

He therefore left a small garrison of men to hold Tumbez as terminal of his only line of communication with Panama, and led his main body on a southerly march along the littoral. His first objective was a suitable site for a camp which might become a town, a place where he could found a colony which would become a base for the conquest of Peru. The march lasted several weeks, partly across rainless desert and partly through fertile, irrigated valleys. Pizarro imposed an iron discipline on his men, rigorously punishing any looting or abuse of the Peruvian villagers. He was everywhere received with the mildness and hospitality natural to the people, and everywhere readily supplied with fresh provisions. At each center of population—there were no great towns here—the same comedy was enacted: public proclamation was made that the Spaniards came in the names of the Vicar of Christ and the Emperor of Spain who required the Peruvians' obedience as Christians and as vassals. Of course, the Peruvians did not understand one syllable of this nonsense; but since their ordinary acts of courtesy were accepted as homage by Pizarro, their conversion and submission to Church and Crown of Spain were solemnly recorded and attested by a notary public with the troops, and everyone was satisfied.

The site for Pizarro's first town was fixed upon in the valley of Tangarara, or Tangarala, and there the town of San Miguel was founded. (The location was later found to be unhealthy, and the town was moved to the banks of the Piura River. Thus, the present city of San Miguel de Piura is the oldest European settlement established in the Tahuantinsuyu.) The men left behind in Tumbez were summoned, the ships sailed round to the mouth of the Piura, timber was felled, stone quarried, and building started. Nothing is more remarkable, in our world of specialized tradesmen, than the manner in which fifteenth-century soldiers and sailors turned their hands to every trade, becoming, at need, masons or wheelwrights, carpenters or plasterers. The buildings raised included a church, a fort and a court of justice. A municipal council of the officials usual in any Spanish town was elected or appointed so that San Miguel had its *regidores* and its *alcalde* before it had any houses. This instinct, manifest in the conquistadors, to have everything orderly and lawful from the beginning is wholly admirable but it is not, as Señor de Madariaga implies, exceptional; much the same kind of conduct is to be noted in the first English, French and Dutch settlements outside of Europe.

The surrounding country was next parceled out among the new colonists, hitherto soldiers, now soldier-settlers. To each settler was allotted a number of native Peruvians as slaves in all but name. The excuse for this outrage, apart from the fact that the practice of *repartimiento* was normal in the Spanish colonies of the New World, is recorded by Pizarro's secretary and cousin with a candor which time has made amusing:

> It being manifest that the colonists could not support themselves without the help of the Indians, the churchmen and leaders of the enterprise all agreed that a *repartimiento* of the natives would serve the cause of religion and tend greatly to their spiritual wel-

fare, since they would have the opportunity of initiation into our holy faith.

In the course of the march to Tangarara and as a result of reconnaissance by parties detached to explore the land and question the natives, Pizarro had obtained some of the information he had so badly wanted. He now knew something of the course of the civil war; he knew its outcome, and he had confirmed that the victorious Atahualpa lay within twelve days' march of San Miguel. But he also knew that the wealth and power of the Sapa Inca were overwhelming, and that, if the bait was far more tempting than he had even dreamed of, the trap was also far more dangerous. It was now perfectly clear that even if he waited at San Miguel for Almagro and the reinforcements he might bring, the force at his disposal would be ridiculously small compared with that of the Peruvians. Moreover, the longer he waited and hesitated to take the initiative, the greater the chance that the Incas would see their danger and exterminate the Spaniards while it was still easy for a small detachment of their army to do so.

There was another reason for quick action. The tropical climate and a life of ease overseeing Peruvian slave labor was lowering his people's morale. A huntsman after dangerous game, he needed a pack of wolves, not house dogs. There was one way to take action and yet avoid direct encounter with the Sapa Inca and his victorious army: a swift march and a lightning blow against Cuzco, of whose greatness and wealth Pizarro was now informed. But supposing he did that, he would still, only a few weeks or months later, have to fight a war against odds so enormous that to hope for victory was fatuous. No, there remained just one chance of success; he must emulate cousin Cortes, march to the Sapa Inca's camp and find means to seize his person and so hold the whole empire for ransom.

Before setting out on this extraordinary adventure, Pizarro had one piece of business to transact. His officers had turned in a quantity of gold and silver ornaments and utensils obtained by plunder or theft or trade. These were melted down and cast into ingots, and the Crown's one-fifth set aside. The remaining four-fifths should have been distributed among his men, but the Captain General persuaded them to let him keep it, promising to repay them from the next lot of loot which fell into their hands. (Morale, and therefore confidence, had been fully restored.) This done, Pizarro gave orders that the colonists left behind were to treat the Peruvians well and to do all in their power to maintain the good will of the surrounding population. The *contador* (accountant general) Navarro was left in charge of the new town while the Captain General, at the head of two hundred men, less than half of them being mounted, set out to find, trick and capture the emperor of a vast and powerful empire who was surrounded by his victorious troops and supported by his councilors and his generals.

Prescott asks us to believe that the great hazard of the enterprise was its charm; and that Pizarro was acting "in the spirit of the knight errant." A curious claim—what did he know of knight errantry, this sometime swineherd, this aging failure barely out of debt to his backers, this desperate adventurer who could not read? He went forth bravely, indeed, with a cool head and a resolute heart. But surely his were the coolness and resolution of a master gambler making a desperate last throw.

6

THE CIVIL WAR

WHILE FRANCISCO PIZARRO was in Spain preparing for the Peruvian adventure, Quilacu Yupanqui was on his way back from Cuzco to Quito with the Sapa Inca Huáscar's threatening message. Unwilling to go without seeing his Golden Star again, he contrived to get a message delivered to the household at Siquillapampa saying that he would, if possible, turn aside from the great north road to the Chinchaysuyu and Quito, and formally claim the girl from her guardian, the Princess Cahua Ticlla, who was the Sapa Inca's sister. The legend of these lovers, curiously interwoven with the great events which were shaking the Tahuantinsuyu, tells us that the girl kept anxious watch for her lover's coming, taking every passing farmer with a *taclla* on his shoulder for Quilacu in disguise. One day Quilacu finally did emerge from a field of man-tall maize in which he had been hiding, and the girl flew to his arms. Quilacu reported to the princess what had happened to his embassy, and he then asked for her niece in marriage. The princess replied, however, that the relations between Quilacu's prince, Atahualpa, and Curi Coyllur's father being what they were, the young people would have to wait. They were obliged to accept this decision; the princess doubtless made it clear that they must not be responsible for provoking her brother still further against Atahualpa. Quilacu continued on his way to Quito to report the outcome of his mission and thereafter to take up a subordinate army command in the division commanded by the Apucuraca Chalcuchima.

A probable reason for Huáscar's increasingly aggressive conduct

151

—and it is clear that he was now regretting the readiness with which he had agreed to his father's wishes regarding the division of the empire—was that he had conceived an ambition to emulate his ancestors and add to his dominions; or such a policy may have been forced on him by the difficulty of remaining at peace when there still remained parts of the known world outside the Tahuantinsuyu and hostile to it. The most interesting possibilities for conquest lay to the north; but it was obvious that Atahualpa himself, pushed by his ambitious Quitu generals, might undertake some military adventures there. The Incap Ranti had at his disposal a whole group of warlike nations, incorporated by Huayna Capac into the Inca system and therefore subject to conscription; they could provide Atahualpa with large numbers of soldiers. It was even conceivable that Atahualpa might conquer so much territory as to create a power comparable in fighting strength, if not in economic resources, to the Tahuantinsuyu itself; and so become, despite his protestations of humble vassalage, a very dangerous rival for world dominion.

Huáscar and his *apu-cuna* probably had the political acumen to see that even if Atahualpa had no such ambitions himself, he was under the influence of his general the Apucuraca Quizquiz; that Quizquiz knew himself to be the ablest soldier in the whole country; that Quizquiz, albeit loyal to the *mystique* of the great Incaic system, was a Quitu and might well consider that the Tahuantinsuyu could not be in safer hands than those of himself and his half-Quitu prince. Huáscar might perceive all this, but he was temperamentally incapable of making properly cool and calculating use of his own intelligence. This is manifest in his treatment of the old prince Tupac Yupanqui; by executing his father's old comrade-in-arms and the empire's valued councilor, and by alienating the dowager *qoya*, Huáscar had committed worse than a crime—he had committed a blunder. For it is perfectly clear that by so doing he had made a party matter of his quarrel with Atahualpa and roused a faction against himself even in Cuzco.

Whatever the origin of that division of society in Cuzco and in other cities throughout the land, into the two moieties *hurin* and *hanan*, that division had by Huáscar's time taken on a distinct flavor of party. We have suggested that the division was of sexual origin, that it reflected some very ancient dominion of women under a matriarchy, and of the later rise to dominion of the male, the warrior. Had it, perhaps, retained even in its sophistication, its decadence, some hints of its origin? It is at least clear from the hints of those chroniclers and commentators whose references to social strife between *hanan* and *hurin* presume prior knowledge in the reader and therefore do not explain enough, that the Hanan party was that of the old queen Rahua Ocllo. In the oldest legends, when Cuzco was founded, the people and quarter of Hanan-Cuzco were the queen's followers, those of Hurin-Cuzco the Sapa Inca's. Possibly, if not probably, the *qoya's* party at court was always the Hanan faction; and one was born to one's political party in Cuzco.

It seems that not only Auqui Tupac Yupanqui but others of Atahualpa's envoys to the court were of the Hanan faction. The Sapa Inca was, of course, a Hurin man. Whether faction entered into his treatment of the envoys, we do not know. But it is clear that his killing of them, and the angry withdrawal of Rahua Ocllo from her son's court, turned all Hanan-Cuzco against the Sapa Inca. The opposition was not overt until the last, tragic scene; but it was there and it was to weaken Huáscar very seriously in his struggle with the north, for it constituted a moral "fifth column" not only in the city but in every province of the land. And when, in what follows, we encounter, as we shall, some very ambiguous conduct on the part of some of the Sapa Inca's principal officers in the struggle with Atahualpa, we cannot help seeing the Hanan faction at work.

Moreover, Huáscar was alienating another powerful party, the Church. He was disturbed—it is more likely to have been his accountants and the Apucama who were disturbed—by the drain on the state's resources of the increasingly important Cult of the Dead. The country had not only one living court to support; it had, grotesquely, the equally elaborate and costly "dead" ones of Huayna Capac, Topa Yupanqui, Pachacuti and possibly several others. That Huáscar planned to reform this is to his credit; but just as his temper disabled him from making use of his own political good sense, so his personality was against him when it came to social and economic reform. His manner was not grave and dignified; it was sullen and excitable. And a reform which another Sapa Inca might have successfully presented as a contribution to the national welfare seemed, when proposed by Huáscar, to be motivated by mere parsimony or by a jealous desire to confine pomp and luxury to his own household. (The state in which Huáscar lived was a curious mixture of magnificence and simplicity; we shall describe it below, as Atahualpa adopted it in imitation of his brother's court and of his father's court at Quito.)

It should be understood what Cuzco meant to any man of Inca blood, let alone to one who might aspire to the throne: Cuzco was to the Incas what Lhasa is to the Tibetans, Mecca to the Arabs, and Paris to all educated Europeans, and what Rome was once to the whole Western Christian world. Cuzco was at once Sacred City, world center, megalopolis, *la ville lumière*; it was religion, learning, sophistication, fashion. Atahualpa, in his northern capital to which he does not seem to have been attached, as his father and grandfather were, felt banished, a mere provincial, even something of an exile. This, no doubt, had something to do with his readiness to fall in with the plans of the war party at court, the party led by the rude veteran Quizquiz. That soldier's Quitu prejudices and half-barbarous contempt for Cuzcan refinements made him see the Inca enemy as an effete tyrant to be destroyed and superseded by a man worthier of empire. Atahualpa saw that he could use the general's feelings in this matter for his own ends.

He began then to surround himself with the pomp and ceremony suitable to a Sapa Inca—hardly to a viceroy, except as a grand show intended to impress the natives and thereby to support the authority of the empire itself. It was not difficult for Atahualpa to find court officers and *pallas* who knew all about etiquette and protocol; for twelve years his father had ruled the empire from Quito, and there were plenty of men and women who knew how to behave when the prince assumed a state equal to his unique brother's.

Atahualpa held court in a room of the palace to which only the women and girls attendant on him had access. These were his "qoya" (who had, of course, no right to that heavenly title), his other wives and his concubines. It was their duty to wait on him at table, to valet him, to act, in general, as his domestics, confidantes and playmates. The male courtiers were all gentlemen of either Inca or *curaca* rank; perhaps there were one or two up-and-coming *yanacuna* whom we may, with a good deal of stretching of meanings and some reservations, think of as the *nouveaux riches* of this court. But it is quite important not to allow the use of this term or other European terms, unavoidable as they are, to give us an impression which is quite misleading. There was, about both the real Inca court and its imitation in Quito, a quality of simplicity which is still not exactly barbarism. We can best explain what we mean by a criticism of Prescott in this context: that great historian tells us that the male courtiers attended on their prince in an *antechamber*, and at once we have visions of an Andean Versailles; but in fact the male courtiers did no such thing; they attended outside the palace halls and chambers in the open air—we should be going to another, but perhaps corrective, extreme, if we said that they "hung about" in the yard. The perceptive reader will understand exactly what we mean when we point out that although the walls of the palace rooms were lined with beaten gold and those rooms furnished with objects of virtu exquisitely wrought by craftsmen who would have found places in Paris or London, yet the palace roof was thatch.

When a courtier or an official on business, or a *curaca* or even a *puric* petitioner, was summoned to the presence, he could not enter it until he had removed his shoes, assumed a token burden and bent his back humbly beneath its imaginary weight. What a pity it is that Swift had never read Sarmiento, Morúa or Garcilaso de la Vega Inca!

The furniture of Atahualpa's rooms and halls was made of wood and was painted red; it consisted solely of low tables and stools, well wrought and severely rectilinear. For ceremonial occasions, the sitting-in-state to hear cases referred to the highest court of appeal, the reception of great tributaries, allies or ambassadors, a throne was used. It was of solid gold and was wrought to the body's shape, yet it, too, was a stool, not a true chair. The palace furniture did not have to be moved about when the Inca princes went on progress; there was a complete suite of it in each palace. The walls, as we have said, were lined with gold, and in some palaces the very stones were mortared together with gold, or at least tuck-pointed with gold lines. The ornaments which gave the rooms color and offset the cold bareness of stone and metal were the exquisite llama-wool tapestry used for various purposes though not for covering walls; some might be footcloths. In addition to these were fine featherwork, ornaments made by the goldsmiths and silversmiths, and the very colorful and beautifully made pottery vessels and ornaments in every style, Inca and provincial, some simply pleasing to the eye, others amusing or even, by our standards, obscene or sadistic, which were as important an expression of art in the Tahuantinsuyu as was porcelain in China.

The palaces were often set in gardens or had gardens into which they opened. It is a great pity that although the Spanish chroniclers marvel over the Inca gardens they do not describe them in detail; they were, as usual, so much interested in precious metal that their attention was always distracted from the living plants to those of goldsmiths' and silversmiths' work, with which the Incas, showing questionable taste, decorated their pleasaunces. A more natural and particularly delightful ornament of Inca gardens were the hummingbirds. For their sustenance the Incas must have planted certain flowering shrubs, among them probably the brilliantly crimson-flowered crinodendron, the fire-tree embothrium, and red and yellow desfontainea, the lovely white-flowered eucryphias. The fuchsias, too, come to us from the Inca domain. But we do not really know what flowers the Inca gardeners planted, for a flower was a flower to most Spaniards; you could neither eat it nor sell it.

In the fruit gardens chirimoya (or cherimoya), avocado and pineapple were grown and were also imitated in gold and silver. There were several kinds of nut trees. Maguey, like coca and tobacco, was grown in plantations, rather than in gardens. Much valued as ornamental trees as well as for their fruits were the molle trees. The juice of the small red fruits was gently squeezed out and mixed with water, and then allowed to ferment, the resultant wine being drunk as medicine as well as for pleasure, sometimes mixed with the *chicha* (maize beer), or with the wine made by fermenting the juice of the maguey, or agave. Reduced by boiling, molle-fruit juice provided the people with a sort of jam. Other delights of the table which Inca gardeners provided were peppers, tomatoes, and possibly strawberries. Among the more useful plants were those cultivated for their aphrodisiac, contraceptive or aesthetic properties; they also included tubers (*Tropaelium tuberosum*), which supposedly had antiaphrodisiac qualities and for that reason were issued to the army on campaign to solve a problem which is as troublesome now as it was then.[1]

Atahualpa ate his meals in solitary state, not in company, for no man or woman, however great, was fit to sit at table with the son of the Sun. The table was spread with a fine cotton cloth and the service was of gold or silver plate finely wrought. Instead of a written menu, there was a display of all the dishes sent in by the cooks. The prince indicated which ones he would eat. The chosen dishes were then held conveniently in front of him by one of the *pallas*-in-waiting, all the time he was eating. If, in the course of the meal, Atahualpa's tunic of fine woolen cloth was soiled by a drop of sauce, one of his ladies went at once to the royal wardrobe for a clean tunic, and the soiled one was removed, the clean one put in its place at once, while he was still at table. But this was perhaps not a matter of etiquette; it may have been so, but Atahualpa was in any case fanatical on the subject of personal cleanliness. The prince's table servants and female attendants were all of "noble" rank. Each team of them did an eight-day stint of duty, and they were under the direction of a sort of Mistress of the Maids, Atahualpa's half sister, a daughter of Huayna Capac.

As to the food served to Atahualpa, it consisted of the vegetables and fruit mentioned above, llama meat, game—including several sorts of gallinaceous birds—duck both wild and farmed, sea and river fish. The principal difference between the prince's food and that of his subjects was in its variety only; perhaps he might enjoy an occasional luxury which was one only by the difficulty of getting it at a certain time of year, or because of the distance it had to travel. But in any case heavy expenditure on food was forbidden to the *puric* by sumptuary laws. Of Inca cuisine we know nothing, whether the dishes were subtly flavored and the sauces works of art as in France or China, or whether the meat was simply fired to make it edible, as in Germany and Spain. But the other applied arts were carried to such heights of perfection in ancient Peru that it is at least possible that their cooks had developed a true cuisine. There is one thing to be said against this, however: Atahualpa, like the humblest *puric* in the land, took his salt in a manner which seems rather uncouth: it was neither ground nor crystallized by condensation, but was served as a lump of rock salt in a silver or golden vessel, and this lump was, from time to time, licked by the diner. There were, for all classes, two meals a day, one between 8 and 9 A.M. and the other just before nightfall.

The courtiers were served, with any guests, in another hall, and they were waited on by *yanacuna*. Each class of specialists, cooks, waiters, et cetera, was provided by a certain village from whose people that class of domestics was always recruited.

Inca beds were very simple and of two kinds: in his highland palaces the prince or the Sapa Inca slept upon cushions laid either on the ground or on a raised platform; in his sea-level palaces, in a hammock, another Peruvian gift to the world.[2] These hammocks were exquisitely fine and delicately netted. In both cases, the covering was a blanket of fine vicuña wool for the Sapa Inca or other great persons, of llama wool for the common people. The Incas did not use sheets, slept naked, and, according to some accounts, always with one foot tucked under the thigh of the other leg, this being for some religious or hygienic superstitious reason.

Whereas the *puric-cuna* wore clothes of llama wool or cotton spun and woven by their women, the prince's clothes and those of other people of rank and consequence were of vicuña. The yarn was so fine and the weaving so exquisite that the cloth had the appearance and texture of silk. This cloth was made up into mantles worn over a vicuña or cotton shirt or tunic. Atahualpa had a special taste for clothes and he was fond of wearing mantles of batskin instead of wool; his batskin mantles are described by the Spaniards as being "soft and sleek as velvet." Brilliantly colorful but rather stiff were ceremonial garments of featherwork, which was not, however, as important as it had become in Mexico. Among people of rank the head was covered; Atahualpa, like his upper-class subjects, wore a *llauta*, a multicolored scarf or shawl of the finest vicuña wound round the head like a loose turban, from beneath which hung the red and gold threads of the *borla* covering the prince's brow and even half veiling his eyes.

We are accustomed to the idea of a city's splendor being the by-product of its commerce. But Cuzco's was a by-product of its religious importance, like that of Lhasa; of its academic importance, like that of Oxford; and above all of its administrative importance, like that of Washington, D.C. Cities as we know them are markets for the goods and services of a nation and perhaps of a continent; they grow rich on the fees and percentages paid to their merchants and bankers and brokers and on the profits of their manufacturers. At one time historians, as if reluctant to admit that a nation could exist, or a great empire could flourish, without trade at all, tried to prove that, despite the socialist system of the Incas, there were merchants and markets as we know them. But Philip Means, in his analysis of the country's daily life, showed that in the whole Tahuantinsuyu there was no commerce as we understand it, no money, no transactions in which broker, banker or agent could play a part. It is true that in Cuzco, and in all towns great or small, markets were regularly held; they were for the exchange of surplus products among the *puric-cuna*; one household might have plenty of maize but no oca; another be rich in sandals but short of woolen cloth. But, excepting for the Sapa Inca and his court in Cuzco, and the Incap Ranti and his court in Quito, only local consumer goods were available; there was no question of the Antisuyu sending its maritime produce to the Collasuyu and receiving mountain produce in exchange. And these markets, large and busy though some of them were, could not enrich a city, for a city's wealth is made by its middlemen, its agents, its importers and exporters and merchants, and of these none were necessary, since the markets were simply convenient places for direct exchange between producers.

It is true that goods in large quantities might be moved about; wool, both raw and manufactured, cotton, maize and other staples sometimes had to be shifted some distance from the place of origin to the state warehouses, or from the warehouses to the place where they were needed for consumption. But this was administrative, not commercial business; a matter of logistics, not trade.

The great size and wealth of Cuzco, then, were by-products of its importance as the center of government, religion and learning. Because that class which was paid out of the Sapa Inca's third of the national product—the civil and military officers, the philosophers, poets and teachers, and the priests—was concentrated in Cuzco, it was there that this wealth could manifest itself in great palaces both public and private. (The reader is referred to the city map on page 161.) Sacsahuaman was the great fortress covering the city on its mountainous side. Huacaypata (the word means "Holy Place") was the city center, and it covered an area of about ten acres. There, on occasions of state, ceremony, holiday, mourning, gathered the Inca and *curaca* élite; it was barred to the *puric-cuna*. Means calls this sacred square "ever the very axis of the empire's being." Entering it from the north is the great Antisuyu road which continues, from the far corner, as the main road to the Cuntisuyu. Hanan-Cuzco, in the right-angled triangle formed by the River Huatanay and the Antisuyu road, with Huacaypata at its apex, was the newer and "smarter" quarter of the city. Hurin-Cuzco, the lower, far more ancient and far holier part of the city, lay between the Huatanay and the Rodadero, south of Huacaypata. Across the Huatanay from the Huacaypata was the Cusipata (the word means "Joy Place"), a twenty-acre open space where the common people forgathered to make holiday or on those occasions which brought the gentry out into the Holy Place. Beyond were the suburban wards, where the people lived, while still more of the city population lived right across town on the far side of the Rodadero and the Collasuyu road.

The somber and massive glory of the city was in its great palaces, royal, administrative, religious and academic. The map shows the probable or certain position of the principal ones. They were all enormous buildings: the *Yacha-huasi*, for example, which we have dared to call the university, covered three acres of land with a five-hundred-foot frontage on the Huatanay. Topa Yupanqui's palace of Puca Marca ("Red Ward") was as large. These figures will give a rough scale for the other great buildings

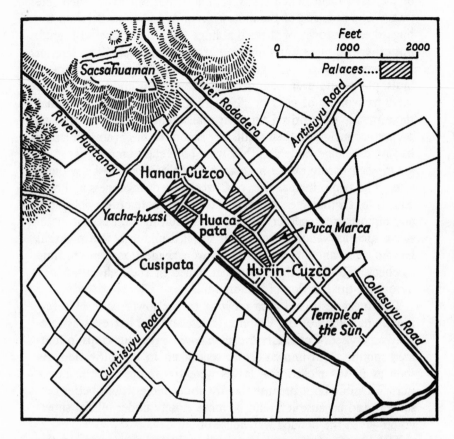

Plan of ancient Cuzco. The *Yacha-huasi*, or Teachers' House, was a
school founded by Inca Roca. *Puca Marca* was the palace of the Inca
Topa Yupanqui.

of the city's heart. Their size was almost, but not quite, their sole merit. The pointing of the almost invisible junctions between the huge dressed stones of these buildings was often done with gold, but otherwise there was almost no external ornament. The interior walls were paneled with gold; finely wrought figures of animals, birds, plants and even men decorated the rooms and halls, for the most part made of gold or silver. It should be emphasized that these metals were prized for their malleability and other physical properties, including their sunlike or moonlike brightness; but they had no exchange value and they were both state monopolies.

One can hardly expect a great metropolitan city to be without vices. The two principal vices of Cuzco were drunkenness and coca addiction. Drunkenness seems to have been more or less obligatory and almost or altogether of religious significance on certain occasions, such as wedding feasts. But social drinking before nightfall had no such sanction, and attempts were made from time to time to check it by laws; these, as usual, failed of their effect, as they have since the Babylon of Hammurabi.

The Incas restricted coca growing to the lower parts of a few mountain valleys of the Eastern Andes, and the harvest was carefully supervised. Coca (*Erythroxylon coca*) gave four crops in fourteen months, and immense care was taken in its cultivation. As soon as it was picked, the leaves were transported to the upper sierra, possibly both because the dry atmosphere would better preserve it and because it would be more closely under official supervision—as in the bonded warehouse of our day.

The chewing of coca leaves, with a little lime to release the alkaloid, enabled the chewer to do without food and perform immense feats of endurance. It was probably given to the *chasquis*, who would run fifty miles a day quite easily. It was also used by the *qoyas* and the Chosen Women, and there are accounts of women dying if they could not get it; an excess of coca, by overstimulation alone, would shorten life and induce despair. The only coca addict to get into history, however, was the old *curaca* to whom Huayna Capac forcibly married one of his sisters who had refused his own amorous advances. In any case, abuse of coca was, if not quite rare, apparently not so common as to constitute a social problem. And, of course, the effects of chewing coca are much less drastic than those of its alkaloid derivative, cocaine.

Under the Incas, the use of coca was permitted only to people of rank and condition. But the Spaniards saw no reason to make much distinction between one class of "savages" and another. It soon became apparent to them that, if the stick was one way of getting an Indian to work, the carrot also had a place, and this carrot was coca. They allowed the royal stores to be raided and coca to be grown indiscriminately. It soon became the money of the native Peruvians. The fact that in its inevitable reaction stage it induced torpor and shortened lives was probably not noticed; certainly no account would have been taken if it had, except when it was too late and the mines were closing because of lack of labor. Coca addiction may well have been a potent factor in the consolidation of the conquest; it was a consolation prize, the "soma" of the Peruvian "Brave New World."

Whether cosmetics were used we have not discovered. But as cleanliness of person and beauty of clothing were highly valued, the people of all classes had mirrors for their toilet: those of the *puric-cuna* women were of polished bronze; those of the *pallas* were finely made of obsidian, pyrites or silver very highly polished.

Such, briefly, was the city of two hundred thousand or two hundred and fifty thousand souls. Such were its power, its amenities and its fashion, which Huáscar enjoyed and to which Atahualpa aspired. If Atahualpa was seeking a chance to quarrel with his brother in order to possess the city, he did not have to make it; it was made for him.

Among the barbarous nations subject to and governed from Quito since the establishment of Atahualpa's principality or viceroyalty were the Huancavilca of northern Ecuador. They had been conquered by Topa Yupanqui before he became Sapa Inca, had revolted from the Tahuantinsuyu with other northern tribes under Quito leadership, and had been reconquered and resettled by Huayna Capac, whose residence in the north, with his army, had kept them quiet. They now broke out into revolt again, this time without the support of their erstwhile allies. It is possible that they had some intelligence of the uneasy state of relations between

Cuzco and Quito and thought themselves safe. But Atahualpa proved more active than the Huancavilca chiefs had anticipated. He drew upon the *mit'a* for regular troops, on the subject tribes for auxiliaries, and with Chalcuchima and Quizquiz as his principal generals, marched against the rebels. It is probable that the prince had the sense to leave the strategy of the war to his two veteran generals and its tactics to the corps commanders, while he himself acted as commander in chief only in name and by his presence with the army. The Huancavilca were brought to battle and utterly routed, suffering such losses as rendered them incapable of further mischief. This was Fortunate Warrior's first supreme command and though it was merely nominal there can be little doubt that his success greatly increased his self-confidence as a soldier, his assurance as a ruler, and his high opinion of Chalcuchima and Quizquiz as generals. At the end of the brief and completely successful Huancavilca campaign he knew, in short, that he might do great things and had the means to accomplish them.

Nevertheless he behaved with perfect correctness as the Sapa Inca's viceroy: he sent to Cuzco a report on the revolt and its suppression. And this he did even though he had, meanwhile, received not only Quilacu Yupanqui's account of his embassy, but still further intelligence of Huáscar's lowering temper and growing hostility. There were rumors that the Sapa Inca was preparing to send an army north to deprive Atahualpa of his principality by force. The rumors were shortly confirmed by the news that Atahualpa had been officially declared an *aucca*, that is, a traitor, by the Apucama.

But there was also encouraging news: the Sapa Inca had broken completely with the Hanan party; and this could only mean that Atahualpa would find powerful friends in his brother's capital. But on the advice of Quizquiz and Chalcuchima, Atahualpa did not immediately take the initiative. He simply waited, apparently in ignorance of his brother's hostile preparations, while Huáscar, far from being appeased upon receiving Atahualpa's dutiful report of the Huancavilca campaign, was angered and alarmed by it, considering that his brother had taken too much upon himself and would now be more dangerous than ever.

When the time came for an open breach with Cuzco, the occasion for it presented itself: the mummy, or it may have been simply an image, of the rival princes' deified father had been placed in the palace and shrine of Tumipampa, leaving the great Cuzcan palace of Amaru Cancha empty even of the dead. Two men of rank from Cuzco, whose names are given probably incorrectly by Sarmiento as Hanan and Atoc, were sent to Tumipampa to offer sacrifice to the dead Sapa Inca's spirit and to bring back to Cuzco all of Huayna Capac's women who were still there. But that palace and shrine were, according to the Quitu, in Quito territory and Atahualpa's bailiwick. It was, therefore, a studied act of hostility when the two envoys failed to pay even a courtesy call on the prince who had now been named a traitor to the state and went directly to Tumipampa without any reference to his government. They set out to return to the capital with Huayna Capac's now rather elderly harem and also what Sarmiento obscurely describes as his "insignia." This was the chance that Quizquiz, if not Atahualpa, had been waiting for. He intercepted the party on the road, arrested everybody, had the two envoys questioned and, deciding that they knew more than they were telling, had them tortured. They then revealed that they had acted entirely on the Sapa Inca's orders and that an army was ready to march against Quito. Manifesting that cruelty of which we have seen an outburst in his father and which was to mar the rest of his career, Atahualpa had the two Incas put to death and their skins used to make drums.[8] Meanwhile spies were sent south to check the information gained; they returned to report that the Inca army was already on the move.

By this time Atahualpa's commanding general had completed his own preparations. Atahualpa had two great advantages over his brother: although the latter could call on the men of the *mit'a* from all four provinces, and was in due course to do so, there had remained in Quito what the chroniclers describe as "the flower of the Inca army veterans." What they meant by this is not clear; it should be remembered that sixteenth-century Spaniards knew, as yet, nothing of the Inca social and political system. Europeans of that time knew four kinds of army: the ancient fyrd, the democratic home guard of free men which Harold Godwinson used against William of Normandy; feudal levies; volunteer adventurer armies; and mercenary armies. Of a conscript army drawn from the whole adult male population, they had no idea. They would have seen an Inca army as a feudal assembly of vassals owing armed service to their local lord. It seems rather unlikely that those men of the *mit'a* assigned to military duties could be kept under arms indefinitely, although we know of no law which entitled them to demobilization short of retirement at fifty. The most probable meaning of "flower of the Inca army veterans" is: that, owing to Huayna Capac's long residence in Quito, the most experienced officers, whether Inca or Quitu, had all their ties in the north and had remained there; and so it was Atahualpa and not Huáscar who had at his disposal the best men to form an officer corps of experienced centurions and senior commanders.

His second advantage was in having the services of Quizquiz, unquestionably the ablest soldier in the empire. We may, perhaps, compare this half-barbarian general to those German soldiers who, in the declining centuries of the Roman Empire, had a nobler, sterner, braver conception of imperial duty than the men of Roman patrician stock whom they first served and then replaced. Quizquiz, then, was the "Romanized" barbarian of this other empire. His colleague in command of the Quitu-Inca army is less easy to place. Chalcuchima is said by some to have been an Inca; on the other hand, the Inca historian Salcamayhua says that he was Atahualpa's maternal uncle, in which case he was a Quitu of princely rank: we believe this to have been the case. Less aggressive in council than his colleague, he was no less consistently successful in action.

As soon as Atahualpa was sure that his brother was sending an army against him, he moved his own force south to meet it. The Sapa Inca did not command his troops in person but remained in Cuzco. He was probably overconfident, regarding his brother as a servant to be punished rather than as a rival monarch to be conquered. He was not even using all the military strength at his disposal, for his brother Titu Atauchi and his general Tampu Usca Mayta were in the far east with a large part of the *mit'a* troops, fighting a campaign of expansion against the savages of Pumacocha, outside the imperial frontier.

The army sent against Quito was commanded by another of the Sapa Inca's brothers, Auqui Huanca,[4] the most unfortunate or the most incompetent general officer in Inca military history. It should be remembered that this prince was also Atahualpa's brother, but probably of the Hurin party by birth.

[Atahualpa, drawing upon his new-found assurance which was a by-product of the Huancavilca campaign, led his own army to the first encounter of the civil war. He met his brother's forces at Riopampa, where a pitched battle was fought, the issue being long in doubt and the casualties heavy. Atahualpa was victorious; we do not know to what extent the victory was his own, but it must still further have enlarged his confidence and opened his ears to his generals' ambitious plans. It was at this stage that the civil war ceased to be, for Atahualpa, a matter of defending his viceregal, semi-independent monarchy of Quito against Huáscar's determination to upset their father's disposition of the empire, and became quite clearly a campaign to conquer the unique office for himself. Atahualpa decided that he would no longer be his brother's Incap Ranti, bearing himself humbly toward Cuzco; he would wear the *borla* and be a god.]

Upon receiving the news of the defeat, Huáscar recalled the army from the east and sent reinforcements to Auqui Huanca. Atahualpa, meanwhile, had withdrawn his army to Tumipampa, where he rested it, taking no action, either because his mind was not yet quite made up or because he had been advised that he would need more troops before taking the offensive.

Although the Sapa Inca sent reinforcement to his commander in chief and brother, he could not curb his own peevish temper and he had been greatly shocked at his defeat; by way of reproach for Riopampa, therefore, he sent the prince a mocking present, a gift of women's clothes. It seems an unwise thing to have done, for in a war between factions both of which might perhaps claim the right there was danger of an insulted general's going over to the other party. But Huáscar evidently knew that his brother's loyalty was to be counted on, and it seems clear that this was of supreme importance, in that the Sapa Inca could not absolutely count on his other generals. But there is some ambiguity in Huanca's position at this time, commanding one brother's armies against those of another. It is possible that Atahualpa did not expect this half brother to put forth his whole strength against him. For it is written that when Huanca, spurred to make a great effort by Huáscar's mockery, marched on Tumipampa and surprised the resting Quitu army, inflicting severe losses on it, Atahualpa, back in his capital of Quito, "was much grieved that his brother Auqui Huanca should have made this attack, for at other times when he [Atahualpa] could have hit him [sic], he had let him go because he was his brother."[5] The prince of Quito had good cause for grief; his army had been caught off guard and had suffered very heavily. Either this is the only instance of carelessness attributable to Quizquiz, or that officer had already set off at the head of the army moving against Cuzco.

Auqui Huanca was never, as we have said, meant for high command. Instead of following up his victory at Tumipampa, he withdrew hastily, as if he had been leading a mere raid and was afraid to compromise his success. Or as if—we make the suggestion with reserve—he felt that he had done enough to satisfy the government in Cuzco but was unwilling to cripple his other brother in Quito. While Atahualpa resumed command of the troops still at Tumipampa, Quizquiz and Chalcuchima, at the head of the army reorganized for aggressive war against Cuzco, were diverted to pursue Huanca; they caught him at Cusipampa, brought him to battle again and defeated him, inflicting, but also suffering, heavy losses.

The people of Tumipampa, and the Canari in general, had always sided with Cuzco, or rather with Huáscar. It will be remembered that the Canari nation was the first of the northern peoples to be conquered by the Incas; after their conquest they had become the most loyal of provincials, unshakable in their respect for the Sapa Inca, and themselves providing some of the best troops and officers of the imperial armies. Atahualpa's victory at Riopampa had not put an end to their resistance, so Atahualpa set about breaking the Canari and forcing them to accept him as Sapa Inca. He conducted this campaign with remarkable cruelty: he used torture freely and, against men of rank, quite illegally. Any place which did not submit unconditionally might expect to have its people massacred, men, women and children. The wreckage which Pizarro was to find at Tumbez was at least indirectly the work of Atahualpa. The town had early declared in his favor, and since his own punitive raid on Puna met with only partial success, he left the finishing of the work to the men of Tumbez. By their subsequent attempt to carry out the conqueror's orders, they brought down on their heads a retaliation from Puna which they were unable to cope with.

Atahualpa's conduct during this campaign is by some attributed to his vindictiveness; there are touching stories of Canari towns sending out their women and children bearing green branches and wailing for mercy, all in vain. But what seems to have been vindictiveness may have been that ruthlessness which makes the born commander, who must be a man capable of refusing mercy if he is to gain his ends.. It is a fact that the treatment of the Canari so terrified the other provinces that, the awful news going before the army, they submitted to and acclaimed him without resistance, as he moved steadily and slowly in the wake of his main army under Quizquiz.

Auqui Huanca led the rout of his army after Cusipampa, successfully withdrawing a good part of it. But his opponent was a man who knew all Caesar's rules, having discovered them for himself. Quizquiz followed as fast as discipline permitted, keeping his rejoicing force well in hand, alert for a chance to finish off his enemy. But he was obliged to halt; for at Caxamarca Auqui Huanca was able to check his retreat, thanks to a large reinforcement sent forward by his brother which met him at that place. The new levy numbered ten thousand men, principally of the Chachapoya *mit'a*; that is, they were again provincial troops, not Incas. But Huanca had evidently had enough of personal campaigning for the time being; he remained with a garrison in Caxamarca and sent the Chachapoyas under their own officers out

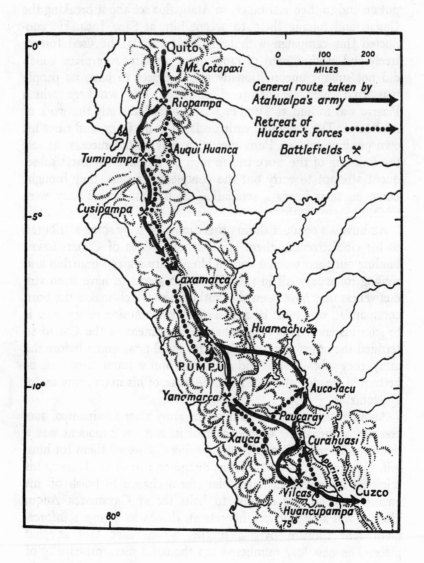

Quito

Mt. Cotopaxi

Riopampa

Auqui Huanca

Tumipampa

Cusipampa

Caxamarca

Huamachuco

P U M P U

Yanamarca

Auco-Yacu

Paucaray

Xauca

Curahuasi

Apurimac

Vilcas

Cuzco

Huancupampa

General route taken by
Atahualpa's army

Retreat of
Huáscar's Forces

Battlefields   ✗

0   100   200
MILES

-0°

-5°

-10°

80°

75

against Quizquiz. That general caught them not far north of the city and almost wiped them out; seven thousand were killed, wounded, or driven to desert—Inca armies took no prisoners, and the Quitu fought in the same spirit. The remaining three thousand rejoined Huanca in Caxamarca and with him and his own troops fell back hastily toward Cuzco. Quizquiz resumed his steady, orderly, ruthless pursuit. Huáscar, informed of this fresh disaster to his armies, sent yet another forward to his brother's support.

It is of some interest to speculate on the number of men an Inca government could mobilize at need. We have adopted, as the probable population of the Tahuantinsuyu, the figure of sixteen million favored by Means.[6] If the population was sixteen million, then it is safe to say that the government could call upon about three million puric-cuna for the mit'a. Presumably not all of them could, even in an emergency, be used as soldiers; there were essential public works and the agricultural economy to be maintained, whatever happened. Nor do we suppose that the Inca administration could have handled anything like that number of men; nor could it have equipped them, however simply. Nevertheless, it is obvious that the Sapa Inca's manpower resources for army call-up were enormous, in practice inexhaustible. If we suppose that only 20 per cent of the men between twenty-five and fifty were called for mit'a service, and of that 20 per cent only 20 per cent assigned to military duties, then Cuzco could field armies of one hundred and twenty thousand men. In the event, armies engaged at any one time were very much smaller. It is quite clear that the economy and daily life of the empire as a whole were only very slightly disturbed by the war.

The third Inca army to be sent forward in an attempt to stop the steady advance of Quizquiz and his colleague is described as large; we do not know how large, however. But it included contingents from every province in the empire. The opportunity to replace Huanca had not been taken, and the new army placed itself under his orders when it checked that retreating general's flight in the province of Pumpu. Huanca stood to fight, and Quizquiz attacked him as he came up with him; for this able old barbarian fully understood that victory has its own momentum which can be lost by caution; tired but consistently victorious troops have frequently proved too much for fresh armies with no tradition of victory. On this occasion, however, the number and freshness of Auqui Huanca's men were very nearly more than the veterans of Riopampa and Cusipampa, wearied by their interminable marching, could handle. Two days of almost unbroken attack and counterattack left the issue still in doubt. On the third day of this battle the imperial force began to show signs of weakness; at this point Quizquiz used his reserves under Chalcuchima, a simple device which had been usual in Inca battles since Pachacuti's day, but of which the fumbling Auqui Huanca seems to have been incapable. Sensing defeat, the Sapa Inca's brother managed to withdraw himself and a substantial part of his army. That he was able to disengage at all proves that Quizquiz himself had realized that his men needed rest. Huanca fell back on Xauca where the latest *mit'a* levy was waiting to strengthen him yet again, men of the Soras, Chancas, Ayamarcas and Yanyos provinces; but still no Incas. This new army was led by yet another of Huayna's sons, brother therefore to both principals and to Huanca; but he handed over his command to Auqui Huanca. Why, at this stage, that unsuccessful general was not relieved of his command is not clear: he would have been under Huayna, Topa or Pachacuti. Probably the government in Cuzco had nobody better; or possibly Huanca's friends in that city were too strong for any other party. And Auqui Huanca was a royal prince, the most difficult of all commanding officers to get rid of.

Huanca joined the reinforcements to the large force of men saved from the last battle. Quizquiz and Chalcuchima were still advancing with what by now must have seemed to the Inca commander in chief the inevitability of a ponderous but quickening landslide. Quizquiz seems, at this stage, to have divided his force into two, possibly hoping to catch the enemy between them. Huanca did not, this time, wait for him but with the confidence conferred by his now very superior force marched out of Xauca to meet that half of the army which was commanded by Chalcuchima at Yanamarca. But by this time Atahualpa's soldiers knew themselves unbeatable and consequently were so. Chalcuchima inflicted a total defeat on Auqui Huanca, caught and massacred the greater part of his army, and drove the unfortunate prince into a panic flight for his life to Paucaray.

At Paucaray he at last found Inca levies under veteran officers, instead of provincial conscripts. But they were commanded by Mayta Yupanqui, victor of the Pumacocha war, and he had the Sapa Inca Huáscar's commission to call Huanca to account. Mayta Yupanqui reproached the prince for his losses. How, he asked, could Auqui Huanca have lost so many battles and so many men *unless he was secretly in concert with the enemy?* With Cuzco divided against itself into Hanan and Hurin factions, and with four or five generations of unbroken victory behind them, the Incas were bound to ask that question. It was probably quite unjust. There might, however, have been this much truth in it: if Huanca was in his heart of the faction opposed to Huáscar and therefore doing his duty against his inclination, he may have been leading the imperial army dutifully rather than zealously.

What, meanwhile, of the principals? [Atahualpa continued his slow march southward, receiving submission wherever he passed, enjoying his parade of power while *quipu* after *quipu* announcing victories came in from his generals. No changes in the administration or the daily life of the countries he put behind him had to be made. Both worked like machinery, and in any case this territory need not be regarded as conquered; for although Quito and the countries of Ecuador were not technically part of the Tahuantinsuyu, the war was not a foreign one, but civil in its character, a struggle between two brothers for dominion over the whole. It may have been more than that, a faction fight. That one faction was identified with Hanan-Cuzco, the other with Hurin-Cuzco, had, we believe, no profound social significance; this was in no sense a revolt of the oppressed against a tyrannical emperor; there was no class distinction between Hanan and Hurin, no question of Hanan being the more liberal party. The whole thing seems to have been merely personal.]

[Huáscar's want of capacity and his uncertain temper, on the other hand, were making him unpopular. In an earlier generation it would have been impossible to consider the matter in such simple terms; the Sapa Inca was God, Son of the Sun. But the sturdy rationalism of Topa Yupanqui and the failure of the old simplicities to satisfy an increasingly sophisticated upper class had resulted in the Sapa Inca's being judged as a man; as such, Huáscar fell short.

His own contribution to the defense of his *borla* had not yet been such as to strengthen his party. He had, as we have seen, alienated a powerful church faction by grumbling that the cost of maintaining the Cult of the Dead was absorbing resources wanted for the war. He seems, however, to have suffered a reaction from this anticlerical attitude, and after the chain of disasters described above, he celebrated an expiatory fast, the *Itu,* by way of penance and to put him into a state of grace such that heaven might be expected to help him. But he allowed his mind to be diverted from the task of recruiting divine aid and giving royal aid to his officers, by a trivial domestic row.

The love affair of Quilacu Yupanqui and the girl Golden Star intrudes into this war in a very odd fashion; the authority for its details is Morúa, who is not perfectly reliable; and it is excessively romantic. But there is enough truth in it to make it worth setting down; and in any case, it provides relief from too much military history.

In the early stages of the battle of Yanamarca, when the outcome was still in doubt, Chalcuchima had used the usual Inca device of throwing in a reserve force when the enemy showed a weakness. The officer commanding the reserve was Quilacu Yupanqui. His attack broke one wing of the Inca army and started the rout, but Quilacu himself was badly wounded. "He fell among a heap of the dead when his men were fully occupied in pursuit of the enemy so that they did not notice the absence of their leader. The tide of battle rolled onward and he was left to his fate."

Meanwhile, Golden Star was in trouble: her aunt and guardian, Cahua Ticlla who had always stood between her and the girl's father, lay at the point of death; and Huáscar, whose passionate love for the first Curi Coyllur, embittered by her murder, seems to have taken a merely possessive form when it came to her daughter, ordered her to marry one of his high-ranking officers, presumably her uncle. Three years had passed since she had seen Quilacu, but her heart was still set on him. In the confusion of the household caused by her aunt's death, she cut her hair short and, disguised as a boy, slipped out and joined the camp followers of Mayta Yupanqui's army as it marched through Siquillapampa on the way to Paucaray.

When Quilacu regained consciousness he saw a boy moving about the battlefield searching among the dead. He called for help and the lad came to him, dressed Quilacu's wounds and helped him down to the bank of a small stream, where he lighted a fire of brushwood. When Quilacu asked the boy why he was thus helping an enemy officer, the lad answered him, "Brother, I am a native of this country. My name is Titu. Ask me no more." Next day Titu took Quilacu to an abandoned hut, where for many weeks he (or rather *she*, Golden Star) nursed the young man through a raging fever and its aftermath of weakness.

Thus, to Huáscar's other troubles, was added the distraction of his daughter's disappearance. She was the last link with his happiest hours and with what had, perhaps, been the best of himself.[7]

To the accusation that he was betraying his trust, Auqui Huanca replied angrily that it was a lie, that he had done his best and could have done no more; and he bade Mayta Yupanqui go out himself against Quizquiz and discover what fighting that unbeatable general was like. While they argued, Quizquiz advanced. Mayta Yupanqui went out against him with his force of Incas and Huanca's auxiliaries. They met at Auco-Yacu where there was a bridge over a river. But here the fighting was sporadic, a series of inconclusive skirmishes. It seems that Mayta Yupanqui was afraid to engage his troops closely with the Quitu veteran and the crack troops of Atahualpa's army. In such fighting as there was, however, the Incas were so severely beaten that their commander lost his nerve. Physically, there appears to be no reason at all why he should not have given a very good account of himself and at least done Quizquiz some serious damage; but by this time the imperial armies had got into that state of hopeless dejection which overcame the French in 1940. It was the reputation of Quizquiz,

Chalcuchima and their troops which won the battle of Auco-
Yacu for Atahualpa and which, indeed, put Mayta Yupanqui into
such a state of terror at the very idea of encountering these cham-
pions, that he soon broke off the skirmishing, disengaged the
larger part of his force, and beat a hasty retreat, marching sixty
miles to Vilca on the road to Cuzco with hardly a stop.

Upon receiving news of his army's victory at Yanamarca Atahualpa hesitated no longer but concluded, rather prematurely, that
the war was won. Without ceremony and at his own hand, he
assumed the *borla*, the *capac-uncu*, and the manners of the unique
office. From Huamachuco he sent word to his generals of what
he had done; and he announced to them that the provinces
through which he had advanced from Quito had all submitted
and received him as Sapa Inca. The readiness with which all the
peoples but the Canari had submitted and acknowledged him as
Unique Inca, Son of the Sun, if it was not simply the outcome
of fear, has significance for our argument that Huáscar's cause
was weakened by a faction in Cuzco. As we have explained, the
highest officers, the *cucuricuc-cuna* and their immediate subordinates were either Incas by blood or *curacas* (there may by this
time have been one or two *yanacuna* among them), and they were
appointed by and responsible to Cuzco. The readiness with which
these civil servants accepted Atahualpa may well mean either
that they knew they would receive support in the capital, or that
they thought Huáscar and his Apucama weak enough to defy with
impunity.

Atahualpa, in his message, seems also to have claimed that he
had been received with rejoicing by the *puric-cuna*; he probably
was, and this welcome was no more significant than that accorded
by modern city crowds to anyone whom the press has proclaimed
to be of consequence. It could mean no more to the *puric*, this
change of Sapa Incas, then a change of Presidents to an American
farm hand; there would still be the same day's work to do, the
same taxes to pay, the same abuses to suffer. There might, however, be some sense in the *puric* rejoicing over a clear victory for
either side, for with the ending of the war there would be a
reduction in the number of men called for *mit'a* service, and of the

proportion of them assigned to military duty. Atahualpa's triumph would mean peace again, and the greatest service any government can render the people is to restore and keep the peace at home and abroad.

Yet, both the classes and the masses of the Tahuantinsuyu must have found cause for anxiety upon Atahualpa's assumption of the *borla*. It might be both natural and politic to insist on the etiquette and protocol proper to a Sapa Inca's court; and a monarch with a shaky claim to the throne is perhaps bound to be stricter in such matters than one whose claim is indisputable. But Atahualpa began at once to reveal in his conduct the uneasiness of his spirit, the want of assurance, which derived, no doubt, partly from his illegitimacy, partly from the knowledge that he was acting contrary to his deified father's wishes, partly from that element of blasphemy involved in making war on the legitimate Sapa Inca. The religious reforms of Pachacuti which had placed the higher worship of Viracocha-Pachacamac above sun worship, and the moderate rationalism of Topa Yupanqui which had given men of parts some freedom to question hitherto eternal verities, doubtless led to a decline in the superstitious awe with which the Sapa Inca was regarded. But although Atahualpa might know with his mind that Huáscar was only a man, blood and flesh of his own blood and flesh, and not a very admirable man at that, yet he might be unable to dismiss entirely from his mind and spirit a feeling of awe for Huáscar's godhead, which he did not really believe in.

It was this manifold uneasiness which led the victorious usurper into excesses of regal pride and which brought out in him, as if in savage defiance of his own conscience, the strain of cruelty we have already noted. Atahualpa insisted upon adopting the unique unapproachableness: no man, however great, might enter his presence shod or unburdened. But he went further; he decreed that no man might address him directly. This had its importance during his first encounter with Hernando Pizarro, when his conduct seemed to the Spaniards so peculiar. In order that communication might be maintained between the new Sapa Inca and his subjects, an *apu* of noble blood was appointed to be his mouth and ears. The title of this officer can best be translated "the Inca's Lord." When Atahualpa sat in state on his golden throne-stool to transact business of state, those persons, civil or military officials, who had business with him, addressed themselves to the Inca Apu and not to the Sapa Inca, who sat impassive, giving no sign that he was seeing or hearing. The Inca Apu then conveyed what had been said to Atahualpa, who told him his decision, which was then repeated to the official in question or to the humble petitioner or appellant in the case. This had, of course, the great practical advantage of giving the Sapa Inca time to think during negotiations.

As to Atahualpa's cruelty, we are obliged to treat the principal accounts of it with reserve. The longest and most detailed of these is to be found in the writings of the half-Inca, Garcilaso de la Vega, and as we have already said, this historian was strongly prejudiced in all his chronicles by his own royal blood. For him. Huáscar, because he was the legitimate Sapa Inca, could do no wrong and Atahualpa must have been a devil to revolt against him at all. On the other hand, much of Garcilaso's account is borne out by at least one other, and unprejudiced, chronicler.

There is no doubt at all concerning his savage treatment of the Canari. It is true that established Inca practice was to offer opponents every chance of repenting of their resistance and, if they did not take the offer, to treat them ruthlessly. But Atahualpa was much more ferocious in his use of this policy than his father or grandfather had been. Moreover, he would not even put up with opposition from his fellow gods. At Huamachuco there was a famous *huacca* consisting of an oracular idol attended by a body of priests, or at least by one priest whose business was to convey the oracle. Atahualpa sent two lords-in-waiting to sacrifice before the *huacca* for the success which had attended his cause; and to consult the oracle about his future progress. The *huacca* informed the two *apu-cuna* that Atahualpa would come to a bad end because he was cruel and bloodthirsty. This may have been an attempt on the part of the clergy to frighten the victor into behaving more gently. If so, it was ill advised. When the oracle was delivered to Atahualpa by his officers, he went with a body of his guards to the *huacca*, armed with a golden "halberd"—presumably a battle-ax. The priest of the oracle, a venerable centenarian dressed in a long, hairy, woolen robe closely embroidered with seashells, came out to meet the Sapa Inca; and Atahualpa, upon learning who he was, struck off the old man's head with his own hand. He and his guards then went in to the *huacca* and beheaded the idol. Afterward he caused the priest's body and the idol and the temple itself to be burned, and the cinders to be scattered; finally, the hill where this *huacca* had resided was leveled.

In Cuzco the legitimate Sapa Inca was by now thoroughly alarmed. He still had large armies at his disposal and he could call up many more men, but their morale and his own had been seriously undermined by repeated defeats; not for centuries had Inca armies suffered decisive defeat, and the shock of meeting with it, even at the hands of a partly Inca enemy, was shattering. Nor could he at first obtain any encouragement from the gods: Huáscar fasted and cleansed himself of sin and consulted all the oracles in and around Cuzco. At first they gave him no hope. But when the clergy got wind of Atahualpa's way with recalcitrant oracles, they decided that even Huáscar was preferable to a Sapa Inca who cut off the heads of pessimistic clergymen with his own hands, and hastily changed their tune. The diviners, the *umu-cuna*, began giving Huáscar a different message from heaven, although the *amautas* of the Cuzco university still maintained a philosophic silence. Huáscar was told that if he took personal command of the army he would be victorious. This seems to have made a great impression on him, for he became suddenly active and decided in his conduct. He mustered a larger army than he had yet fielded and meanwhile learned from his intelligence service that the enemy's main body, under Quizquiz and Chalcuchima lay at Curahuasi near the great bridge over the Apurimac, and was moving thence off the main Cuzco road onto the road to Cotabamba to the west of it. Quizquiz, wise as ever, was not going to expose himself to a crossing of the Apurimac bridge which could easily be defended by a score of Incas or even destroyed by the Sapa Inca's authority. The Quitu general had therefore decided to approach Cuzco by the roundabout route; and as a consequence the final battles of the campaign were fought in the province of Cotabamba.

Huáscar decided to attack Quizquiz in front and on both flanks at the same time. The Apucuraca Arampa Yupanqui was given command of the men drawn from the Collasuyu, and the Antisuyu *mit'a*, the Charcas, Chuys and Chileans, with orders to march through the Omasuyu country and get between Quizquiz and the Apurimac bridge. He was to hang on to the Quitu flank, harassing the enemy without engaging him closely. A second corps of the army was composed of the survivors of Prince Huanca's series of defeats, now jointly commanded by that unfortunate general and his principal critic, Mayta Yupanqui with a third general, Ahua Pauti, to arbitrate between them—a thoroughly bad appointment all round. Huáscar, as commander in chief, himself led a third corps, probably of Inca and *curaca* elite troops. Auqui Huanca's orders were to march into Cotabamba and fall upon that flank of the enemy which lay farthest from the Apurimac. It was Huáscar's intention to use his own force for the frontal attack. Unfortunately for him, this perfectly sensible plan was abandoned as a result of a premature and partial victory over part of Atahualpa's force.

The swiftness with which Huáscar, once roused, had acted made Quizquiz's task of getting at Cuzco without using the Apurimac bridge more difficult. The old barbarian found himself with Huanca between him and the river, Arampa Yupanqui on his right, encamped on the heights commanding the valley, and the Sapa Inca himself, facing him *in* the valley. He therefore decided to draw all three Inca armies into battle himself, and thus to give his colleague Chalcuchima a chance to lead a detachment against Cuzco in a forced march by way of Chumpivilcas. This typically aggressive plan was tried and failed. It seems clear that Quizquiz simply did not have enough men to carry it out; he was very heavily outnumbered. And in the second place, the element of surprise failed; Arampa Yupanqui, having received intelligence of a strong detachment under Chalcuchima on the move toward Chumpivilcas, himself marched to cut it off and caught it in a ravine leading from the plain called Huancupampa. After fierce fighting with heavy casualties on both sides, and the death of Tomay Rima, second in command of the Inca force, the Quitu were forced to retreat into their main body.

Meanwhile, Quizquiz had seized the initiative from Huáscar in the Cotabamba valley and made a frontal attack. Just before this attack was launched, a runner came in with the news of Arampa Yupanqui's victory over Chalcuchima. Huáscar turned to the officers of his staff and said, "The Colla have won this victory. Behold the obligation we now have to emulate our ancestors!" The Quitu attack was repulsed with losses, the Sapa Inca counterattacked, and Quizquiz was forced to retreat, badly mauled.

Chalcuchima had fallen back along the ravine in which he had been caught, onto the plain of Huancupampa. There Quizquiz, likewise retreating, joined him. And there they would have halted to rest but Huáscar, inspired by success, called a new ally to his aid: fire. He had the dry grass of a *pampa* set aflame; the fire spread with appalling swiftness, part of the Quitu army was trapped, many of Atahualpa's men were choked by smoke and burned, and Quizquiz was forced to withdraw his whole army across the Cotabamba river, to put water between himself and the fire.

It was at this point that Huáscar missed the military training he should have received as a boy had his father not withdrawn to Quito and given all his paternal care to Atahualpa. In the conduct of the battle of Cotabamba he had given clear proof of that common sense, quickness of decision, and ingenuity, which were inherent in his family. It is obvious that he had the makings of a soldier. But he had had no experience. Moreover, because the Tahuantinsuyu proper had been at peace throughout his lifetime, and all the serious fighting had been confined to the extreme north, all the experienced generals were on the Quitu side and Huáscar had nobody to advise him, or nobody of the same mettle and status as Quizquiz or Chalcuchima. It is true that Arampa Yupanqui had fought a successful action against Chalcuchima, but under conditions where all the advantage lay on his side; there is no reason to suppose him an experienced strategist, and in the action he had won, the tactics to be adopted would have been obvious to a boy playing at war. Mayta Yupanqui had fought a successful war against savages; we know from his history that such warfare does not teach a man to face a civilized enemy technically his equal. As for poor Prince Huanca, his advice would clearly have been worse than useless. Huáscar should have followed up his success at once, as Quizquiz could have told him. Yet, it is possible that his failure to do so was due not to a want of military common sense, but to the fact that the fire he had kindled to help him may, at this later stage, have become a serious hindrance by serving to protect the enemy. Whatever the reason, Huáscar failed to advance. He celebrated his victory and shifted his entire force onto the highest land in the neighborhood—a sensible move; but that was all he did, and Quizquiz was given time to recover and to rest his army.

That general, meanwhile, either from spies sent into the Inca camp, or from Hanan fifth-columnists within it, learned that there was a plan to keep his attention engaged with the main body of the Inca army on the heights while a strong detachment deployed through a ravine to surprise him. There is said also to have been a plan to kill or capture both Quizquiz and Chalcuchima by a sort of limited-objective commando raid through this ravine. An officer named Tupac Atao was sent scouting with a small detachment down the ravine in question, while the Sapa Inca Huáscar in person—"whom the gods would destroy . . .!"—as the oracle had commanded, led five thousand picked men in Tupac Atao's wake.

Having been warned, however, Quizquiz had men hidden and watching. They sent word back as soon as Tupac Atao's advance party was sighted, and Chalcuchima led a detachment into the ravine where he was able to form an ambush. As a result the Inca advance party was destroyed to the last man, and its commanding officer, badly wounded, was captured. That officer had evidently been ill-chosen. Either he was of the Hanan faction in his heart or he broke under torture; at all events, he talked, and Chalcuchima was informed of the five thousand men, led by Huáscar, who were advancing along the ravine. He sent an urgent message for help to his colleague, who came in person at the head of a strong detachment. Again an ambush, on a much larger scale, was formed. Chalcuchima led one force up the ravine toward the advancing Incas, and hid it on the hillsides well above the point at which the corpses of Tupac Atoa's vanguard lay sprawled on the ground. Huáscar and his five thousand were allowed to advance down the ravine well past Chalcuchima's hidden force. When the Incas came to the bodies of their vanguard, the Sapa Inca lost his nerve or came to his senses, and ordered a retreat, but as soon as the Incas tried to fall back up the ravine, Chalcuchima broke from ambush and fell on them. Huáscar then tried to continue down the ravine, whereupon Quizquiz launched his own attack from hiding. Both attacks were pressed with ferocity; the five thousand were all killed, wounded or scattered. [Chalcuchima himself led a flying wedge against the Sapa Inca's litter and guard, reached the litter and dragged Huáscar from it. "Thus," writes Sarmiento solemnly, "was taken prisoner the unfortunate Huáscar Inca, twelfth and last tyrant of the Inca sovereigns of Peru, falling into the hands of another and greater tyrant than himself, his people defeated, killed, scattered."]

Not quite true; a powerful Inca army commanded by men of the royal house still lay intact on the heights above Huancupampa. It now became Quizquiz's object to defeat it with a minimum of casualties on his own side. To this end, while the royal prisoner was placed under a strong guard, Chalcuchima took his place in the imperial litter. The object of this was to prevent the Inca army from retreating in good order and before Quizquiz could smash it. The Incas, watchful on their heights, saw their Sapa Inca's litter approaching, escorted by five thousand men, and supposed his trick to have succeeded. It had been arranged that when Chalcuchima gave a certain signal, Quizquiz would attack. But it would be better to have the Incas in a panic than in their ranks. As soon as Chalcuchima was near enough, he released a wounded Inca prisoner who crossed to his own people and warned them that Huáscar had been taken and that the man in the litter was one of the enemy commanders. The news broke them, as Quizquiz had known that it would; and at the very moment when the Quitu

EL DOZENO INGA
TOPACVCIGVALPA
GVASCAR INGA.

acabo Reyno ar
murio en anda

quispus ynga
comenzo a cuypar y murio

antamarca

challcochimaynga
guascar

Huáscar, the Inca, is held captive by his half-brother's troops.

launched their attack, the Incas broke and fled. They were cut down and massacred as they ran. Prisoners were not taken, but an exception might be made for a man of rank: Titu Atauchi, one of the Sapa Inca's brothers, fell into Chalcuchima's hands. At the hamlet of Quiuipay, about two miles from Cuzco, Quizquiz ordered the pursuit to cease, and set up a headquarters, placing Huáscar under guard in one of the houses.

Some of Atahualpa's soldiers, released from duty, climbed the hill Yanina to look at the city they had come to take. There they could see and hear the lamentations of the Cuzcans, and on their return to camp they reported to their superiors what they had seen. Quizquiz thereupon sent a message to be proclaimed in the city, which bears singular witness to his independence of spirit and rude candor. He bade the inhabitants cease their outcries; they had nothing to fear; it was well known that this was a war between two brothers for the gratification of their own passions. Those who had helped Huáscar had done no wrong; they were in duty bound to help their Sapa Inca. And he, Quizquiz, would pardon them in the name of the Great Lord Atahualpa. Presently he would order them to come out of the city and do obeisance to the statue of Atahualpa to whom the general referred in his message and thereafter as *Ticci Capac* ("Lord of the World"). And the title was not misleading; for a few days or weeks, a single monarch was, indeed, lord of the known Andean world.

In due course, the more considerable citizens, marching in their *ayllus*, did come out to Quiuipay. There they were marshaled and seated on the ground, surrounded by the northern army. From them Quizquiz took all the senior officers who had fought against him in the war, and the High Priests Chalco Yupanqui and Rupaca, who had crowned Huáscar with the *borla*. These being secured as prisoners, Quizquiz addressed the assembly: they had, he said, raised Huáscar to be Inca *though he was not the heir*; they deserved death for having opposed the Sapa Inca whom the Sun guarded and kept. But in the name of the Ticci Capac he, Quizquiz, would pardon them.[8]

There followed a somewhat unedifying scene of recriminations. The Cuzcan Incas, terrified for their lives, loudly acclaimed Atahualpa as Sapa Inca and called on the Sun to grant him long life. The dowager *qoya*, who was present, turned on Huáscar her son and publicly upbraided him:

> O unfortunate! Thy cruelties and evil deeds have brought us to this pass. Did I not beg you not to kill or maltreat your brother's ambassadors?

With these words the old lady went to her son and struck him in the face.

There was worse, much worse, to come. Atahualpa, now holding his court at Caxamarca, received his general's report of victory and of the prisoners taken, and a request for orders. While a reply was awaited, Quizquiz carried on a distasteful campaign of vilification and mockery of Huáscar, in public, which was clearly designed to complete the poor wretch's exposure to the people as a mere man, and a failure at that; and to discredit the Hurin faction in Cuzco. We do not believe that the old man was actuated by malice; it is notable that he allowed no looting in Cuzco, restrained his troops from abuse of the citizens, and in general behaved like a civilized and responsible agent of a legitimate government. The treatment of Huáscar was, then, politic. From his first public announcement following the victory, Quizquiz had begun the work of establishing his master's legitimacy by discrediting Huáscar's.

Sitting in public, the commander in chief had all the prisoners brought before him, and in the presence of Cuzco's leading men he declared that Rahua Ocllo, the dowager, who was present, had never been Huayna Capac's wife but only his concubine. She was no *qoya* but a "vile woman." [9] At this the Quitu soldiers, doubtless well-drilled by their decurions, pointed derisively at Huáscar and some of them bade the Incas, "Behold your Lord! who said that in battle he would turn fire and water against your enemies!" And as these unhappy men lowered their heads in horror and shame, Huáscar was taken and bound in a hammock and carried before Quizquiz who asked him, "Who, of those present, made you Sapa Inca, there being others better and more valiant than you who might have been chosen?" The implacable dowager *qoya*, far from being driven to her son's side by insults to her status, again upbraided Huáscar, saying that he deserved all that was happening to him because of his cruelty to his kinsmen. With a dignity in adversity equal to his courage in war when he could no longer avoid fighting, he bade her be silent and ordered the two high priests to answer their conqueror's question. Chalco Yupanqui then said to Quizquiz, "I raised him to be lord and supreme Inca by command of his father Huayna Capac and because he was the son of a *qoya*." Quizquiz replied that he was a deceiver and a liar. Huáscar next, despite the indignity of his position, proudly told Quizquiz, "Leave off these arguments. This is a question between me and my brother and not between the party of Hanan Cuzco and the party of Hurin Cuzco. We will investigate it and you have no business to meddle between us."

Both commanders were enraged at Huáscar's dignity. He was sent back to prison and kept there until Atahualpa's order to confine him in the fortress of Xauca was received. While the new Sapa Inca's orders were awaited, the Hurin men of Cuzco prayed in their temples and homes, "O Viracocha! O Pachacamac! who gavest life and favor to the Incas, where art thou now? Why dost thou allow such persecution to come upon us? Wherefore didst thou exalt us if we are to come to such an end?" The complaint is a familiar one. All these things were recorded by the *amautas* who witnessed them, using their *quipus*, and were afterward told to the priest Sarmiento.

When Atahualpa received his general's report in Caxamarca, he sent his orders to Cuzco by a kinsman and senior official who was an Inca but doubtless of the Hanan faction, Cusi Yupanqui. The orders were simple and atrocious: Huáscar was to be imprisoned in the Xauca fortress, but no kinsman or friend of his was to be left alive. Cusi Yupanqui was given or assumed some discretion, but on the whole he carried out these orders exactly. Although this kind of conduct is new in Inca history, it is not particularly surprising; Atahualpa knew that he had no legitimate claim to the throne and that almost any descendant of Topa Yupanqui and any of his sister-queens, of Huayna Capac and any of his sister-queens, of Huáscar and any of *his* sister-queens, had a better claim than himself. To ensure his own position it was clearly advisable to exterminate every possible claimant, old, young or still in the womb. And from the list of people who were in fact killed it is clear that this was his object.[10]

Cusi Yupanqui arrived in Cuzco, and Quizquiz handed over the prisoners—all the members of Huáscar's several families and many prominent Hurin men. Cusi Yupanqui had poles erected beside the road to Xaquixahuana over half a mile in extent, and from them he hanged all Huáscar's wives and their children. To make perfectly clear what he was aiming to accomplish, he had unborn children removed from the womb and hanged separately. (Neither the late Marshal Stalin nor the late Adolf Hitler thought of this refinement when they were clearing away rivals to their respective thrones, though both of them killed far more individuals.) With these, Cusi Yupanqui, that conscientious officer, hanged all Huáscar's elder sons. The number of Huáscar's children hanged was eighty; it should be remembered that the Sapa Inca began to beget children in his teens and could have as many women as he liked. Cusi Yupanqui was intent upon exterminating not only unquestionably legitimate heirs, but children who, having a claim equal to Atahualpa's, that is through the father only, might grow up to assert it just as Atahualpa himself was doing.

Yet this massacre was incomplete; we know that one of Huáscar's sons, Manco Capac, escaped and was crowned as a puppet monarch in due course by Pizarro. Presumably this prince was absent from Cuzco at the time. We know also that another, Paullu, was spared by Cusi Yupanqui. This prince had been imprisoned and nearly starved to death by his father for seducing one of the royal concubines. (She was buried alive for it.) He contrived to persuade Cusi Yupanqui that his punishment had been for belonging to the Hanan party, and for some reason this was accepted and he was allowed to live. This and still more the sparing of Huáscar are extremely odd, for it was, surely, from them that the greatest danger threatened. In the case of Paullu only one explanation seems possible: the people hanged were child-heirs or women with embryo heirs in the womb; that is, heirs of whose future capacity no man could judge. But Paullu was old enough to be judged and either Cusi Yupanqui or Atahualpa must have decided that on evidence of character, health or past record, this prince was not to be feared. It is rather thin, but we can offer nothing more substantial.

But why was Huáscar spared? It may well have been Atahualpa's intention to kill him later. It is arguable that Atahualpa was still superstitious enough to shrink from killing the Sun's son; or that Huayna Capac's wishes still had weight for him so that he planned still to share the empire in name while making sure that he kept the real power in his own hands and the future power to his own sons. There is some evidence for this. But the readiness with which he had Huáscar killed when it seemed absolutely essential to get him out of the running, makes such arguments difficult to sustain. We therefore think that Huáscar was kept alive, and perhaps Paullu also, for a simple, political reason: it was necessary to have him as live bait in order to bring lurking members of the Hurin faction into the open, so that they, too, could be killed.

The family having been disposed of, it was also necessary to crush the Hurin faction in the state and the city. Among its leaders were the priests and household of the deified Topa Yupanqui's mummy. The work of dealing with them was handed over to the army, that is to Quizquiz, probably because it entailed blasphemy of the most frightful kind and the old general was no Inca but a Quitu. The priests and servants of both sexes were hanged and the mummy itself was burned. A certain, not large, number of leading men and women of the Hurin party were hanged; and a number of Hurinist or legitimist *curacas* of Chachapoya and Canari nationality.

It makes Cusi Yupanqui's purpose quite clear that such of Huáscar's concubines as were not pregnant and had borne no sons were spared. The operation was, in short, one of policy and not of sadism. Yet if there was no malignant cruelty in the killing of the Hurin Incas, there was surely malignant cruelty in forcing Huáscar to witness the whole atrocious business, and to watch as his sisters the *qoya* Miro and the lovely Chimbo Cisa went to their brutal death, the *qoya* with his child in her arms and another in her womb. It is no wonder that Huáscar then called upon God, "O Pachacamac Viracocha, Thou who showed favor to me for so short a time, and honored me and gave me life, dost Thou see that I am treated in this way, and seest Thou in Thy presence what I, in mine, have seen and see?" And a Quechua poet with a true insight into that fallen ruler's feelings makes Huáscar curse the lesser gods:

> *Lying huaccas,*
> *Cruel and devilish enemies,*
> *Cause of my misfortune,*
> *Of my deception,*
> *Of my failure!*
> *I have adored*
> *These enemies of Cuzco's king*
> *With all my power,*
> *With great sacrifices,*
> *With human sacrifices*
> *To you, you greedy robbers*
> *And cruel enemies of my soldiers.*
> *Cursed shall you be for what you have done.*
> *No longer will any of my descendants,*
> *Not even the tiniest girl child,*
> *Nor my royal grandchildren,*
> *Call upon you.*
> *Serving still Tonapa the Tarapaca* [11]
> *Of Viracocha the Creator,*
> *Albeit indignant,*
> *I eternally curse you.*

Atahualpa in Caxamarca, meanwhile, was making his preparations to set out for Cuzco, take possession of that city and there be crowned ceremoniously by receiving the *borla* from the hand of the Sun-god priest. As he was about to start, a messenger arrived from Tumbez, sent by the *curaca*. The message reported the arrival of the Spaniards. This news was probably no great surprise. Apart from the contacts already mentioned, a trading raft out of Tumbez, laden with gold, silver, mirrors and cloth, had been met by the pilot Ruiz off the coast of Panama.[12] It is likely that the Peruvian government was better informed of Spanish movements than has been generally conceded. Their beards and their horses were particularly described and the *curaca* suggested that their chief man, Pizarro, might be the God Viracocha. But we cannot suppose that a man who had received his religious education at the hands of men who wrote and who chanted the hymns we have quoted above was much impressed by that suggestion. The word *cocha* means "sea," and doubtless what the *curaca* really said, and what was subsequently misunderstood by the Spanish clergy, was something about "men from the sea." We do not believe that Atahualpa at any time believed that he was dealing with supernatural beings in his intercourse with the Spaniards. He put off his departure for Cuzco, but he did not, it seems, send orders for the foreigners to come to him. He simply waited, as if for Destiny to arrange a meeting. The name of Destiny was, in this instance, Francisco Pizarro.

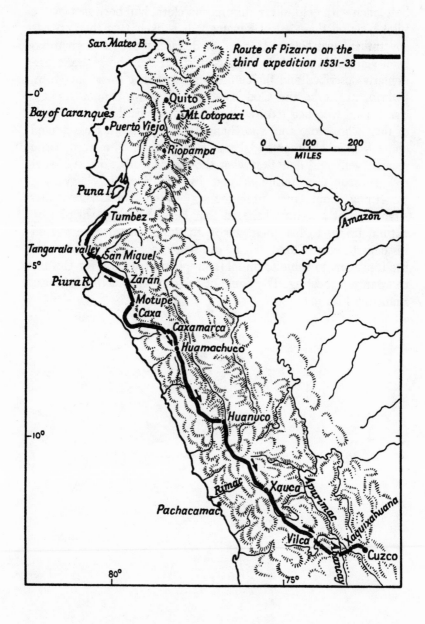

San Mateo B.

Route of Pizarro on the
third expedition 1531-33

—0°

Bay of Caranques

• Puerto Viejo

• Quito
▲ Mt. Cotopaxi

• Riopampa

0   100   200
MILES

Puna I.

Tumbez

Tangarala valley
San Miguel
—5°

Piura R.
Zarán

Motupe
• Caxa

Caxamarca
• Huamachuco

Amazon

Huanuco

—10°

Rimac
Pachacamac
• Xauca

Apurimac

Vilca
Xaquixahuana
Cuzco

Yucay

80°   75°

7

ATAHUALPA
AND HIS EXECUTIONER

FOR FIVE DAYS after crossing the Piura River from San Miguel, Pizarro and his men marched through lovely valleys rendered fertile by the mountain streams and by the skill of their inhabitants in the craft of irrigation. The weather was favorable, the going easy, provisions plentiful and varied; the welcome given to the Spaniards, who were kept strictly in hand by their leader, was friendly in both hamlets and towns; the attitude of the people could not have been more reassuring. The invaders were now in country where civilization was ancient and among people who had, on the whole, enjoyed centuries of peace and who were, accordingly, pacific. Nevertheless the adventurers glanced nervously at the formidable fortresses which they observed in every place of importance.

Had Pizarro been literate, had his cousin, Pedro, or the Friar Valverde been men of intelligence and breadth of mind, we might have had some account of what the Peruvians made of these ironclad foreigners and of what these foreigners observed on the march. As it is we have very little; but we can dismiss as highly improbable the theory, of largely clerical origin, that the Peruvians took the Spaniards for gods, "*viracochas*."[A people who had developed the subtle and sophisticated worship of Pachacamac with its elevated ideas of the unknowableness and ubiquity of God, its high ethical code, its confession, penances and absolution, its fasts and rituals, its hymns of resignation, would not have taken a troop of soldiers—albeit white, bearded, and mounted on animals hitherto unknown to science—for heavenly visitors.]

On the fifth day of the march, when a halt had been called for a general inspection in one of the beautiful valleys of this country, Pizarro was able to confirm his disturbing impression that there was disaffection and dangerous grumbling among his men. Conditions which would have produced high spirits and contentment among professional soldiers under discipline were not good enough for Pizarro's rough and independent adventurers kept in order by persuasion only. How much longer was this marching to continue? What about those dangerous-looking fortresses? Were they not walking into a trap? The spirit of the malcontents might be contagious—Pizarro had already had bitter experience of working with scratch troops. He decided on one of those bold strokes which made him so remarkable a leader.

In a similar difficulty, Cortes, his model, had burned his boats, thus leaving his men no alternative to advance. But only land lay between Pizarro's fainthearted troublemakers and the relative safety of San Miguel. Pizarro mustered the men and told them that they were now come to a critical juncture in their adventure and that no man should go further in it who could not do so with all his heart; those who now repented of their boldness and wanted to be back in San Miguel were perfectly free to return there and to take up their share of land and their *repartimiento* of Indios. Nine discreet men took advantage of this offer, four foot soldiers and five mounted. These were the principal malcontents, and by thus allowing them to quit the venture Pizarro was strengthening his hand. He was, at the same time, depriving the rest, who tacitly committed themselves to follow where he led, of justification for future complaint; they had had their chance to back out and had refused it.

The march was resumed, and in another five days the Spaniards came to the town of Zarán, in yet another fertile valley, but this time among the hills, for Pizarro and his party were beginning to climb the slope of the Andes foothills. At Zarán, as elsewhere, the leader noted that there was a shortage of adult males among the population: Atahualpa had been calling up the *purics* liable to *mit'a* duty to enlarge his army. The *curaca* of Zarán was prepared for the Spaniards' coming; he received them courteously and made them free of the local *tambo*, or resthouse. It will be recalled that such were to be found at regular intervals on all the highroads of the Tahuantinsuyu; and as they were large enough to accommodate the imperial suite when the Sapa Inca went on a progress, there was ample room for Pizarro's one hundred and sixty-eight men.

Pizarro and his officers had expected to come up against Atahualpa before this, but they still had no real news of him. However, they learned from the *curaca* of Zarán that there was an Inca garrison at Caxas, not far away in the hills. Pizarro detached a small party under Hernando de Soto (the gentleman who was later to help Quilacu Yupanqui and Curi Coyllur, and when the latter was widowed, to take her for his mistress) to reconnoiter Caxas and see if he could get in touch with some Inca of rank. A week passed without news, and Pizarro was becoming uneasy, his men restless, when de Soto reappeared accompanied by an Inca acting as ambassador from Atahualpa, with a small but adequate suite of minor officers. This envoy, whose name we do not know, brought Pizarro an invitation to visit the Sapa Inca in his mountain camp, and a present of two fountains carved in stone to represent fortresses, some fine woolen cloth embroidered with gold and silver, and a vessel containing duck flesh, specially treated and seasoned and powdered, which was used by Incas of consequence—as a perfume or cosmetic, say our authorities; but what kind of scent it had, we do not know.

The reader may wonder at the failure of the Inca government to halt and arrest the intruders, that curious tolerance or seeming indifference with which it suffered the Spaniards to wander about the country. And it does seem incredible that a mysterious party of armed foreigners was not called to account by the authorities of a highly civilized and very highly organized country. It would not, we believe, have been allowed to happen in any previous reign, or if the country had not been involved in a civil war. We have said that the life of the Tahuantinsuyu ran like machinery, despite the war; machinery will run for some time with nobody at the controls. Atahualpa at Caxamarca had not yet taken over the controls of state. Moreover, there was no precedent for dealing with such an event as the Spanish invasion. Furthermore, the only subjects of the Tahuantinsuyu attacked by the Spaniards had been the people of Puna, themselves enemies to Atahualpa, and to all other subjects of the Sapa Inca the Spaniards had behaved pacifically and honestly, so that Pizarro seemed to be conducting himself like a valuable ally. There was also the possibility of getting hold of European iron weapons; there was, finally, Atahualpa's intense curiosity about these foreigners whose coming his father had foretold with anxiety.

The Inca ambassador's real purpose was to gather information for his master. Pizarro realized this, but he did all in his power to flatter the man, urging him to stay with the Spaniards as long as he liked. Conversation was made easy by the presence of Felipillo and of another young Peruvian who had accompanied Pizarro to Spain and had been taught Castilian. The Inca ambassador, having collected all the information he could, took his leave and departed to make his report. He took with him by way of gifts a cap made of crimson cloth and some glass jewelry of no value. He was also the bearer of a message to the Sapa Inca: the Spaniards came from a great prince who ruled beyond the sea; the fame of Atahualpa's victories had reached them and they were come to pay their respects and to offer their services against his enemies. They would present themselves before him with the least possible delay.

The Inca ambassador had shown much curiosity about the Spaniards' weapons and armor and he had paid careful attention to them. This is important, because it is likely that one of Atahualpa's motives for dealing so freely with the Spaniards and for letting them come to him was a wish to study and perhaps buy and copy their weapons. As an able ruler advised by experienced officials he must have anticipated trouble with a resurgent Hurin faction; indeed, he was trying to bring that trouble into the open by keeping his brother Huáscar alive. Furthermore the empire's recent history must also have made him expect frontier trouble. Finally, if we suppose that the Incas knew more about the Spaniards in Central America than we have any way of knowing, that they knew the superiority of their weapons, the ferocity of their character, and the cunning of their leaders, then some of them may have seen that in the end the Tahuantinsuyu would have to fight for its life against these technologically brilliant ruffians, and in that case, it would be as well to do it with their own weapons if possible; we know that it would not have been possible for the Peruvians to copy Spanish arms, for they had no iron and, even if they were to find it, did not know how to smelt and handle it, but there is no reason why their leaders should have realized this.

If Pizarro had hoped to find throughout Peru the same disorder as he had found in Tumbez, he was disappointed. De Soto told him that on arriving in Caxas he had met with regular troops and with hostility; he had explained his pacific intentions; he had then been received with courtesy; he had found the country at peace and under law—several men, for example, having been convicted of an assault on some Virgins of the Sun from a neighboring convent, had been executed during his residence in Caxas. De Soto had been received by an Inca official of high rank in Caxas on treasury business and from him he learned something of the Inca social state. He had also learned that Atahualpa was indeed at Caxamarca taking the baths (the place then as now was famous for its warm springs) and that a large part of his victorious army was with him.

De Soto had not confined his mission to Caxas but had gone on to Huancupampa and there found himself in a city of stone houses and public buildings instead of adobe bricks. One of the great Inca highroads passed through the town; it was splendidly paved with dressed stone and carried across the river on a bridge, and it was shaded by willow and molle trees planted to make traveling pleasanter. To the same end, some of the irrigation channels, lined with masonry, were carried beside the road, to cool the air with running water and slake the traveler's thirst. De Soto saw posthouses and resthouses at regular intervals along the highway. He visited one of the state warehouses and saw that it was well stocked with grain, cloth and clothing. It was explained to him that the army could call on such stocked supplies all over the country and whenever these were needed. He noticed the administrative posts manned by officials at all the entrances to the town and took them for octrois, or local excise offices. In short, de Soto had to report a far more highly developed economy and far more highly organized and sophisticated social system than Pizarro had probably anticipated. And while this gave him a more splendid idea of his prospective prize, it also gave him anxious pause, for the task before him seemed to grow more difficult with every piece of information that came in.

Pizarro showed none of the anxiety he felt as he led his men out onto the road to Caxamarca, but he was praying that reinforcements would reach him before he had to encounter the Sapa Inca. He was, in fact, hoping that Almagro had reached Tumbez and San Miguel, and would soon catch up with him; this is made clear by his conduct at the next halt—and by the fact that before leaving for Caxamarca he sent a messenger back to San Miguel with details of his proposed movements. He took the same opportunity to send back the presents he had received from the Sapa Inca and such articles of local manufacture as had been obtained on the march, probably by barter. Some of the vicuña woolen goods were sent back to the Spanish court, where some of these materials were pronounced finer than silk.

The Spaniards marched south through cultivated country watered by irrigation channels—the *tierra caliente*—until they arrived at Motupe in a fruitful green valley among the foothills of the cordillera. Here were signs that the war had produced abnormal conditions; not only had three hundred *puric-cuna* been called to the colors but the *curaca* of Motupe had gone with them as their officer. It is unlikely that Pizarro recognized this as exceptional. There was no reason to halt at Motupe, especially as Pizarro had told the Sapa Inca that he would press forward with a minimum of delay. Nevertheless, he now called a halt of four days, giving no explanation. His purpose was to give the hoped-for reinforcements time to come up with him. There was no sign or news of them, however, and he pushed on again, marching through flat, sandy country well provided with irrigation works, until he came to a broad and turbulent river, a difficult obstacle, which flowed across the Spaniards' line of march.

At no time did Pizarro allow himself to be lulled by the Peruvians' smiling manners and gentle welcome into trusting them. He behaved as if he felt that his own secret purpose must be suspected by the people he planned to betray into slavery. He very well knew that no European monarch would allow himself to be approached by a band of formidably armed foreigners of unknown provenance; and he was, consequently, unremittingly suspicious of a trap. He saw that if there was any intention of holding up his advance, this river was the very place for it; and if the Peruvians opposed the river crossing, he would be in a very ugly position. He therefore sent Hernando Pizarro across with an advance party, to seize and hold a bridgehead. This operation was accomplished in darkness, and on the following day Pizarro and the main body crossed the river on rafts made by felling trees and lashing them together, the horses swimming alongside. Far from resisting his landing, the people on the far bank fled in terror, and the Spaniards had to pursue them in order to catch a prisoner who could give them information. We do not think that this means that the social order had collapsed; these people were simple peasants in a countryside remote from any urban center. It is true that they knew of the Spaniards' coming; but the actual sight of their fierce, bearded faces, their iron clothes and their swords, their harquebuses and their horses, was too much for them.

Hernando Pizarro caught a prisoner but he could get nothing out of the man, who sullenly refused to give the whereabouts of the Sapa Inca and his army. Hernando therefore had him tortured, whereupon he broke and said that Atahualpa was still near Caxamarca with his whole army in three divisions, that he knew of the Spaniards' approach, and that he was decoying them into his camp in order to destroy them or to have them in his power. Why Pizarro, when this information was passed to him, should have been worried, is not clear; he himself had informed the Sapa Inca of his approach; and Pizarro can hardly have supposed this frightened peasant to know anything of Atahualpa's intentions. What seems to have worried him was the discrepancy between the prisoner's information—which may have been invented on the spot as an expression of resentment—and that obtained from the local *curaca* after the people had been sufficiently reassured to come drifting back to the village. This minor official told Pizarro that he had himself visited the Sapa Inca's camp, that it was not at Caxamarca at all but at Huamachuco fifty miles south of it, that this was a fortified town, and that the army with Atahualpa numbered at least fifty thousand men.

Pizarro decided to make sure of the truth. He asked one of the Peruvians who had been with him all the way from San Miguel to go into the Inca camp as a spy and bring back information. The man refused. He seems to have considered secrecy quite unnecessary, and he suggested that he be sent openly to Atahualpa as an emissary. The man seems to have been some kind of petty *curaca* by rank and perhaps saw himself becoming quite a great man as a result of this mission. Pizarro agreed; the Peruvian was to tell the Sapa Inca that the Spaniards were still on their way to him, that their conduct to Atahualpa's subjects had been uniformly pacific and honest, and that they trusted his to them would be the same. The emissary was told to note whether the passes on the road through the mountain were manned or guarded, and if so how strongly, and in general to keep eyes and ears open for evidence of hostile preparations against the Spaniards. With the Peruvian messenger were sent three runners to be sent back with intelligence to the advancing Spaniards.

These precautions having been taken, the march was resumed and three days brought Pizarro and his men under the lee of that mighty wall of mountains beyond which lay Caxamarca, an ancient city like a palace in a walled garden. The nearer and lower slopes were covered with dense evergreen rain forest, bright with epiphytic orchids and even more brilliantly colored birds. Here and there was a cultivated terrace and a few houses of adobe and thatch. Above towered the naked rock of the mountains, penetrating the clouds. The way through this barrier was by a series of narrow and tortuous passes each higher than the last. From the military point of view the place was a nightmare; no superiority of cunning, experience, arms or courage could have availed even a large disciplined army, let alone a small band of soldiers of fortune against a few score brave men defending the passes. If those passes were defended by the Sapa Inca's fifty thousand, an attempt to march through them would be mere suicide.

Over the mountains lay a stony path beset with difficulty, hardship and danger; but at right angles to it ran one of the empire's great highways, wide enough for six men to ride abreast, firm and smooth, and pleasantly shaded by molle and willow trees so that it was a cool avenue all the way. A number of his men urged Pizarro to take this easy and pleasant way directly to Cuzco, rather than the hazardous and laborious path to Caxamarca. Had Pizarro given way to these weak sisters there can be no doubt what would have happened: the Spaniards would have walked into a formidable combination of Quizquiz, Chalcuchima and their Quitu veterans; either the old barbarian general would have combined with the Hurinists to defend the sacred city against the aliens, or the Hurinists, seeing in Pizarro their savior, would have involved him in war with Quizquiz. That officer was no easygoing, overconfident Atahualpa; the Spaniards would have been wiped out. Atahualpa would then have had time to establish himself as Sapa Inca and get the country under control. And the Spaniards who came in Pizarro's wake would have found themselves opposed by a united empire, a warlike Sapa Inca, at least two brilliant commanders, and possibly some European weapons.

But Pizarro was a true leader. He saw that the hard way must be taken. He pointed out to his men that they had everywhere announced their intention of visiting the Sapa Inca in his camp. If they now failed to do so they would be branded as cowards and earn the Sapa Inca's contempt.

> Let every man of you take heart and go forward like a good soldier, nothing daunted by the smallness of your numbers. For in the greatest extremity God always fights for his own; never doubt that he will humble the pride of the heathen and bring him to the knowledge of the true faith, the great end and object of the conquest.[1]

Both the reasons given for sticking to his plan and the speech made to his men are rather thin, not very convincing, although there was, from the Spanish point of view, something in both of them. The fact is that Pizarro knew that he had just one chance of success in an enterprise which, judged by ordinary standards, was impossible of accomplishment—he must emulate Cortes; he must seize the person of this empire's emperor and so hold the source of power. Once again Pizarro was able to persuade his men to follow him by the harder way. Says Oviedo in his *Historia de las Indias*:

> *Todos digeron que fuese por el camino que quisiese i viese que mas convenía, que todos le sequirían con buena voluntad e obra al tiempo del efecto, y vería lo que cada uno de ellos haría en servicio de Dios e de su Magestad.*

But Pizarro was as prudent as he was brave; as the adventure proceeded he seems to have grown in stature; he was learning the trade of leadership all the time, an astonishing achievement for a man now in his sixty-first year. Small as his number was, he divided it into two parties: he himself led the forward party of forty horse and sixty foot; Hernando remained at the base of the mountains with the other threescore men, covering his brother's rear until he received orders to advance.

The Spaniards had hitherto been marching over *tierra caliente* not much above sea level and in an equatorial climate, and through foothills of inconsiderable altitude. As they made their painful way along the steep path into the mountains, a path which skirted terrifying *quebradas* (the immensely deep fissurelike abysses which distinguish the Andes), which clambered over obstacles forcing the cavalry to dismount and lead their frightened horses, and which penetrated narrow gorges between towering cliffs, the men began to suffer from cold and altitude. Most people suffer some discomfort at eight thousand feet, and sickness at about ten thousand; the Spaniards had to cross passes higher than ten thousand feet. The scenery, too, became forbidding, as they passed from the forest of tropical hardwoods, through a wide belt of somber conifers where nothing stirred and no bird sang, and so up into the region of naked rock or alpine scrub, their progress followed with sinister interest by hovering condors, those huge scavenger birds of the cordillera.

It was increasingly obvious that every next turn in the path might, and indeed should, conceal an ambush of well-armed mountain troops. When the leading men came in sight of a lowering fortress dominating the path, they could not fail to assume it manned, and to think that here, at last, was the trap they had been lured into. They found it deserted and nothing could have been better for their morale. The soldiers became convinced that their leader was right; the Sapa Inca could have no intention of opposing their advance. Even Pizarro himself was now so sure of this that he sent back orders to Hernando to strike camp and follow. He himself soon came to a second, larger fortress of colossal masonry, likewise unmanned, where he decided to pass the night. At this point one of the runners sent with the messenger to Atahualpa arrived in camp to say that the way was clear and unguarded and that another embassy was on the way from the Sapa Inca. Pizarro immediately sent off a dispatch to his brother telling him to hurry; he did not want the Inca ambassador to see him with so few men. Hernando was not far behind and joined the main body in good time.

The Inca government's ambassador was a man of the highest rank, was accompanied by a suite, and was bringing a present of llamas for the Spaniards. He welcomed the strangers in his master's name and wanted to know when they expected to be in Caxamarca, so that preparations could be made to receive them. Pizarro now at last had firsthand intelligence of the Sapa Inca's movements: Atahualpa had been at Huamachuco but had gone thence to Caxamarca for the baths. From the ambassador, Pizarro also received a clear account of the recent civil war and its outcome.

The ambassador gave such an account of his master's power and prowess as drove Pizarro into corrective boasting. He admired, he said, the Sapa Inca's military success and had no doubt that he was the greatest of Inca warriors. But he was as inferior to the white men's emperor as a petty *curaca* was to him; and as proof of this discourteous assertion he told the ambassador how a few Spaniards had overrun the American continent subduing nation after nation. It is not to be supposed that the Inca was much impressed; as a diplomat he showed awe and admiration; as a diplomat he knew brag when he heard it. And the boasting of Pizarro can have meant little to a man who knew nothing of any country outside the Tahuantinsuyu whose vast extent and enormous resources were familiar to him as a member of the administrative caste. Nor could such boasting have given him a very high idea of the Spaniards' manners; it was bad form among the civilized American Indians. Pizarro went on to say that having heard of Atahualpa's fame he and his men had come to take service with him and if well received were willing to "postpone their passage across the country to the opposite seas."

Two more days of marching through difficult passes at high altitudes followed. Many of the Spaniards must have suffered mountain sickness. Then began the descent. Shortly thereafter another ambassador or messenger arrived from Atahualpa, with another message of welcome and more llamas. This gentleman was an old acquaintance, he was the high official who had met Pizarro down in the valley. The Spaniards noted with quickened greed the golden cups in which his attendants served him with *chicha* while he was in their camp. While the ambassador was still with the Spaniards, that messenger whom Pizarro had sent forward to the Sapa Inca, a man it will be recalled of *curaca* rank but not an Inca, returned from Caxamarca, saw the Inca being made much of by Pizarro, and flying into a terrible rage would have assaulted the man had he not been restrained. His reason was that he had been very shabbily treated in the Sapa Inca's camp. He had been refused access to the Sapa Inca on the ground that Atahualpa was keeping a fast and might not be disturbed; and when he tried to insist, he got off with his life only by threatening that the Spaniards would treat the Inca in their camp exactly as their own envoy was treated in the Inca camp.

We have here a perfect example of the kind of conduct the Spanish presence was to give rise to not only in individuals but in communities, tribes and factions. The Spaniards came to represent, at first unwittingly, hope for malcontents. Their intrusion into the body politic of the Tahuantinsuyu acted as a catalyst in precipitating revolt among those who had cause—good, bad or indifferent— to resent the Inca dominion. We have seen something analogous happen on a much vaster scale in our own time: the entry upon the scene of world politics of the United States and the U.S.S.R. gave heart to nationalists in the colonial empires of the old European powers, enabling them to assert their independence. The *curaca* envoy employed by the Spaniards, whose protection he made sure of, behaved with an insolence he would never have dared to exhibit before the Spaniards arrived in Peru. He went on to warn Pizarro before the Inca's face that Atahualpa's intentions were hostile; the Spaniards, he said, were being drawn into a trap.

To all this the Inca ambassador replied contemptuously. He made it clear that the fellow chosen by Pizarro as his envoy was of insufficiently high rank to be treated with consideration at court. And he had not even been provided with proper credentials. Had he carried credentials it was possible that the Sapa Inca, out of courtesy to the foreigners, would have interrupted his fast to receive the *curaca*. For it was true that Atahualpa was fasting and it was simply not safe for his officers to disturb him when he was engaged in such religious exercises. The *curaca* envoy had likewise made a great to-do about the size of the army with Atahualpa; but there was nothing in the least exceptional or surprising about that, considering that the empire was still on a war footing. Finally, the envoy had said that Caxamarca was abandoned by its inhabitants as if that too were something sinister; it had been cleared of its inhabitants to make living quarters available to the Spanish guests.

Pizarro believed little of this, for it was his plain duty, the part of mere common sense, to distrust the Sapa Inca and his government. But it was likewise the part of common sense to avoid an open quarrel with him, for by quarreling he would probably lose the chance to betray and entrap him. Pizarro's intentions toward Atahualpa being what they were, he was bound to assume that Atahualpa's toward him were no better, and to pretend to others that he believed all the Sapa Inca's fair promises. He therefore accepted the ambassador's explanations and sent him back to Caxamarca with assurances that the Spaniards would not be far behind him.

The descent of the mountains, although hard going, was easier than the ascent had been, and a week's steady marching brought

Pizarro and his men within sight of Caxamarca's green and prosperous valley. It was a place of intensive horticulture in a temperate climate. This walled garden, as we have called it, was an oval plain fifteen miles by nine, and its *puric-cuna* made an immediate impression on the Spaniards by the superiority of their dress and the cleanliness and comforts of their houses. A wide, shallow river supplied both covered aqueducts and open irrigation channels with ample water. The small but beautifully regular town of Caxamarca, of straw-colored adobe and pale-gray limestone, looked, we are told, "like a sparkling gem in the dark skirts of the sierra." From their heights the Spaniards could also see, identifiable by its permanent plume of steam, the baths made famous by the patronage of several Sapa Incas. But if these pleasant sights were glanced at, it was another, not so agreeable in Spanish eyes, which held their attention: several miles of hillside above the town were covered with the regular lines of snow-white cotton tents composing a vast military camp of a very large army under good discipline. Here is what one of Pizarro's officers wrote touching this spectacle:

> It filled us with amazement to behold the Indians occupying so proud a position. So many tents so well appointed as were never seen in the Indies till now. The spectacle caused confusion and something like fear in the stoutest hearts. But it was too late to turn back or display the slightest sign of weakness, since the natives in our own company would in such case have been the first to rise upon us. So, with as bold a countenance as we could, after coolly surveying the ground, we prepared for our entrance into Caxamarca.[2]

This, incidentally, reveals that Pizarro must have recruited on the march enough Peruvians, presumably more or less disaffected to the Inca government, to be dangerous if not kept in awe. Doubtless he had, here too, the example of Cortes in mind, although for him there was no possibility of taking a whole anti-Inca nation into alliance.

Prescott tells us that whatever may have been Atahualpa's feelings when he saw the martial cavalcade of the Christians, as with banners streaming, and bright panoplies glistening in the rays of the evening sun, it emerged from the dark depths of the sierra, . . . he could hardly have felt such confidence in himself as not to look with apprehension mingled with awe on the mysterious strangers who, coming from an unknown world and possessed of such wonderful gifts, had made their way across mountain and valley in spite of every obstacle which man and nature had opposed to them.

We are not of Prescott's opinion. What cause for apprehension was there in the sight of fewer than two hundred men, albeit ironclad and mounted on animals, when opposed, if opposition was in the Sapa Inca's mind, by his own tens of thousands? As for awe, the feat of marching had been much less remarkable than hundreds such performed by much greater bodies of men when Atahualpa's father, grandfather and great-grandfather were conquering their empire. What obstacles had been opposed to the Spaniards by men? As we have seen, none whatever; on the contrary they had been encouraged to come. As to the natural obstacles, they were contemptible to the Incas by reason of their familiarity. The men who built the road over the mountains were hardly likely to be impressed by the feat of marching along it. No; curiosity and excitement were Atahualpa's most probable feelings on the occasion.

What followed is singular, however. It was as if the Sapa Inca had passively allowed rather than actively bidden the Spaniards to come to him; but the entire want of any kind of reception may have been intended to put the Spaniards in their place and show them that they were not regarded as very important. Pizarro, having formed his men into three companies and battle order, advanced steadily on the town. Not a soul came to meet him, either to welcome or to challenge. He entered the town, a considerable place, having normally ten thousand inhabitants, but now it was entirely deserted; not a dog stirred in the streets, not a child appeared at the doorway of a house, not a soul lingered in any of the public buildings of fine masonry and timber roofs. And not a sound was heard—only the hollow clatter, made by the Spaniards themselves, of horseshoes and boot leather on stone paving.

Plan of Caxamarca.

Caxamarca was a watering place because of its hot springs; it was also a garrison town. Apart from the houses of the people there was a Convent of the Sun, a temple in a grove, a fine fortress dominating the town and defended by a spiral wall which wound three times round it. The military quarter consisted of barrack dwellings, some of them spacious halls, surrounding a triangular parade ground which Hernando Pizarro describes as vast, dominated by a fort from which a stone causeway led across meadows and a stream to the tented camp of an imperial army.

Although it was late afternoon (November 15, 1532) when Pizarro entered Caxamarca, and although it now began not only to rain but to hail and to be very cold, Pizarro was too nervous to go into quarters and wait till the morrow, doing nothing or waiting for a move from Atahualpa. He decided to find out at once the Sapa Inca's state of mind and feeling about the Spaniards. While the majority of his men took shelter in the barrack quarters, Hernando de Soto was sent, with fifteen other horsemen, to the Inca camp. On second thought Pizarro detached another twenty horsemen led by his brother Hernando Pizarro, to back them up.

The Spanish cavalry galloped along the causeway to the Inca camp. The distance was not more than two miles. They were then among the tents where Inca soldiers off duty stood about and watched in silence and doubtless some amazement as the Spanish cavalcade swept past at the gallop, trumpets sounding brassily. The area under tents was crossed and divided by a stream over which was a wooden bridge; it did not look strong enough to bear mounted men in armor, and the troop of horsemen dashed into and through the water. They were deliberately riding showily, of course; and the astonishment of the watching Peruvians must have been gratifyingly manifest. The far bank of the stream was guarded by a body of Inca soldiers under arms, but they made no attempt to interfere with the Spaniards. De Soto drew rein and his interpreter, Felipillo, asked the way to the Sapa Inca's own quarters. The way was pointed out without cavil or question.

Atahualpa was not himself under canvas but in a lightly built and graceful pavilion of timber with an open gallery running all round it; it was evidently a permanent, not a temporary, structure, a sort of miniature summer palace, for it opened at the back into a garden. The pavilion walls were decorated with a pattern in gleaming white and colored plaster, and in front of it stood the imperial bath, a large stone tank supplied by aqueducts with both hot and cold water brought from the medicinal springs. The Spaniards found the courtyard of the pavilion crowded with Incas and *pallas* of rank, attendant upon Atahualpa. The Spaniards distinguished the Sapa Inca without difficulty, for whereas the rest of the company were gayly and colorfully dressed, his own garments were austerely simple; moreover, he wore the *borla* beneath his *llauta*, its fringe down to his eyes. He was seated on a low stool and about him, in order of rank, stood his great officers of state and army. The ceremonious quality of the occasion was expressed in stylized grouping and attitudes which made an impression on the Spaniards.

It was a part of Atahualpa's court pose, a part of etiquette in fact, to appear grave and conscious of power by a schooled nobility of bearing and deliberation of gestures, to dismiss all expression or motion whatsoever from the countenance, so that nothing could be guessed of the Sapa Inca's feelings by studying his face. Even on this occasion, when confronted by a spectacle so novel and redoubtable as that presented by thirty-five mounted, armored, fair-skinned, bearded men, a spectacle such as had never been seen in the whole history of the Tahuantinsuyu, not a flicker of feeling enlivened Atahualpa's handsome but unmoving countenance.

The body of horse having been halted, Hernando Pizarro, de Soto, and two or three others walked their horses up to the Sapa Inca. Hernando Pizarro, bowing respectfully from the saddle but not dismounting, informed Atahualpa that he came as an ambassador from his brother and commander, to inform the Inca government of their arrival in Caxamarca. They were subjects of a great king across the sea and they had been brought to Peru by the fame of the Sapa Inca's military prowess and to teach him the true faith, which they professed. Hernando then delivered an invitation from Pizarro to Atahualpa to visit the Spaniards in their quarters. It was a part of Pizarro's brilliant handling of the appallingly dangerous situation into which he had deliberately led his men, to treat Atahualpa with the respect due to a brave soldier and a great

king while clearly implying, by an attitude of courteous conde-
scension, that the courage, power and importance of his own prince
were incomparably greater than those of the Sapa Inca.

The interpreter Felipillo, either with the same kind of deliberate
insolence as had inspired the *curaca* envoy's attack on the Inca
ambassador in the Spanish mountain camp, or from ignorance of
court etiquette, addressed his translation of Hernando's speech
directly to Atahualpa and not to the Inca Apu. The Sapa Inca sat
still and unresponsive as an idol, with his eyes on the ground. It is
obvious that, even if this had not been his normal practice, it would
have been necessary in this case, for had he responded with attention he would have been at the usual disadvantage of a seated man
in converse with a mounted one, and would have had to lose face
by raising his head and eyes to the Spaniards. And since, for whatever reason, he was not willing to quarrel with them, he could not
order them to be dragged from their horses and forced to do
obeisance. There was, too, something huge, overpowering, over-
bearing in these ironclad, towering, multiple beings, man and beast
united, which by contrast emphasized the smallness, slightness,
frailness of Peruvian flesh and blood and cotton and wool;
Atahualpa and his advisers must have felt a little like men in the
presence of a large and powerful and unfamiliar machine which
may, if mishandled, blow up in their faces. But some response to
Hernando's speech was clearly necessary. The Inca Apu answered
in a single, curt phrase which Felipillo translated *"Buen está"* (it is
well).

The anonymous author of the account of this meeting,[8] who
was an eyewitness, being one of the cavaliers escorting Hernando
Pizarro, says that Hernando found this embarrassing and discon-
certing. It was certainly rather an anticlimax and altogether inconclusive. We have, even now, no satisfactory idea of what was
passing in Atahualpa's mind and the minds of his advisers.
Hernando, infusing voice and manner with the utmost respect and
courtesy, and addressing himself directly to Atahualpa, now begged
that monarch to do him the honor of speaking to him with his own
mouth. Atahualpa broke his rule to do so; he did not raise his eyes
but a smile touched his lips and he spoke. Felipillo translated:

"Tell your captain that I am keeping a fast that will end tomorrow. I will then visit him with my principal officers. In the meantime, let him occupy the barracks on the square and no other building, until I come, when I shall order what is to be done."[4] We cannot escape the conclusion that on this as on other occasions the fast was diplomatic in the sense that a statesman's illness may be diplomatic in our own polity.

While he was speaking, Atahualpa at last raised his eyes to look not at his interlocutor but, with the only sign of faint interest he had yet permitted himself, at Hernando de Soto's charger, which was champing the bit and behaving restlessly. De Soto is said to have been the finest horseman of the Spanish expedition; now, observing the Sapa Inca's flicker of interest, he set spurs to his horse, wheeled, galloped onto the field before the courtyard and went through an impressive exhibition of horsemanship designed to show off the animal's powers and his own complete control over them. He concluded it by galloping his horse right up to Atahualpa and pulling it up short onto its haunches so close that the Sapa Inca's clothes were splashed with foam from the bit. By not a flicker of an eyelash did the Lord of the World betray awareness that anything was happening, much less fear, but sat unmoved, unmoving, composed as granite. Nor did his officers flinch. But some soldiers who had started back, disconcerted, from de Soto's dashing passage, were subsequently arrested and put to death for having shown fear.

Attendants, *yanacuna* of the imperial household, now appeared with refreshments for the visitors. As the latter were under orders not to dismount, the food was refused but the drink accepted. It was *chicha*, handed to them in large golden cups by girls of Atahualpa's household; and having drunk this stirrup cup the Spaniards took a respectful leave and cantered over the causeway back to Caxamarca. The impression made on them had greatly depressed their spirits. They had now seen for themselves that the Sapa Inca was a civilized monarch wielding immense power; that they were up against no congeries of half-savage tribes temporarily united under a war chief, but a great and highly organized nation with a large and apparently well-disciplined army. Both Hernando

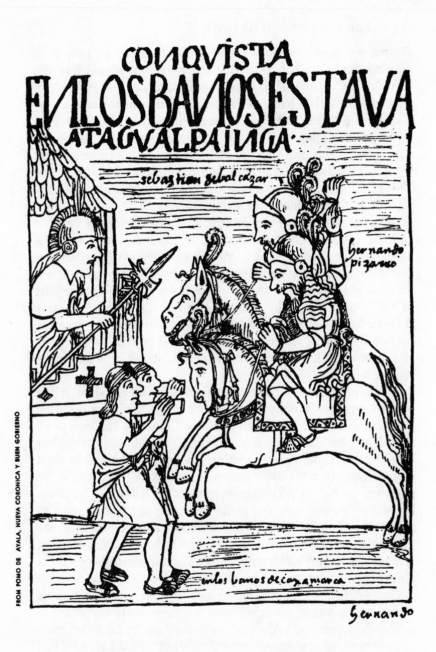

Hernando Pizarro visits Atahualpa and shows off the paces of his cavalry.

Pizarro and the anonymous author of the *Relación* we have been drawing upon, make it clear that the men who returned to the barracks in Caxamarca did so in a spirit of gloom and foreboding, regretting that they had put themselves at the mercy of a power they were too few and weak to resist, instead of waiting for reinforcements. They say, too, that their comrades in Caxamarca soon caught their own spirit of despondency, which turned to fear when, night having fallen, they saw the campfires of the Inca army all over the hillside—". . . *no parecía sino un cielo muy estrellado*" (looked like a sky thick with stars).

Although Caxamarca was deserted by its citizens, there were, as we have noted, numerous Peruvians in Pizarro's train, and it is probable that Atahualpa had sent others as servants to attend on the Spaniards. Among these Peruvians there were many spies acting for their government. In the course of the night they sent reports to the Inca camp. Pedro Pizarro[5] says that they told Atahualpa that the Spaniards were in such a state of fear that they were involuntarily making water in their clothes. It is likely that reports of this kind made Atahualpa overconfident in his conduct on the following day.

If Pizarro shared his men's consternation he did not show it. His own courage was reinforced by the knowledge that he was within immediate reach of his objective. He had flown in the face of all probability; he had driven himself and his men to overcome great obstacles and endure great hardships; by so doing he had brought himself close to a fantastic success very unlikely to be the lot of any man so late in life; after sixty years of failure he now saw himself within one bold and perfidious stroke of the viceroyalty of an enormous and very rich empire. It was enough to make any man's eloquence persuasive, and Pizarro had never been wanting in words. He called his men about him and addressed them. As has always been customary, he invoked Providence, pointing out that as God was fighting on the Spanish side the overwhelming number of the enemy was of no significance whatsoever. He succeeded in raising the spirits and rekindling the enthusiasm of his followers.

The time had now come to reveal to his officers the plan he had in mind and following which he had brought them and their men and himself over those terrible mountains from San Miguel. In putting this over to them—his plan to entrap and hold the Sapa Inca and therefore the source of all power in Peru—the desperate situation into which he had deliberately led them was a positive advantage. It was useless for them to think of retreating now; the fact that the mountains, in which the number and experience of the Sapa Inca's troops could catch and destroy the Spaniards with great ease, lay between them and anything like safety, was equivalent, as an argument in favor of extreme boldness, to Cortes's boat-burning. If the Spaniards retreated now, they would be showing fear and consequently inviting the Peruvians to attack them. If they merely did nothing, just waited for Atahualpa to take the initiative, they would give the Incas and their people time to discover that the Spaniards were only human (if they did not know it already), to realize that they were but few, to resent the impertinence of their conduct in seizing Peruvian territory on the coast, to resent also the impertinence of their political and religious demands on the Tahuantinsuyu, to realize that it would be better to exterminate them at once than wait for their number to be increased by reinforcement, to conclude that the army had better be ordered to destroy the strangers. Thus, the plan to seize the person of the Sapa Inca was presented to the officers whom Pizarro had called to a council of war as being now the only thing left to be done.

Like all leaders of men, all successful demagogues (Pizarro was that as well as a soldier), the Spanish captain knew that he could count on two ordinary human weaknesses among his officers: short and confused memories of past speeches; relief at having decisions taken for them. In getting his people into their present dangerous corner, Pizarro had assured them that the Sapa Inca's embassies of good will and friendly welcome were sincere, and that the warnings of those Peruvians who had told them that Atahualpa meant them no good, could be ignored as coming from partisans hostile to the Inca yoke or favorable to the party of Huáscar. Now he told them that the same embassies had been designed to lure them to their deaths and that the same warnings had been perfectly honest and sound. No reader who follows politics will be surprised to learn that not a voice was raised against this inconsistency. Pizarro then added a further argument for quick and decisive action: the army under Quizquiz now in Cuzco might very soon move north to rejoin the Sapa Inca in Caxamarca. The leader's extraordinary plan was accepted without a murmur and the officers went about their duty of setting a good guard for the night.

The day set for betraying Atahualpa's misplaced confidence or for calling his bluff, as Pizarro now represented the case, was Saturday, November 16, 1532. The vast triangular parade ground of Caxamarca's military quarter was, as we have said, delimited by buildings, many of them great halls having wide, high doorways opening into the square, and dominated by a small fortress. Pizarro put his artillery, two small cannon of the kind called falconets, commanded by Pedro de Candia, into the fortress, to enfilade the parade ground. His cavalry he divided into two parties, one under Hernando de Soto and the other under Hernando Pizarro; and he placed them in two separate large buildings or halls which had wide openings or doorways onto the square. The main body of the infantry was similarly concealed in another hall. Twenty men of them were, however, picked out and reserved to act under Pizarro's immediate orders as occasion should require. Orders were to remain on the alert under cover until, the Sapa Inca having entered the square and a falconet having been fired by way of a signal, they were to rush out and fall on the Peruvians whom Atahualpa brought with him, while Atahualpa himself was seized and made prisoner by Pizarro's special party. De Candia would receive a signal from Pizarro, the waving of a white scarf, to fire the opening shot of the massacre.

Preparations were very thorough. Both eyewitness accounts tell us that the steel breastplates of the cavalry charges were festooned with bells to add to the noise they would make when charging, that Pizarro himself inspected all arms, that a lavish meal was served to the men, and finally that, by way of spiritual preparation for one of the most atrocious acts of bloodthirsty treachery in recorded history, mass was celebrated by Father Valverde and his curates, and, no doubt, all communicated. It is necessary to point out that in this there was no hypocrisy; the Incas were heathen and as such they were damned. The destruction of a few hundred or thousand Inca bodies, as a means of bringing a few million Inca souls to Christ, was a good act, a religious deed. We, casting our minds back over our own history for the past quarter of a century, find ourselves regrettably unable to sniff at this. It was with a sense of righteousness, of holiness, that the Spaniards in Caxamarca barrack square that morning called in song upon their God to arise —*Exsurge domine!*—and judge His own cause. And hearing the chorus of manly voices thus raised to heaven, the officiating clergy must have felt that not vainly had their long night been spent in prayer.

The strain of waiting which now followed must have been extremely disagreeable. Not for hours did the Spanish scouts report a bustle of preparation in the Inca camp. Late in the forenoon a message was sent to Pizarro saying that since Pizarro's men had gone armed to the Inca camp, Atahualpa would come with his escort fully armed to the Spanish camp. The purpose of this message can only have been to prevent a misunderstanding that might cause the Spaniards to attack under the impression that they were being attacked. Pizarro was disturbed; he had planned a massacre, not a battle; yet a battle had always been a possibility and there was nothing he could do to prevent it. He therefore sent back a message to say that the Inca might come as he liked, he would be received "as a friend and a brother."[6]

At noon a large body of Peruvians was seen marching under discipline along the causeway which connected the camp to the military quarter of Caxamarca. It was preceded by a swarm of servants, a working party, whose job was to sweep the road before the imperial litter borne high on the shoulders of bearers who were themselves all of Inca blood and high rank and escorted by a guard of nobles so gorgeously clad and decorated with gold and silver that, Pedro Pizarro says, "... *lo que reluzia con el sol*" (they shone like the sun). Meanwhile a large detachment of the Inca army was deployed over the fields through which the causeway passed.

Next came an unpleasant shock for Pizarro. Half a mile from the town and at a moment when the tension before action must have been at that disagreeable peak which all men who have fought will remember, a halt was called to the Inca procession, and Pizarro observed with astonishment that preparations were being made to pitch tents and form camp. An explanatory message shortly arrived to say that the Sapa Inca would remain where he was that night and would not visit the Spaniards until the morrow. Nothing could have been worse; men and horses had been waiting in a state of tension since dawn; further delay would mean their relaxation into the nervous flabbiness of anticlimax. Pizarro sent back a message deploring Atahualpa's decision, saying that elaborate arrangements had been made for his reception—which certainly was true—and that he was expecting the Sapa Inca to sup with him that night. Atahualpa turned the whole business into a story which only Sophocles could have done justice to, by allowing this message to change his mind. The order to pitch camp was countermanded and yet another messenger was sent by the Sapa Inca to say that he would come after all, that he would leave his army outside the town, and that he would enter it only with an unarmed escort and his suite; he would spend the night in the Spanish camp; let the House of the Serpent be prepared for his accommodation. This house was one of the buildings on the barrack square, distinguished by a snake carved into the stone of its walls.

Some difficulty has been made by historians over the Sapa Inca's changeable conduct at this time. We see none. His feeling for the Spaniards was one of intense curiosity. He did not fear them, although he was impressed by them. To make quite sure that they would respect his person and understand his power, he moved a large body of troops down so that they overawed the town. He believed in Pizarro's protestations of friendship and good will because he could not conceive of any man's being so mad as not to value them in the circumstances. Even if he suspected that the presumptuous foreigner had evil designs on the Lord of the World, he could hardly suppose that the man would assault him at a moment when he was protected by a large and well-armed force of trained soldiers. His projected halt within half a mile of the camp may have several explanations; he may have been trying to decide between conflicting advice from his *apu-cuna;* he may have been tired; he may have thought morning a better time for the meeting than afternoon; he may have received a bad omen from one of the clergy. His change of mind was, we believe, partly a gesture of royal courtesy and partly a demonstration to his own people that he was afraid of nothing on earth, not even a thing so alarmingly unfamiliar and even grotesque as ironclad, hairy-faced white men on ironclad, iron-shod beasts. A Sapa Inca with a perfect right to the *borla* would not have found it necessary to flaunt his courage; Atahualpa had won the throne by war and he still had to keep it.

Shortly following Atahualpa's latest messenger, the several hundred sweepers entered the great square, singing at their work as was customary. Their singing did not sound harmonious in Spanish ears; it bore no resemblance to any music they had ever heard, and their own nervousness made it sound like some diabolical cacophony. Servants of higher rank, some in a livery of white-and-red check, others in pure white, followed the sweepers and were followed in their turn by a first detachment of royal guards bearing no weapons and dressed for ceremony. They wore a sky-blue livery and ornaments of gold and silver; their ear lobes being distended by gems, it was clear that they were of Inca blood or *curaca* rank. The Sapa Inca's litter must have been excessively heavy for its noble bearers, since its throne was made of solid gold, while its chassis was paneled with gold and silver and decorated with featherwork. Atahualpa had put off his austere fasting clothes, and was richly attired. Pedro Pizarro says that he was wearing his "crown" (that is, the *borla*) and round his neck a collar of very large emeralds, gems which the Incas obtained from their northwestern province, the Esmeraldas.

The movement of the imperial suite as it entered the square was orderly, well-drilled, almost choreographic; the ranks of servants and noble guards wheeled right and left to open the way for the imperial litter and its escort of high officials. Atahualpa, looking down upon the multitude, wore, says Pedro Pizarro, an air of sedate and dignified composure, like one accustomed to command. He crossed the square in silence, still followed by more courtiers,

The Spanish version of the meeting in the square of Caxamarca between the Spaniards and Atahualpa. The priest Valverde explains the Scriptures; Felipillo interprets; Pizarro and Almagro wait, apparently in submission.

servants and simple onlookers, until there were between five and seven thousand Peruvians in the square, which Pedro Pizzaro reported as being larger than any in Spain.

As not a single Spaniard was in sight, Atahualpa called a halt and asked where the foreigners were. (He also added, Pedro Pizarro tells us, that "they are a pack of thieves and ought to be killed.") One of his staff replied that they were hiding, being afraid of the Supreme Inca—the usual case of telling an autocrat what he enjoys hearing. As if entering on a cue, the Dominican Vicente de Valverde now appeared, approaching Atahualpa with a Bible in one hand and a crucifix in the other, and accompanied by Felipillo. The Friar, speaking through the interpreter, told the Sapa Inca that he was under orders to expound the true faith, for which purpose, he added, the Spaniards were come to Peru.

Nothing in the whole extraordinary story is more admirable and more difficult for us to understand than the willingness of the Spaniards, in the service of Christian faith and charity, to leave it to God to prevent bloodshed, if He would, by performing a miracle. This curtain raiser to a bloody massacre was not a trick; it was not designed to distract the Sapa Inca's attention nor to make the surprise attack more devastating. It was exactly what it purported to be: an attempt to settle the business between the Incas and the Spaniards by a miracle of conversion and submission. As such, it was made at considerable risk to the whole project and to Spanish life and limb. Valverde, whose courage was as finely tempered as his mind was narrow and fanatical, stood there surrounded by five thousand Peruvians who, for all he knew, were hostile and might react to his evangel with bloody violence. Undaunted, he proceeded to explain the creation of man, his fall, his redemption by Jesus Christ, the crucifixion, ascension and doctrine of the Trinity. How long this took him, what Felipillo made of it in Quechua, and how much Atahualpa understood of the Friar's intention, we do not know. The interpreter did not do very well with the last part of the sermon; he said that the Spaniards worshiped three gods and one god, which made four gods. But the prince understood very well when Valverde went on to his sequel and conclusion: the Pope, holding authority over all princes and powers by virtue of his succession to that Peter who, as he had already explained, had been left as Christ's viceregent on earth, had ordered the Spanish emperor, greatest of secular monarchs, to conquer and convert the peoples of the western world; and Francisco Pizarro was come as the emperor's officer to carry out that order. Therefore Valverde implored the Sapa Inca to "receive him kindly," to renounce the error of his religious ways, to embrace Christianity and thus ensure his own salvation, and to acknowledge himself a vassal of Charles V, in which case the emperor would aid and protect him. But if this plea was rejected, then Atahualpa would be treated as an enemy of Spain and of Christendom.

Thus was God given His chance to perform a miracle of mercy; we do not doubt that had He taken it, had Atahualpa promptly descended from his litter, received baptism at Valverde's hands, and done homage to Carlos Quinto's general for the Tahuantin-suyu, not a drop of blood would that day have been shed. But, as usual, the devil was brisk, if he it was who put into Atahualpa's mouth an answer which reveals that Felipillo's translation had at least conveyed the principal points of Valverde's exposition and plea. For, scowling darkly down on the priest, the Sapa Inca said:

I will be no man's tributary. I am greater than any prince upon earth. Your emperor may be a great prince: I do not doubt it, seeing that he has sent his subjects so far across the waters; and I am willing to hold him as my brother. As for the Pope of whom you speak, he must be mad to talk of giving away countries which do not belong to him. As for my faith, I will not change it. Your own god, as you tell me, was put to death by the very men he created. But my god still looks down upon his children.

He then asked Valverde by what authority he made his demands, whereat the Dominican pointed to the Bible in his hand. Atahualpa took it from him, turned over a few pages then threw it con-temptuously on the ground, saying, "Tell your people that they shall account to me for their doings in my country. I shall not go from here until they have given me satisfaction for all the evil they have done."[7]

What, really, had Pizarro and his men expected from this *démarche?* Was it, despite what we have suggested, an example of that diplomatic dishonesty for propaganda purposes which consists in offering the adversary peace on terms which one knows in advance he cannot possibly accept? Almost certainly not. Almost certainly Pizarro had, at great risk to the whole plan, wanted to make sure of God's will; if He wished to spare the Peruvians, He had only to cause Atahualpa to submit. If a modern general thus offered the Almighty an opportunity to show mercy by performing a miracle in heathen hearts, he would clearly be a grotesque hypocrite; it does not follow that Pizarro was such himself. But from what happened next, it is clear that while the laymen may have hoped for and even perhaps expected a miracle, the Dominican, better acquainted with heavenly manners, had no such expectation and had been acting under orders to keep the record straight. He picked up the Bible—he had been shocked and angered by the contempt with which the Sapa Inca had treated it—hurried back to Pizarro and said, "Do you not see that while we stand here talking to this haughty dog, the fields are filling with Indians? Fall on at once! I absolve you!"

At that, Pizarro, taking up a white scarf, made the prearranged signal to Candia in the fortress, who discharged one of his cannon. Pizarro and his men, the other officers and their following, gave the war cry "Santiago and at them!"—a slogan which in the course of years was to signal death or mutilation to tens of thousands of Americans—and hurled themselves with the murderous fury of released tension upon the huge, soft body of humanity that crowded the square. Let the reader imagine himself one of a crowd of five thousand collected for a demonstration. Suddenly, without warning, two cannon open fire on the crowd; at the same time, fifty guards, with swords and lances working like pistons and flails, charge into the throng, and infantry pour out on the double, firing muskets as they come. Such was the situation of the Peruvians, with one qualification: there was but a single entrance to the vast square, and that was quickly barred. As the Peruvians, terrified by the echoing thunder of cannon and musketry, and by the clouds of sulphurous smoke which rolled over them and darkened the setting sun, fled in panic toward the only way of escape, they were cut and shot down in such number that a pile of dead closed the way to safety and left the living trapped by the Christians whom they had come weaponless to welcome to their country. At one point, where the press of people driven to the wall was greatest and terror of death at the periphery of the crowd most powerful, one hundred yards of adobe and stone wall suddenly gave way to the pressure of panic-stricken bodies and opened a great breach to those who could run. But the Spanish cavalry, maddened with blood lust, pursued the fugitives into open country and cut them down.

The Sapa Inca's escort had been a ceremonial, not a military, guard. With the exception of some silver maces carried by certain officers, the guardsmen were unarmed. Some chroniclers, trying to mitigate the Spanish crime, have said that the Peruvians carried arms under their clothes; but since not a single eyewitness saw any such arms in use and all agree that the Peruvians made no armed resistance, we can dismiss that as a fable. The Incas and *curacas* of the imperial escort had, in fact, only one way of defending their prince; they could thrust their unarmed and lightly clad bodies between the Sapa Inca and Spanish steel. They did so, in hundreds; they clung to the sword arms of the Spaniards and even dragged a few cavaliers from their horses; and as each such living impediment to regicide and deicide fell dying of his wounds, another took his place, with a disregard of self that is well-nigh incredible, but thoroughly attested.

[In the whole course of the massacre only one Spaniard was wounded: Francisco Pizarro.]It happened in defense of the royal life which he needed as a hostage for the empire's good behavior. Some of his men, made desperate by the sheer quantity of butchering still to be done, and fearful that the Sapa Inca, within his fence of living bodies, might still escape, decided that it would be safer to kill him than to risk losing him. He was still in his litter, still on the shoulders of his bearers, still swayed and tossed, stunned with horror and fear, as the dense mass of living, dying and dead reeled and staggered from the butchers' knives. Those Spaniards who had determined to kill him made a fierce charge to cut their way through his people and get at him. Pizarro saw what they were about, fought his way with his own company as near as possible to the litter, and in a great voice which carried above the clamor cried out, "*Nadie hierra al Indio so pena de la vida!*"—"Let no man, for his life, strike at the Inca!" He flung up an arm to shield the litter and was wounded in the hand by a blow intended for the Sapa Inca.

The hideous struggle about the litter became more violent as twilight fell over the reeking square. The Spaniards slashed and stabbed their way through the living and palpitating wall of bodies about their prize, until they could strike at the bearers themselves; one was cut down, then another; the litter toppled at last, and Atahualpa was flung out. Pizarro and his company were waiting for this, they caught him, surrounded him and, taking him at once out of harm's way (though not before one Miguel Estete had torn the *borla* from his brow), secured him bound and under guard in one of the buildings.

The panic of such people as managed to escape from the slaughter yard communicated itself to the troops in the meadows beyond the town as soon as it became known that the Sapa Inca was taken. Only night, falling fast in the low latitude of Caxamarca, put an end to a massacre in which every Spaniard had, in the space of less than an hour, taken between ten and thirty undefended Peruvian lives. This remarkable achievement of sheer hard work was modestly attributed by the Spaniards themselves to their Heavenly Father.

That night Pizarro and Atahualpa kept their engagement; the Sapa Inca supped with the Viceroy of Peru, while outside in the square lay the bodies of three or four thousand dead to which the condors would attend in the morning, while the abattoir stench of blood fouled the air breathed by victors and vanquished alike. To such trifles as these it is not customary and perhaps not fitting for great men to pay attention, and the conversation at supper was urbane. It is said by the Spaniards that Atahualpa accepted his defeat with the Quechua equivalent of "*Fortuna de guerra*"; and he confessed—or so Felipillo conveyed to his masters, and they were very eager to believe him—that, fearless of the Spaniards because they were so few, he had lured them to Caxamarca with every intention of using the service of the best, seizing the weapons of all, and putting the less serviceable foreigners to death.

We may properly use some reserve in noting this confession. There is at least some reason to believe that Felipillo may have been a malicious rascal with a personal grudge against his Sapa Inca. Then, too, this judgment may be a by-product of the white-washing of Pizarro by his family and the Spanish authorities. Another possibility is that Felipillo was under orders from Pizarro to give an anti-Atahualpa slant to his interpretation of what the Sapa Inca was saying. Finally, although Felipillo may have learned Castilian well, the difficulty of translating from Quechua, a language so utterly alien in roots and construction and which had shaped the Peruvian mode of thought to a form hardly communicable in a European tongue, was very great.

8

THE LAST OF THE INCAS

THE SITUATION in the Tahuantinsuyu following the capture of Atahualpa was altogether extraordinary. The wealth, industry and civil peace of that great empire had been very little disturbed by either the civil war or the seizure of its effectual emperor by a band of Spanish plunderers. It was still a balanced, working economy. But a number of forces were at work pressing one against the other in such a tension as to paralyze all political action; the Tahuantinsuyu was held briefly in a state of rest, but it was as precarious as that of a house of cards.

It must be repeated here, for emphasis and by way of reminder, that all power, all authority, all political virtue were vested in the person of the Sapa Inca. Caxamarca was surrounded by troops, although they were mostly inexperienced young men of the *mit'a*, for the veterans were with Quizquiz in Cuzco. Even so, they could, by the mere superiority of their number, have overwhelmed the Spaniards and set Atahualpa at liberty; they did not do so because they were not bidden or directed to do so. The *puric* had almost no conception of himself as a citizen of a great empire except by reference to the duties he owed the Sapa Inca, the state personified; politically, he was as much use without the Sapa Inca as the hands would be without the head. There were only two men in the Tahuantinsuyu who could move the *puric-cuna* to violent, properly concerted action: Atahualpa and Huáscar. The latter was Atahualpa's prisoner and unable to act; the former, in Pizarro's

227

hands, knew that the first casualty in any war to liberate him for which he might give the signal, would be himself. Even in Mexico, it had taken a long time and extreme provocation to make the people rise against the Spaniards at the risk of causing their chief Moctezuma to be put to death; in the Tahuantinsuyu, devotion to the Sapa Inca was far more intense than that of the Mexicans to their leader, and government far more centralized.

Had Pizarro killed Atahualpa at once, Quizquiz and Chalcuchima might immediately have released and restored Huáscar, and there would then have been a Sapa Inca free to act against the enemy, to animate the body of the country and allow it to rid itself of the Spanish pest at least for a time. Or if Atahualpa and Huáscar had been put to death by their respective jailers at the same moment, then the high priest and the army would, in concert, have been free to crown Manco, or perhaps Atahualpa's brother Toparca, or even Prince Titu Atauchi; and by thus restoring the country's incarnate will, they would have made its nationhood effective. But while two men lived who both found recognition as Sapa Inca, and while they were prevented from acting, then so must the whole empire be prevented from acting.

The tension was made all the greater by the urgency, which many leading Incas must have understood, to act quickly. If the Inca grip on the provinces was relaxed for long, then the provinces, led by native princes who could not know that in exchanging an Inca for a Spanish master they would be exchanging a "despotism of predictable demands and justice for one of limitless demands and justice reserved to their oppressors,"[1] would fall away. They might even revolt or ally themselves with the Spaniards to their own ultimate bane.

How much of this remarkable situation was understood by Pizarro, we do not know; but his conduct implies that he understood a great deal of it. He did not treat Atahualpa as a mere prisoner of war, and he made no attempt to keep him incommunicado. Atahualpa, in his captivity, was treated with proper respect; he was allowed to have his courtiers and his women about him, to maintain the etiquette and protocol of the court, to communicate freely with his subjects and to issue his orders and decisions exactly

as if he were staying with the Spaniards for his own pleasure—
except that he was not allowed to leave his quarters. Pizarro, in
short, whether by political intuition or by a clever appreciation of
the situation, did exactly the right thing from his point of view.
By allowing his prisoner freedom of all but the person, he deprived
the Incas in Cuzco and the *curacas* in the provinces of any excuse
to rally round Huáscar or some other son of a *qoya*, and march
against Caxamarca.

Yet this policy, if policy it was, had disadvantages. In theory,
Pizarro's next move must be to march, with his prisoner, on Cuzco
and occupy that capital, placing Atahualpa as a puppet on the
throne; it was there that treasures as well as power were concentrated. But if he did so, he would expose himself to attack, which
he could not be absolutely certain would never be launched, by
Quizquiz. Furthermore, he would be moving, still unsupported,
deeper into the country, farther than ever from his base. He knew
also, or thought he knew, that the present passive acceptance of
the situation by the Peruvians could not continue. Always, he had
the example of Cortes in mind: had not the Mexicans at first
acquiesced in Moctezuma's captivity, but later recovered their
nerve, risen, and nearly destroyed a much greater force of Spaniards, who were aided by a whole nation of native allies, than he,
Pizarro, though he probably did have native allies, could muster?

Nevertheless, to Cuzco he must soon go. He therefore sent an
urgent summons for reinforcement to San Miguel, together with
a detailed report of his success. He hoped that by now Almagro
would have arrived from Panama and would at once march to his
support. Pizarro set himself to wait and his men to turning one of
Caxamarca's public buildings into a church.

At some time during that term of days when he was waiting for
the Spaniards to cross the mountains, Atahualpa must have sent
an order to Quizquiz that his half brother Huáscar was to be taken
from the fortress of Xauca and sent under strong escort to Caxamarca. We do not know what his purpose was; he may have
intended to kill Huáscar, but this is by no means certain and is
even rather improbable. We have already given one reason for
keeping him alive, and Atahualpa may still have intended, as we

have already hinted, to reconcile the Hurin men and respect the deified Huayna Capac's wishes by sharing the empire, at least in appearance, with Huáscar. There is, indeed, some slight evidence that he had this course in mind; an Inca of rank pointed out to a Spaniard of consequence a certain boundary mark which, he said, was to have marked the limit separating Huáscar's domain from Atahualpa's after a treaty between the brothers. But this small incident is hardly conclusive and it provides no matter for substantial discussion.

When the officers bringing Huáscar to Caxamarca reached Andamarca, they heard of Atahualpa's capture by the Spaniards. They therefore remained in Andamarca, no great distance from Caxamarca, waiting on orders and events, stricken, like all else in the Tahuantinsuyu, with paralysis of the will. Huáscar, while he did not enjoy the amenities in captivity which were his brother's lot, nor the freedom to communicate with his erstwhile subjects, was not so rigorously guarded that he could not get messages in and out. It is possible that the people with whom he was in touch were men of such high rank as to overawe his jailers; for, from what followed, it is clear that, while they knew what was going on and even knew what their prisoner and his friends were saying to each other, they did not put a stop to it, but contented themselves with reporting it. As soon as Huáscar heard of Atahualpa's capture by the Spaniards he saw that it might be made into an opportunity for himself. But no obvious course of action immediately suggested itself; a close captive, he was in no position, even had he the necessary will and courage, to rouse the empire, or at least the Incas, Colla, Canari and other dependable nations, against both the Spaniards and Atahualpa. But what seemed a good opportunity to get the Spaniards to help him to freedom was made for him by Atahualpa himself.

This came about in the course of Atahualpa's own efforts to recover his liberty and assume the full government of the empire. For Atahualpa, too, fully realized the urgent need to act swiftly. Living with the Spaniards, he had soon observed that, while they apparently were zealous in their avowed purpose to convert him and his subjects to their faith, their motive for conquest was far more powerful; they had an incomprehensible lust for gold, silver and precious stones—incomprehensible to him because, although he, like his fellow Peruvians, valued these things as beautiful and enduring materials for craftsmanship to work in, and as symbols of solar and lunar brightness, he had no idea of the value arbitrarily attributed to them in the Old World, no idea of a money economy. However, it was his concern not to understand the Spanish greed for gold, but to exploit it. In short, it occurred to him to try to purchase his freedom.

Having come to this conclusion, he took an early occasion to say to Pizarro that in exchange for his liberty he would cover the floor of the room they stood in with gold. This being received with incredulity, he raised his bid: he would fill the room with gold as high as he could reach. Pizarro was not as incredulous as his subordinate officers; he had been told, and he enjoyed believing, that Cuzco was roofed, and its principal buildings were tiled, with gold, that its tapestries were woven of gold thread. In any case he could lose nothing by agreeing. He was not the man to hesitate to make a promise which he had no intention of fulfilling; and he was even ready to sign a contract with Atahualpa undertaking to free him in exchange for a large roomful of gold. There was nobody who could force him to keep to the contract; Atahualpa was hardly in a position to take his case into a Spanish court of law.

A contract was, therefore, drawn up and signed: Atahualpa was to fill a room twenty-two feet long by seventeen feet wide,[2] to a line nine feet from the floor, with gold. The gold was not to be melted down but was to retain the form in which the goldsmiths had cast it; another, smaller room was to be filled twice over with silver; in return for this, Atahualpa was to be set at liberty; and he was to have two months in which to collect this, the largest ransom ever offered to or demanded by any brigands in all the history of extortion.

Just as soon as this contract had been made and couriers had been dispatched to Cuzco and other principal centers with orders that the gold ornaments and parts of the fabric of temples, palaces and public buildings were to be sent to Caxamarca, Huáscar was informed of it. He acted promptly: he sent a message to Pizarro saying that Atahualpa, never having resided in Cuzco, had little idea of its wealth in gold, silver and gems, and that he, Huáscar, would offer a far greater quantity of these commodities for his freedom, than Atahualpa had offered for *his*.

Pizarro may or may not have been impressed. What was obvious to him was that he could exploit the brothers' rivalry. He therefore told Atahualpa that he proposed to have Huáscar brought to Caxamarca, and there to judge which of them had the better right to be Sapa Inca. And he added, with all the shrewdness of a snide lawyer, that according to such information as he had, Huáscar and not Atahualpa was the legitimate monarch. Atahualpa had already been warned by the officers in charge of Huáscar that their prisoner had contrived to make the Spaniards an offer for his freedom. He now became very much alarmed; if Huáscar were brought to Caxamarca, Pizarro would soon see that he would make a much more biddable puppet than Atahualpa. The Spanish general would then have no further reason to keep his prisoner alive. Atahualpa would lose not only the *borla*, but his life. There was one thing to be done, and he did it: he sent an order to Caxamarca that Huáscar was to be put to death at once. It was done, probably by drowning the unhappy prince in the Andamarca River.

With a cunning which would have done credit to Pizarro himself, Atahualpa pretended to be astonished and indignant when the news of Huáscar's death was brought to him; and he feigned deep grief when, sending for Pizarro, he told him the news. Pizarro was so taken aback, and the idea that Huáscar might be dead was so unwelcome to him, that he flatly refused to believe it.[3] It *could not* be true, because it did not suit his plans. Atahualpa insisted that it was true; he added that his officers, fearing that Huáscar might exploit the country's anomalous situation to escape, had killed their prisoner on their own initiative. This lie is of the greatest interest, since it implies two things: first, that Atahualpa had quickly learned the sort of people the Spaniards were, what kind of things they might do in given conditions, and therefore what kind of lies they would believe; and secondly, that Pizarro did not yet know, and Atahualpa realized that he did not yet know, what sort of men he was deal-

THE LAST OF THE INCAS / 233

ing with. For nobody knew better than Atahualpa that his explanation of the murder was, from a Peruvian's point of view, absurd. No Inca officer would in any circumstances have taken so much on himself. Greatly put out, Pizarro had inquiry made and soon found that he had been told the truth. He was tolerably sure that even if Atahualpa's officers had put their prisoner to death without their master's authority, they could have done so only in anticipation of his known wishes; but if Atahualpa denied this there was nothing Pizarro could do about it.[4]

Meanwhile, porters were arriving from all over the empire with the Sapa Inca's ransom. But the collection of the gold and silver was slower than Atahualpa had anticipated; weights of individual items were often great; a single temple or palace ornament might weigh seventy or eighty pounds. The distances, too, were great, and a man or a llama could not carry much at a time. Nevertheless, as the days passed, the guarded store of treasure increased, and it began to look as if Atahualpa would be able to fulfill his part of the contract. But, their appetite for precious metal growing with their foretaste of it, the Spaniards began to nag their prisoner for the dilatoriness of his servants; they made no allowances for distances or any other difficulties of collection and transport. Still fearful for their lives in the midst of this mysterious empire which they had invaded, the more so now that they had before them the prospect of great riches, they became a prey to nervous terrors and were soon suspecting every delay in bringing in the treasure as being contrived by Atahualpa to gain time to organize, in secret, a rising against them. Might he not be sending, together with the order for gold and silver, an order to prepare for insurrection against the foreigners?

Pizarro, unwilling to quarrel with Atahualpa himself, since he valued the Sapa Inca very highly as a pledge for the empire's good behavior, was nevertheless compelled by his people to tax their prisoner with treachery. His officers, he said, had warned him that the neighboring town of Huamachuco had been chosen as a military rendezvous for the Sapa Inca's secretly mobilized army. Atahualpa heard this rigmarole with surprise and denied it with scorn. His answer, as recorded by Pedro

Pizarro, is interesting in that it confirms what we had said about the helplessness of the Tahuantinsuyu when deprived of its Sapa Inca:

> Not one of my subjects would dare to appear in arms or raise a finger without my orders. You have me in your power. Is not my life at your disposal? What better security can you have for my fidelity?

Then, after explaining the greatness of the distances over which the gold and silver had to be carried; and that, for example, whereas the system of posts could get a message from Caxamarca to Cuzco in five days, the same journey would take a laden porter as many weeks, he went on:

> But that you may be satisfied I am acting in good faith, I wish you to send some of your own people to Cuzco. I will give them safe conduct. When they are there they can superintend the carrying-out of my orders and see with their own eyes that no hostile movements are in preparation.

Pizarro at once agreed to do this. It would, in any case, suit him well to have some of his men spy out the promised land. He made, however, the mistake of sending some of the basest men of his company, which is saying a good deal. He was probably unwilling to weaken his force by detaching men he could trust. He had already had to detach a small party of cavalry under his brother Hernando, sending them to Huamachuco to see whether there was anything in the rumors of Inca mobilization. There was nothing; the town was quietly going about its ordinary business, the citizens were friendly and welcoming. Hernando reported accordingly, by courier, and in return received his brother's order to continue on his way another three hundred miles to the city of Pachacamac on the coast, a great religious center which was said to be fabulously rich and where the pickings should be good.

It is very likely that the religion of Pachacamac and its syncretism with sun worship had made great progress with the Incas before its center was conquered by their army and incorporated into the Tahuantinsuyu. At all events, the cult, and the shrine itself, were respected at the time of that conquest; and while the Incas might still refer publicly to the Sun as their god, their deeper religious feelings were concentrated upon Pachacamac, Creator of the Universe. The shrine, moreover, increased in importance as the principal place of pilgrimage, and the principal oracle, the Delphi, for all the peoples of the Tahuantinsuyu. And as the pilgrims brought offerings, Pachacamac became as rich as Delphi was and the Vatican still is. It was for this reason, and at Atahualpa's suggestion, that Hernando was sent to the holy city. The Sapa Inca was anxious to get his hands on the temple gold before the priests buried it or spirited it away.⏋

Hernando's journey was the most interesting and revealing yet made by the Spaniards in Peru. He was amazed by the quality of the road on which he traveled from Huamachuco, and praised it as far superior to any road in Christendom. In places, however, the journey was hard going, for spurs of the cordillera had to be crossed. The steeper ascents had been cut into steps which made them not less but more difficult for horses; and although the way was protected by heavy stone balustrades at dangerous places, the abysses were terrifying. The wooden or stone bridges across the smaller rivers were easy enough, but the suspension bridges across wide rivers and deep gorges looked, to alien eyes, dangerously flimsy; however, the troop of horses passed over them in perfect safety. Well-farmed land and vast herds of carefully tended llamas were observed all along the route, and the road passed through numerous prosperous villages and small towns. In the mountains, as in the tropical lowlands brilliant with flowers and birds, the Spaniards were treated with hospitable kindness and were generously supplied with provisions and with porters to carry their gear. On arriving in the considerable city of Pachacamac, however, they were forbidden access to the great complex of temple, shrine, monasteries and presbyteries which completely covered a conical hill, a sort of Vatican City or Potala. Hernando and his men forced their way in and climbed to the holy of holies at the summit of the hill. Here the priests again barred their way, but were terrified into flight by a sudden earthquake shock which might topple the great buildings at any moment. The Peruvians took this for a threat by their god to destroy the blasphemous foreigners; the Spaniards saw it as encouragement from the same source, to destroy the devil in the holy of holies. This, when they entered it, turned out to be a small, dark place, foul with the stench of sacrificial çarrion. The idol, in the darkest corner, man-faced but of monstrous form, was dragged into the open and was smashed to pieces. As the god showed no sign of blasting the alien for this rough treatment of his image, the Peruvians, with their usual good sense, concluded that the interlopers were under his protection; therefore they made no attempt to interfere or protest when the Spaniards cleaned out the holy of holies and, setting a cross in the idol's place, did their best to consecrate it as a Christian chapel. Moreover they listened submissively while Hernando, albeit no evangelist, addressed them on the error of their ways and taught them to make the sign of the cross, armed with which one was even able to destroy the image of god with impunity.

For the temple gold, however, Hernando had come too late. A quantity stated as eighty thousand *castellanos* (about eight hundred pounds) was indeed secured, but the priests, forewarned of Hernando's coming, had made away with the greater part, and Hernando was distracted from any attempt he might have made to recover it by the chance to secure something even more valuable; he was informed that one of Atahualpa's two great generals, Chalcuchima, was at Xauca, not an impossible distance from Pachacamac. If his person could be secured, as his master's had been, one of the greatest threats to the Spanish future in Peru would have been eliminated. Hernando was told that Chalcuchima was a close kinsman of the Sapa Inca and, for that reason as well as for his military ability, stood highest of all men in the empire. True, he was not alone at Xauca; he lay there encamped with an army of thirty-five thousand troops. But by this time Hernando was beginning to learn something about the way in which the Tahuantinsuyu worked; he seems to have grasped the fact that, while civil and military officers could carry on with routine duties unhampered by the Sapa Inca's captivity and thus keep the machinery of state in motion, they could not possibly take any initiative. The Incas and *curacas* comprised, as we have said, a bureaucracy—an ideal contrivance for the repetition of sanctioned and necessary tasks of administration, but by its nature unfit for unsanctioned action. While Atahualpa lived and issued his orders, albeit from captivity, Chalcuchima was not a dangerous enemy, though he might at once become one if Atahualpa were dead. Thus, Hernando's plan to secure the person of the general, while it was bold, was not foolhardy.

Peruvian roads were hard on horseshoes; the journey to Pachacamac had worn those of Hernando's troop so badly that the horses' hoofs were suffering, and the road to Xauca was rough. No iron, and presumably no bronze, was to be had, but there was plenty of silver. The Peruvian smiths had no difficulty in shoeing the Spanish horses with that metal, under Spanish direction. It answered well; and to ride horses shod with silver doubtless satisfied that yearning for panache which distinguished the men of the Renaissance. There was no economist in the party to see in this use of silver a somber portent of what would happen to the value of that metal, with the consequent gross inflation of commodity prices, when the treasure the Spaniards were collecting reached Spain.

Xauca, fortress and garrison town, was a great city.[5] Chalcuchima lay with his army some miles outside the town. At first he refused to meet Hernando Pizarro, but he was persuaded to change his mind. Hernando was not thinking of repeating the Caxamarca *coup de main*. He had a better plan: He told the Inca general that he bore an order from Atahualpa to Chalcuchima requiring him to present himself in person at Caxamarca. What was Chalcuchima to think and do? He was in a position to destroy the Spaniards, but he had no orders to do so. He knew that his Sapa Inca was a prisoner of these white men of unknown provenance and extraordinary powers; but he also knew that Atahualpa was still effectively ruling the country and might, for all he knew, be in some sort of alliance with the foreigner. Had Hernando had Quizquiz to deal with, the story would have been different; the old Quitu, as his subsequent career makes clear, was a man of more independent character; and as a "barbarian," he was probably less respectful of forms and more concerned with the substance. Chalcuchima, on the other hand, was a gentleman, an aristocrat, a member of the royal family, a pillar of the Hananist establishment. He agreed to obey the Sapa Inca's "order"; it did not occur to him that Hernando was lying; and there is not the least need to invoke, as Prescott does, an entirely imaginary superiority of the white man's will power over the red man's, to explain this obedience.

The Spaniards marched back to Caxamarca on their silver horseshoes and with their eighty thousand *castellanos* of loot, accompanied by Chalcuchima traveling in great state, borne in a litter and escorted by a numerous suite. He was everywhere received with a servile deference which it was his own turn to display when he was introduced into Atahualpa's presence. The Spaniards noted with the utmost amazement that Atahualpa showed no emotion of any kind whatever as his kinsman, friend, general, and greatest subject was introduced into the room. The Sapa Inca coldly bade this great nobleman welcome, while the latter, for his part, gave every sign of being deeply moved by a loyal affection manifest beneath his protocolar humility of bearing.

While the events described above and in Chapter 7 were occurring, Almagro was on his way at last to join the "Viceroy." That he had been an unconscionable time about it was not his fault. Hampered by want of cash and credit, he had had great difficulty in acquiring three small ships and one hundred and fifty recruits. He set out for Peru late in 1532 and early in the cruise south was joined by another fifty men sharked up in Nicaragua by his agents. His force thus numbered one hundred and fifty foot and fifty horse, well found in gear. Although his pilot was Ruiz, the voyage was slow and tiresome, the ships being bedeviled by calms, storms and contrary winds. As usual, the men, a scratch lot, soon lost heart and were shortly beginning to clamor for a return to Panama, for they could hear nothing of Pizarro as they coasted southward. But Almagro had sent a small advance party to Tumbez and at the right moment it rejoined the flotilla with news of Pizarro's colony of San Miguel and of his march into the interior. In December 1532, a month after Atahualpa's seizure in Caxamarca, Almagro and his two hundred arrived in San Miguel and dispatched news of their coming to Caxamarca.

As we know, Pizarro's entourage, led by Hernando, were hostile to Almagro and determined to make mischief between him and Francisco if they could. It was doubtless owing to loose talk by these mischief-makers that Almagro not only was told of Pizarro's fabulous success, which transformed the whole picture of the enterprise, but also was informed that, having accomplished it alone, Pizarro had no intention of sharing the proceeds and was determined to rid himself of Almagro if he got the chance. Some of the San Miguel colonists actually warned Almagro not to put himself into Pizarro's power as it might cost him his life. Pizarro's relations were not the only mischief-makers, however; Almagro had with him a secretary called Perez who, presumably to ingratiate himself with the Viceroy, sent a private note to Caxamarca telling Pizarro that Almagro had no intention of putting himself and his men at Pizarro's disposal, but proposed, rather, to conquer an independent kingdom for himself. Pizarro, out of generosity or as a matter of policy, ignored the letter from Perez and sent his old partner a warm welcome and an invitation to join him at once. Almagro was not the man to nurse a suspicion; by nature openhearted, he was well content with this and prepared to set out for Caxamarca. While his preparations were in hand, he was informed of his secretary's treachery—we do not know by whom, but possibly it was by Pizarro himself—and, before setting out on his march, he hanged Perez out of hand.

Almagro reached Caxamarca in February 1533. Greetings on both sides were warm and excited. For the moment everyone was happy, except Hernando Pizarro; and Atahualpa, whose feelings were those of a farmer who sees a second swarm of locusts arrive to join the first.

Moreover, according to Cieza de León, the Sapa Inca's spirits were further depressed by a sinister portent. A comet, or a large-tailed meteor, was pointed out to him in the night sky by some of the Spaniards who kept him company from time to time, Hernando de Soto being his best friend among them. Atahualpa watched it for some time in silence, his expression growing solemn. At last he turned to the white men and, with a grave sadness in face and manner, he told them that a similar sign had appeared in the heavens just before the death of his father the Sapa Inca Huayna Capac. This heavenly sign made a deep impression on him; and, although he recovered his spirits from time to time and could still speak and act with decision, that impression remained, so that in thoughtful moments, when he was not distracted by the need to talk or act, he seems to have given up all hope in the future, though he still resisted every effort by the Dominicans to interest him in post-mortem prospects of bliss or to frighten him with the prospect of post-mortem burning.

In the month of May the three men sent to Cuzco returned to Caxamarca. They had thoroughly enjoyed themselves, bullying and looting with impunity. Men of the basest antecedents and rendered arrogant by the gentleness of their victims, they had been armed with the Sapa Inca's authority so that nothing they demanded could legally be denied them. They had been carried the whole six hundred miles along the great highways to the capital in *hamacas* borne by relays of porters relieving each other at the *tambos* along the route. The "obsequious devotion" of the people—Prescott's phrase—at every town and village on the way, and notably in Cuzco, where the three Spaniards were received with politic public rejoicing probably about as spontaneous as the welcome arranged by a good public-relations firm for some modern star of stage or politics, has often been interpreted to mean that the Peruvians took them for creatures of a superior order. No such interpretation is necessary; the Sapa Inca was in the power of these aliens and, moreover, he had issued the clearest orders that they were to be treated with deference. A week spent in Cuzco did not enable the three emissaries to see the whole of that great city, but it gave them ample time to discover that accounts of it had hardly, if at all, been exaggerated. For example, they found the exterior of the great Temple of the Sun to be completely covered with plates of gold, probably the only large building in the history of architecture ever to be faced with that material. They refrained—again on orders from the Sapa Inca— from looting the gold and jewels from the royal mummies which were kept inside the temple, but they insisted on stripping the gold from the building itself. The Cuzcans showed some disinclination to despoil their own great national temple, but the Sapa Inca's orders could not be flatly disobeyed, although there were occasions when they could be evaded. Seven hundred gold plates were removed, but the gold cornice which ran completely round the building had to be left; the builders' work had been so good that it could not be removed without pulling down half the building.

On their return to Caxamarca the three men complained to Pizarro that the Cuzcans had been dilatory in stripping their city of its gold and evasive in answering questions about other sources of gold and silver. They had avoided showing the Spaniards some of the richest buildings in the city. This report bore out a general and growing suspicion that the people, notably the clergy. were ceasing to co-operate with the gold seekers, and that gold and silver from the temples were being hurriedly secreted. The fact is the three low-bred ruffians whom Pizarro had foolishly sent to Cuzco had behaved with intolerable insolence to the Cuzcan gentry, with repulsive rapacity to everyone, and with such total disregard of native feelings that they had forced their way into a Convent of the Sun and raped some of the nuns. Even the disciplined and obedient citizens of the Tahuantinsuyu had revolted, at least to the extent of opposing a passive and sullen resistance to orders which they could not legally disobey.

Nevertheless, the three envoys brought back much silver, and 200 *cargas* (probably about 6,000 pounds) of gold, an amount sufficient to raise the level of the gold in the marked room so near to the nine-foot level which, for Atahualpa, represented freedom, that he could begin to hope again—he had still not fully realized the sort of people he was dealing with; he had not yet learned that the Spaniards had no respect for contracts made with heathen. His training had not been such as to fit him to understand them; true, he had put his brother and all of his brother's family to death, but he was not a man to break his word.

Although the gold collected still fell short of the contractual amount and the term of the contract had not yet been reached, the rank and file of the Spaniards began to clamor for a share-out. Some wanted to return home, enriched with present gains; most wanted to push on to Cuzco where still greater riches no doubt awaited them. Both parties agreed that there was no time to lose; waiting for the gold to come in merely gave the Peruvians time to hide it and the Incas time to make up their minds to rise against the Spaniards as the people of Anahuac had risen against the invaders in Mexico. The argument which weighed with Pizarro was that favoring an immediate advance to Cuzco; not until he had the capital in his hands would the Viceroy feel secure in his conquest, not until then could he really set about that conquest in a systematic manner. He therefore agreed to share out the gold at once, and march to Cuzco.

The Sapa Inca's ransom was still, of course, in the form of objects of virtu or domestic utility, products of the goldsmith's exquisite art such as vases, urns, ewers, plates and dishes and cups, figures of men, animals and plants, fountains and models. The pieces which seem to have made most impression upon such of the Spaniards as were capable of appreciating a work of art were the representations of maize, the grains and the cob being of gold, the foliage sheath and the tassel—the male part of the inflorescence—of silver and silver thread. Such representations may probably, by the date in question, have been made merely for ornament, but in earlier times, when the material had been clay rather than gold, they were of religious significance. It was an ancient and beautifully modeled ear of corn which enabled the historians of this plant to confirm their theory of its origin.[6]

In order to share out the gold it was necessary to melt it down and cast it into bars of equal and convenient size. Before this was done, the Viceroy selected some pieces of the finest workmanship for immediate dispatch as part of the royal fifth to

Madrid. Pizarro had two reasons for making this decision: he wanted, by showing Charles the quality of the Peruvian people as it was manifest in their craftsmanship, to glorify his conquest and therefore himself; and he needed an excuse to get rid of his brother Hernando who could be sent to Spain in charge of the gold and to report to the emperor in person on the progress of the conquest. Hernando Pizarro, albeit useful in some ways, was making a nuisance of himself. At the time of Almagro's arrival he had sullenly refused to join in the warm welcome extended to his brother's old partner and friend. And although Francisco had later persuaded Hernando to apologize to the old soldier for this discourtesy, Hernando continued to show, quite openly, that he considered Almagro a greedy interloper who had no right to any share in the wealth or honors of the enterprise. He treated the man who, by loyal support for years had made Pizarro's success possible, as if he were some sort of importunate hanger-on. Almagro, of course, bitterly resented this. A serious quarrel, which might cost the expedition half its men, was to be anticipated, and there might even be fighting between the two factions. Better to lose Hernando than Almagro and his two hundred soldiers.

There was yet another reason for getting rid of Hernando: that attribute of his character which made him resent, except in his brother, such thrusting upstarts as Almagro, also made him sensible of the tragedy in fallen grandeur; he was touched by Atahualpa's situation, treated him with deference, and might object to the plan which Francisco had made for the Sapa Inca's future. It is said that, when he heard that Hernando was being sent back to Spain, the Sapa Inca "wept, for he knew he would then have to die." In any case, Hernando was—apart from de Soto—by far the best man to send to Madrid and to present Pizarro's report at court. He had, when he chose, the manners of a gentleman and an air of breeding totally wanting in most of Pizarro's followers.

The melting down and recasting of the gold was done by Peruvian smiths and took a month of unremitting toil. At the end of that time it was possible to weigh and calculate the value of Atahualpa's ransom. The weight was 1,326,539 *pesos de oro*. In any case, the gold part of the ransom paid by Atahualpa and his people for his freedom was equal to not less than eight million dollars. The silver collected was 51,610 marks, which is approximately twelve tons.

Trouble blew up over the division of this loot, certainly the largest swag ever procured by any band of brigands in all history. Almagro's men claimed a share, while Pizarro's insisted that they alone had risked their lives to seize Atahualpa, that they alone were parties to the contract with him, and that they alone should, therefore, be paid. The argument seems to have been settled between the leaders with remarkable ease: Almagro's men were to be satisfied with a token sum, 20,000 *pesos de oro* (about a tenth of a ton of gold; approximately one pound per man), with the promise that they could look to the future for their fortune. This left fewer than two hundred men to share over five million dollars. After the royal fifth had been made up to its full value, counting the objects which Hernando was to take to Madrid, cavalrymen of Pizarro's company received about $50,000 each; foot soldiers $20,000 each, more or less, according to some system of merit used by Pizarro and generally accepted. Pizarro himself received about $300,000 plus the golden throne of Atahualpa, itself worth another $125,000. Hernando got about $200,000 and de Soto $100,000. Presumably Almagro, as one of the three original partners in the undertaking, got his share; the third partner, Luque, was dead, but his heir and assignee, the Licentiate Espinosa then living in San Domingo, probably received his part also, for there is no record of any unsatisfied claim on the part of Luque's heir. Pedro Pizarro's comment on the division of the gold[7] is: "In this the Marqués was very Christian, for he deprived no man of any part of the treasure he merited."

The ransom having been disposed of, it remained to deal with the man who had paid it.

It seems to us obvious, despite whatever may be urged in his defense, that Pizarro had by this time decided to make away with his prisoner. When the question of Atahualpa's future was raised, he stated his policy in one curt and not too cryptic phrase: *". . . y esto tenía por justo, pues era provechoso."* The Sanhedrin and the Roman government took the same view in the case of an even more distinguished prisoner: what was expedient was to be considered just. It was a policy which was to be adopted by all European governments engaged in imperialist adventures for four centuries, and as such its conception is not the least important of the Viceroy's acts. Pizarro might, moreover, plausibly argue that in killing Huáscar and his whole *ayllu* Atahualpa had not only signed his own death warrant but also justified it. With two claimants to the throne alive, Pizarro could divide and rule. But to set at liberty the only surviving and already generally recognized Sapa Inca, a man, furthermore, who was a successful soldier, who commanded the loyalty of two very able generals each of whom had thirty or forty thousand men ready and under arms, would be madness. It would be raving madness in that Atahualpa now knew by personal experience how very human, how far from being superior beings, the Spaniards were. If Atahualpa were to be released, the whole machinery of the Tahuantinsuyuan government, still running well, would be at his disposal immediately, and at least four of the empire's most aggressive nations. He might then be expected to exact a terrible revenge for the humiliations inflicted on him and his country; and perhaps to make the conquest of Peru forever impossible.

On the other hand it would be difficult, if not impossible, to continue keeping Atahualpa a prisoner. The fact that, in recent weeks, the Peruvians had shown increasing reluctance to give up their gold and silver might be interpreted as evidence of rising irritation. If a really determined effort were made to rescue the Sapa Inca it might succeed; it would at least succeed in killing a great many Spaniards of a very small company. The threat of such an attempt must entail detaching more men than could be afforded for guard duties; this would become impossible in the course of the difficult march to Cuzco.

There was a third and stronger reason for murdering the Sapa Inca. The Spanish leader had now seen and tested for himself the paralysis of the great bureaucracy of the Tahuantinsuyu when deprived of its head. It was true that the death of

Atahualpa might set free certain generals and certain princes of the royal *ayllus* to take a hostile initiative; but their attacks would not be concerted, they would surely soon be quarreling among themselves, and the more discontented provinces would refuse to accept their authority. It is also at least possible that Pizarro already had some knowledge of Toparca, Atahualpa's brother, and knew him to be a young man without character or experience, but of the blood royal and the son of a *qoya*—in short, a far more suitable puppet Sapa Inca than Atahualpa would ever make.

Atahualpa, in fact, was now showing his independence of spirit by demanding his freedom. In talk with Hernando de Soto, the only Spaniard whose patrician breeding made him the Sapa Inca's social equal, as it were, and a congenial companion, Atahualpa pointed out that it was solely due to Spanish impatience that the full sum of the gold contracted for had not been collected; and that, in any case, nobody could claim that the ransom was inadequate—gold had only an aesthetic value in Atahualpa's eyes, but he had seen what it meant to his captors, and he knew perfectly well that he had paid a stupendous ransom. The Spaniards must now keep their side of the contract and release him without further delay.

De Soto was of the same opinion, for he had the misfortune to be a man of honor, and he communicated the Sapa Inca's argument to his leader. Pizarro's answer was evasive: there were serious difficulties; they would have to see. It is probable that Pizarro could not bring himself to expose his necessary and villainous decision to a man he admired, loved and trusted and who would be horrified by it. A necessary attribute of leadership is the willingness to commit crimes on the community's behalf and be damned for it; a leader in military and political adventure must be a moral scapegoat in the service of his lust for power and of his community's success. But he may, as a man, be very unwilling to expose his own necessary baseness in so many words to those of his followers whose higher, more sentimental, "unrealistic" code of behavior he admires, despises, and cannot afford to emulate. And he may even feel obliged to seem a more honest man than he is, by going through motions which quiet his conscience and provisionally set his worthier followers' minds at rest, but which are, as he knows in his calculating mind if not in his heart, meaningless. Pizarro went through this comedy, a commonplace in politics, by causing his notary to draft and his heralds to publish a document in which he acknowledged that Atahualpa had fully discharged his obligations under the contract. Logically, this should have been followed by Atahualpa's release, but the Viceroy declared—"off the record," as we should say now—that, for the sake of those four or five hundred Spanish lives for which he was responsible, the Sapa Inca must be kept a prisoner for a little longer, until the Spaniards had been strengthened by further reinforcements.

In this piece of politic hypocrisy, Pizarro's hand was strengthened by a convenient revival of the rumor that the Incas and, in fact, the whole empire were preparing to rise and attack the Spaniards. In many of its details this rumor, growing hourly until it became a specter haunting the whole camp, was ridiculous. It might, for example, be common sense to fear that the Quitu were mustering and would shortly send a huge army to rescue their prince; but it was simply absurd to believe that thirty thousand Caribs were marching to join it. They had to be Caribs, however, for as cannibals those tribesmen inspired a particular horror in the Spaniards. In the absence of any evidence, it is usual to attribute this and like rumors to Huáscar's party (the Hurinists), some of which were in the Spanish camp and were, of course, bitterly hostile to Atahualpa; but more specifically the rumors are attributed to the interpreter Felipillo, because that young man had an ax of his own to grind. Felipillo, it is said, had fallen in love with, and had been caught making love to, a girl of Atahualpa's household, a royal concubine. Atahualpa, when informed of this, was furiously angry; this was the worst of all the humiliations and outrages he had suffered. And, as Atahualpa told Pizarro, the proper legal punishment for this offense was the execution of Felipillo and his entire family. Although the interpreter was too valuable a man to be sacrificed to the captive monarch's rage, and although Pizarro could hardly, in any case, punish the young man for a crime which his own followers were committing daily, Felipillo naturally would not feel safe while Atahualpa lived; he may reasonably be suspected, therefore, of having spread rumors tending to cause the Sapa Inca's ruin.

But there is another probability seldom considered by historians: that Pizarro used Felipillo to spread rumors that would enable him to put a better face on the judicial murder which, as we believe, he now had in mind. Political and military leaders frequently convince not only their followers, but—what is both more remarkable and much more dangerous—themselves, by their own propaganda. We have only the far from disinterested Spanish testimony for it that Felipillo regarded the Sapa Inca with "malignant hatred." At all events, somebody contrived to shape the rumors of a rising so that they pointed to Atahualpa himself as the archinspirer and leader of the movement. Chalcuchima, still with the Spaniards, was questioned; he knew of no such preparations, and he dismissed the whole story as an obvious fabrication which, of course, it was, and which we feel tolerably certain Pizarro knew it to be. However, he next confronted Atahualpa himself with the story, in the form of a direct accusation. He charged Atahualpa with "treason," a singular choice of word. Atahualpa's reply was interpreted to him as follows:

> *Burlaste commigo? siempre me hablas cosas burlas? Que parte somos yo, i todo mi gente para enojar a tan valientes hombres como vosotros? No me digas esas burlas.* [You are joking? You are always pulling my leg. How could I or my people think of plotting against men as valiant as you are? Spare me your mockery.][8]

This answer is attributed by Pizarro's secretary, at least for the record, as an example of cunning the more remarkable "in a barbarian" in that it was delivered naturally and with perfect composure as if Atahualpa really thought that Pizarro was joking. He may at least have hoped that he was, but he probably had no such illusion; he knew, he remembered, only too well what he had felt, thought and done when his own state prisoner, the Sapa Inca Huáscar, had become a source of embarrassment. Why should Pizarro feel, think or act differently now that his state prisoner, the Sapa Inca Atahualpa, had become a source of embarrassment? It is, perhaps, a pity that he failed to qualify as a hero of a tragedy by Corneille by accepting with noble resignation the fate he foresaw; as it was, he proved himself human by continuing to strive with his jailer for his life, pleading that he was a poor, helpless captive who must become the first casualty in any insurrection on his behalf, and pointing out that while he remained docile no man in his dominions, where the very birds hardly dared to fly without his permission,[9] would raise a finger against the Spaniards.

Whether or not Pizarro had started the rumors which were to make it easier for him to kill his prisoner, it is certain that they had now got out of hand. His men, made fearful and therefore cruel by wealth, were convinced that a huge Inca army was gathering at Huamachuco, one hundred miles from Caxamarca. Something like panic ran through the Spanish ranks; guards were doubled, horses kept saddled, cannon charged and manned, and ferocious threats uttered against the prisoner. Almagro's men, who had got only a minor share of the ransom and were anxious to press on and do some really serious looting, openly advocated putting Atahualpa to death out of hand. He had become a nuisance. In this they were supported by the representatives of the Spanish Establishment, the royal treasurer Riquelme and other crown officials; these men, so little to the taste of Pizarro that he had sent them all back to San Miguel once, had returned under Almagro's wing. They now asserted that the interests of the Crown required the death of Atahualpa.

Pizarro, in short, had now succeeded in bringing about the state of affairs he had sought to contrive, and which, as a leader, a moral scapegoat, it had been his duty to contrive. He was being urged by his subordinates to commit the crime he knew was necessary, which they would subsequently repudiate. He could now start on the next act of the comedy and pretend to resist them; the records are just what they should be, showing the *Gobernador* "visibly" unwilling to consent to Atahualpa's death.[10] This piece of acting had one serious disadvantage: he received strong support in his apparent resistance to the common clamor from the few among his followers—and not so very few as will presently appear—who were men of good heart and good will, and these were led, of course, by Hernando de Soto. Yet even this embarrassing support could be turned to account: if murder was to be done, such softhearted characters were best out of the way. Seeming, therefore, to act in the most reasonable manner, Pizarro ordered de Soto and a party of horsemen to go to Huamachuco and see whether there was anything in the rumor which was now exciting the troops to a point where they might become unmanageable. By this means, the leaders among the men who wished to save Atahualpa were got out of the way, so that he could be disposed of without trouble. But the opposition to the murder had been underestimated.

Whether by convenient accident or design, no sooner were de Soto and his men out of the town than the rank-and-file clamor for Atahualpa's blood became irresistible. We suspect that this was because it was not hoped, but feared, that de Soto would report all quiet at Huamachuco. Pizarro was "obliged" to give way and to bring Atahualpa to trial immediately.

For, of course, there was no question of simply sending one of the more ruffianly soldiers, with a promise of subsequent absolution from Valverde, to cut the Sapa Inca's throat. The Spaniards, as Señor de Madariaga has told us, were passionately law-abiding. We have had some experience in our own time of their way of respecting the law; the late J. V. Stalin, for example, was much addicted to it.

The Sapa Inca was brought to trial on twelve charges. The one real charge, of course, was that he had attempted to "raise an insurrection" against the Spaniards—in short, that when attacked he had defended himself. But as, in fact, he had not done so, and Pizarro knew perfectly well that he had not done so, Pizarro and his clerical and legal advisers took the usual course in such cases and multiplied the charges to get a nice, long indictment. The other charges, with one possible exception, were, and could not but be, ridiculous; they amounted to accusing the Sapa Inca of behaving according to the laws and customs of his country and his office; he had "squandered" the public revenues;

Mel Gibson

he had practiced "idolatry"; he had been guilty of "adulterous practices"; he had usurped the crown and murdered his brother Huáscar.

As in Stalinist Russia in our own times, the trial was mounted with an ostentation of correct forms. Pizarro and Almagro presided as judges; there was a public prosecutor to put the Crown case; and an advocate was assigned to the prisoner to defend and advise him. The indispensable Felipillo was well to the fore; when Quechua answers made by Peruvian witnesses failed to lead toward the predetermined verdict, he translated them with alterations which his own hatred and fear of the prisoner, or perhaps his orders, suggested to his quick mind.

By way of comment on the indictment and trial, of which no detailed account remains, it will be sufficient to quote the old Spanish authority, Oviedo, who was by no means pro-Inca but was a man of integrity. He calls the indictment "a badly contrived and worse written document devised by a factious and unprincipled priest [that is, Valverde], a clumsy notary without conscience, and others of like stamp, who were all concerned in this villainy."

It is typical of the whole comedy that *before* a verdict was arrived at there was a heated discussion, apparently in court, as to whether it would or would not be a good thing, and an expedient thing, to kill Atahualpa. After a majority had concluded that it would be, then and only then was Atahualpa solemnly found guilty on all counts in the indictment. The sentence, probably because one of the charges was idolatry and Father Valverde had his word to say, was that Atahualpa was to be burned alive in the public square of Caxamarca. As there was a serious risk that de Soto might return in a few days, perhaps even on the morrow, and as he would, of course, report that there was no substance whatever in the charge of attempted insurrection, the execution was timed for that same night. Pizarro insisted that Valverde sign a copy of the judgment, which that bishop did with the terse comment that "the Inca deserved to die in any case."

It does very great credit to the hearts if not the heads of a minority of the Spaniards still present in the camp—apparently no less than ten per cent of the total roll—that they resisted and protested against this judicial crime in every way open to them. It was an act of great moral courage. These brave men pointed out that death after a fraudulent trial was in indifferent return for all the favors they had received from the Sapa Inca, who, for his part, had had nothing but evil from them. They exposed, in so many words, what everybody knew and few would admit, that the evidence brought against the prisoner was farcical or contrived. They even had the courage to deny that the court had any legal standing whatsoever, much less any right to judge a king in the heart of his kingdom. If, they said, Atahualpa must be tried, then let him be sent to Madrid and tried by the Emperor Charles. (Which, though brave, was still nonsense, since Charles had no more right to try Atahualpa than to try the King of England.) The answer these protestants received was scarcely forthright: Atahualpa had been tried and found guilty, let him be burned; and let those who opposed the verdict and sentence of the court beware lest, when an account of the proceedings including the present debate reached Spain, the emperor discover who were his loyal subjects and who were, as we should say, the subversive elements. Yet even this threat could not intimidate the party of the just; the argument became so furious that it looked as if it would end in violence; it actually ended, however, with the protestants entering and signing a written protest against the indictment, trial, verdict and sentence.

We have not always, in the course of this narrative, been able to write of Pizarro's men with unstinted admiration. But it must here be admitted that the number of communities of any kind, anywhere and at any time, in which ten per cent of the members are ready to stand up for justice and mercy, at some risk to themselves from the majority and from the Establishment, is very small indeed.

Atahualpa had been in no doubt about the outcome of the trial: he recognized it for what it was, and he said, before it began, that he expected to be convicted and killed. But it is a device common to all men everywhere to declare that an evil must come to pass as a means of ensuring that it will not. It is painful to have to record that when he was told of the court's sentence—Pizarro had the grace to undertake that communication in person—Atahualpa broke down. He turned to Pizarro with tears in his eyes and asked, "What have I done that I should meet with such an end? And at your hands, who have met with nothing but friendship and kindness from my people, with whom I have shared my treasures, and who have received nothing but benefits from me." He pleaded for his life, offered guarantees of safety for every Spaniard in the country, and to double the ransom he had already paid—a senseless offer, this, since his captors had every intention of looting the whole empire systematically in any case; it was what they were there for.

Pizarro is said to have been "much moved." No doubt he was. He had learned his trade of leadership too well to upset his plans in order to spare the life of a man he had consistently wronged, but it does not follow that he enjoyed his own wickedness, nor that the heartlessness of a leader in pursuit of power was an attribute of the man himself in the presence of his victim. He turned away from Atahualpa's pleading; seeing which, the Sapa Inca recovered his courage and his normal appearance of perfect composure.

The execution took place after dark and by torchlight. A trumpet summoned the whole company to witness the spectacle. Atahualpa had been kept, for some time, chained hand and foot like a felon. In his irons, then, he was led into the square, where the flickering and smoky torchlight cast sinister and shifting shadows over the faces of his oppressors; it must have seemed to reveal at last the full blackness of his captors' hearts. As the priest Valverde had been the first, so he was the last of the Spaniards to hold speech with Atahualpa, and on this same spot. The Dominican had long been trying to convert the prisoner to that religion of love and mercy now to be demonstrated in a manner commonplace in Spain but novel to the Tahuantinsuyu. Atahualpa had listened to him patiently and answered him intelligently, but he had taken no real interest in the priest's arguments. Valverde now made a final appeal; he waited until Atahualpa was bound to the stake and the fagots piled about his feet ready for the fire, and then he held up the Cross and called upon the prisoner to receive it and so save his soul. To convert an emperor some small concession to mercy might be worthwhile, might even, one day, be worth an archbishopric and a red hat. The Dominican therefore offered the Sapa Inca a bargain: let Atahualpa accept baptism and in return he should die by the garrote instead of by fire.

It was clear to Atahualpa in his hideous extremity, in the lurid and shifting half-light of the reeking torches where he endured alone and friendless his last hour of agony among men as implacable to him as he had been to Huáscar, that by speaking a few words and submitting to a few gestures quite meaningless to himself and to his god, he might spare himself the atrocious pain of death by fire. He asked if Valverde's offer was in good faith— he had no reason to trust Spanish promises, but he accepted Pizarro's confirmation of the offer and agreed to be baptized.

They gave him Juan as a Christian name, in honor of John the Baptist, whose day it was, August 29, 1533. He told them that he wished his body to be sent to Quito, where it was to lie beside his mother's ancestors. And because there was no man of all that company to whom he could turn but his executioner, he implored Pizarro to take his children under his protection. That done, his face became as impassive as it had been when he gave audience; while the rest watched as best they could in the lurid torchlight and murmured their *credos* for the salvation of Atahualpa's soul, he who filled the office of common hangman took the new Christian and bound him, seated, to a stake; passed a noose of rope over stake and head and having adjusted it nicely to the throat put a stout stick through the loop and twisted it slowly until the face of the Unique Inca, Son of the Sun, and Lord of the World, became a congested and hideous mask with starting eyes and protruding tongue; and Atahualpa, heir to the generations of Manco Capac, departed this life. With him died the Tahuantinsuyu and the independent existence of a noble race of men.

EPILOGUE

IT IS DOUBTFUL whether any more frightful disaster can befall a nation than to fall into the hands of a Great Man, or Hero. The affliction which even brought misery, want and political ruin to the Athenian empire and left the Athenian culture crippled was that great man, that honorable and high-minded patriot, Pericles. Far worse was the fate of Peru, for her Great Man, her Hero, was a foreigner, and a man who, in all but soldiering, was not even moderately competent. Her native Heroes had been moderate men, as we have seen; the Tahuantinsuyu had been remarkably fortunate in her kings. With the death of Atahualpa, Peru was to discover what it was like to suffer the dominion of a European hero.

We have told the story we set out to tell and are not concerned with what happened thereafter. But since those who are not familiar with Spanish colonial history may wish to have some idea of the aftermath, we offer this epilogue.

When de Soto returned to Caxamarca with his report of all quiet at Huamachuco, he sternly reproached Pizarro for executing Atahualpa. It had been, in his opinion, a crime. There followed an unedifying brawl between the Governor and the Bishop of Cuzco, each trying to avoid responsibility for the murder, and each accusing the other of misleading him.

Pizarro now needed a puppet Sapa Inca. Manco Capac was not readily available and was, in any case, an unknown quantity; therefore, a brother of the late Sapa Inca, Toparca, was crowned with the customary but now empty rites. The Spaniards, their puppet, and General Chalcuchima now marched at last on Cuzco. This advance was resisted by Peruvian skirmishers under the general command of Quizquiz. They were driven off but as the Spaniards could not get at their leader and as they were suffering serious casualties and annoyance, they took their revenge by putting Chalcuchima in irons. When the puppet Sapa Inca Toparca suddenly died, Chalcuchima was accused of poisoning him and was burned at the stake. Bishop Valverde had less success in his bargaining with this loyal and gallant gentleman than he had had with Atahualpa. Chalcuchima dismissed the Dominican's threats of hell and promises of heaven with the icy remark that he did not understand the religion of the white men. He did not give his torturers the satisfaction of weakening even in the agony of the fire. He died with the name of Pachacamac on his lips.

When the Spaniards were between Xauca and Cuzco, Prince Manco Capac, after a token resistance, arrived in their camp, claiming the *borla* and their protection. He received both; his monarchy was a hollow mockery. The whole country fell into wild disorder, the remote provinces revolted and declared themselves independent, the *mitmac* colonies broke up, the herds, farms, plantations and gardens were neglected. The Peruvians, having learned from the Spaniards to value gold, started looting and hiding treasure. But even now they continued to resist the notion of private property; it was a new and difficult concept for them. An immense part of the treasure thus snatched from under Spanish noses was, according to tradition, placed in a common and cleverly hidden fund in the care of *amauta* patriots. It is said that when, in the eighteenth century, an Inca revolt under Tupac Amaru of the royal house, was attempted against the Spanish colonialists, the prince was allowed to draw upon this secret fund; for all we know, the rest of it still waits for a man able to make good use of it. Addiction to coca became widespread and drunkenness commonplace. As stores were recklessly consumed and cultivation and irrigation were neglected, famine appeared in the land for the first time in many centuries; and the plagues introduced by the Spaniards killed off hundreds of thousands of Peruvians.

The looting of Cuzco and other places taken by the Spaniards yielded even more gold than had been extorted from Atahualpa. We have already referred to the shocking effect which this had on the lives of the people of Europe. In Peru the effects in the growing Spanish communities were, of course, more immediate; the inflation of commodity prices was fantastic. Converting the figures into present-day values, a bottle of wine cost $1,700, a pair of shoes $850, a good horse $7,000. It was not long before grain was more valuable than gold. One effect of this severe inflation was that creditors hid from their debtors lest they be paid off in worthless gold. Pizarro, who had succeeded brilliantly as a military adventurer, was proved utterly incompetent as a ruler, unable to control his associates and subordinates or to give even an approximation of good government to the miserable Peruvians.

Cuzco did not fall intact into the Spaniards' hands. Although members of the royal Inca house proved to be broken reeds and although Chalcuchima had been murdered either by burning, as we have described, or, according to other accounts, by being thrown alive into a hole in the ground, Quizquiz continued to resist. The armies that he was able to mobilize were not able to defeat the Spaniards, but they could and did inflict casualties on them; and the Peruvians burned their sacred city rather than let it fall undamaged into enemy hands. Thus the Cuzco which Pizarro took was a ruin. But even more disastrous than Pizarro's inability to give government to the Peruvians was his inability to control his own officers, or to enforce, against rival adventurers, the royal authority which he had received. For example, an attempt was made by Pedro de Alvarado, based in Guatemala, to seize Quito for himself. Civil war between the Spaniards at this stage was averted when Pizarro bought off this new adventurer for 120 thousand pesos of gold.

But money could not settle the differences between Pizarro and his family on the one hand, and Almagro on the other. Backbiting, plotting and brawling between the two sides became more and more frequent. In theory the major difference between them was settled by the Royal Capitulations of Charles V which stipulated their respective spheres of authority: Pizarro was given a territory defined by a coastline of 270 leagues and all that lay inland from it; Almagro's territory was to be the country inland from a coastline of 200 leagues, south of Pizarro's. Very roughly, Pizarro got Peru, and Almagro got Chile. It was not possible to define the frontier, however, and a violent quarrel broke out over the ownership of Cuzco. This was patched up before Almagro went to Chile, but on his return from that region, he occupied Cuzco, and war broke out. The Governor entrusted his brother Hernando with the job of retaking Cuzco. Hernando Pizarro defeated Almagro at Las Salinas in 1537, captured his brother's old partner, and had him garroted. This was despite a promise made by Francisco Pizarro to Almagro's son by an Inca wife, that Almagro would be spared.

The Pizarros paid for this broken promise, and the price was high. Hernando, it is true, suffered only a long term in prison when he returned to Spain, and his imprisonment was so far from being strict that he seems to have carried on a normal social life and to have fathered a child by a noblewoman in the course of it. But Francisco paid with his life; Almagro's followers adopted their old chief's son, known as Almagro el Chico, as their leader, attacked the Governor's house, and put him and his defenders to death. The conqueror left several "widows," the most interesting being Inés Huayllas Ñusta, daughter of the Sapa Inca Huayna Capac, and Atahualpa's sister. This lady had borne Francisco two children, a boy, who died, and a girl, Francisca, who was his heiress; her fortune must have been a considerable one, and it was kept in the family, for the girl was married to her uncle Hernando after he came out of prison. Their children founded the line of the "Marqués de la Conquista." This title is extant still, and doubtless there are noble Spaniards living who carry within them the genes of the royal Incas. Francisca, however ill-bred on the male side, was of ancient royal blood on the distaff side; she had the manners of a great lady and did Hernando much credit when presented at Court in Madrid.

Hernando de Soto, best of the conquerors, and Francisco Pizarro's associate in the founding of Lima, remained loyal to his chief; it was he who, with the Bishop Berlanya, fixed the frontier between Pizarro's government and that of Almagro, who was got out of the way during this delicate operation by a mission to Chile. Thereafter, de Soto undertook the conquest of Florida, and died on the banks of the Mississippi at the age of forty-two, of a fever. The fate of that other loyal and noble soul, the Quitu soldier Quizquiz, was worse. His attempts to drive out the Spaniards met with some small successes while Pizarro was distracted by the Alvarado incident in the north; but as soon as Alvarado had been bought off, it was possible to turn on Quizquiz with a large force. It was commanded by one Benalcázar, who inflicted a total defeat on the old imperial commander in chief. He was ready and able to continue the struggle; but his officers and his men had by this time lost heart, and realizing that there would be no peace for anybody while the fiery old patriot lived, they chose one of their number, an officer named Huaypallca, to assassinate their leader. It is impossible to blame them; there is a point beyond which ordinary men are not willing to go on suffering for the nobility of a Hero. Quizquiz was stabbed to death with a dart. It is not clear, however, that his asasssins gained much from his death; they had suffered as soldiers in a hopeless war; now they had to suffer as slaves or fugitives in a hopeless peace.

The catastrophes which afflicted Peru are not in themselves an answer to one great question: Atahualpa having been murdered, why was the resistance to his murderers so ineffective? The reasons must be sought in the Peruvians themselves. First, there is the natural weakness of a highly centralized nation beheaded; without the Sapa Inca the Tahuantinsuyu was a twitching trunk. Next, there is the discontent of the conquered provinces; not only did they revolt, as we have explained, but they often allied themselves with the Spaniards. Then there is the ordinary human discontent at the injustices suffered under any government and the usual vain expectation of better things under a new one; the Peruvians were not to know that they were stepping out of the frying pan into the fire, and it is possible that the *mitmac* colonists were as hostile to the Peruvian government as Siberian exiles to the

Russian governments. But above all, there is a kind of paralysis induced in the Peruvians by the unprecedented and nerve-shattering ferocity of the Europeans, the quality before which other civilizations went down like ninepins from the sixteenth to the nineteenth century. The Peruvians were used to war, but it was a war conducted according to strict rules, it was relatively mild and humane, and victory was wisely and economically used. They now found themselves opposed to a new kind of human being who waged war *à outrance*, inspired by a terrifying religion which enabled them to use treachery, hypocrisy, cruelty, torture and massacre in the name of a God of Love; who were indifferent to the suffering they inflicted and superhumanly stoical in bearing suffering which their own conduct entailed for themselves; superhumanly, that is, from the South American point of view.

It is true that the Church and Crown of Spain repeatedly ordered good treatment of the Indios and that some of the clergy, notably the saintly Las Casas, did their best to mitigate the ferocity of the conquerors; but we know from current history how impossible it is for home governments to impose decent behavior on *colonos* except by force of arms, to which, for example, the United States government repeatedly had recourse in the nineteenth century in forcing frontier settlers to respect Indian rights. Moreover, despite men like Las Casas who was far ahead of his time, Spanish Catholicism was, by Peruvian standards, atrocious. As we have seen, the Peruvian worship consisted in propitiation of the lesser gods, iconolatry, and a profound and prayerful humility in their attitude to the Almighty. In this respect, and even, as we have described, in certain rites and practices, it closely resembled the religion of the Spaniards, who propitiated the saints, worshiped relics and other idols, and abased themselves before their triune Almighty. But, whereas the Inca Church was relatively humane in its practices, forcing no conversions, absorbing rather than suppressing alien cults, and practicing human sacrifice, if at all, then with such moderation that it certainly sacrificed fewer victims in a year than did the Church of England under the first Elizabeth, the Spanish Church was horrifyingly different. It forced conversions by torture and fear of death, it suppressed alien cults with ruthlessness and, in its numerous autos-da-fé, it practiced human sacrifice by means of burning, the most painful of deaths, on a vast scale. It is necessary to stress this fact because a religious excuse is frequently offered for the destruction of native Peru by the Spaniards. It is true that the Spaniards sincerely believed that they were serving their god by such practices. It will help to explain the Spanish state of mind and spirit if we quote from Solorzano Pereira writing for the edification of his fellow Catholics:

> Heresy, the nature and perversity of those who follow it, are such that if it be not rooted out from the very beginning, not only will it be pernicious to religion, but will also subvert and pervert the political state of the kingdoms altogether. Therefore, no Catholic and well-governed republic should tolerate even that the question of whether a diversity of religions may be permitted in it should be so much as discussed, which a few so-called political thinkers have put forward.

Spanish inhumanity in other respects must have been something quite new and terrifying to the Peruvians. We have seen how, during several centuries, the welfare of every subject of the Inca had been assured by the state. Works of irrigation, land reclamation and terrace building steadily increased the area of land under cultivation, so that food and fabric supplies were maintained sufficiently ahead of population increment. Every man, woman and child was provided with work and, in exchange, with food, clothing and shelter, justice, and facilities for religious worship. Men and women taken off the land for public works or military service were paid the equivalent in goods to what their work as cultivators would have produced. Great care was taken to ensure that no man worked beyond his strength. In our own civilization heads of state and Church have often called themselves the shepherds of the people; so did the Incas, who were known, among other titles, as *michec* ("shepherd"). But they seem to have been unique in actually behaving like shepherds—that is, in knowing their own interest and treating their sheep well; the shock of the change-over to a competitive system must have been appalling.

The successful and stable paternalism of the Inca state was, with the advent of the Europeans, replaced in practice and whatever might be decreed in Spain, by a complete disregard for the people, so discouraging to the Peruvians that they withdrew into a stolid fatalism. Not only were their barest wants not provided for but also their accumulation of wealth in stored food and cloth, in vast herds and in fertile soil and carefully conserved water, was all dissipated. The Spanish disregard of ordinary humane behavior and for the future welfare of the people was incomprehensible to the Peruvians, and it induced in them the ultimate despair, a despair from which they do not seem to have recovered. They were enslaved, tortured, and worked to death to provide the Europeans with gold. They were infected by the newcomers with tuberculosis, measles and smallpox. It must have seemed to these wretched people that they had fallen into the hands of all-powerful devils, for their conquerors were for the most part heartless and, moreover, clearly mad, since they mistook gold for wealth and valued it above the heart's blood of a great nation.

There is yet another reason for the despair into which the former subjects of the Sapa Incas fell after the Spanish conquest. There is, clearly perceptible in all things, a pattern in the universe. To this symmetry and grace, man has given the name of beauty; in the science of aesthetics he has studied and adored it for thousands of years; it is as apparent in the form of a leaf, the life cycle of an insect, the markings of a cat's fur, as in a panorama of mountains or a view of the stars. Men, aspiring in their own creations to emulate this beauty, are impelled to impose patterns not only upon inanimate material in their applied and fine arts, but upon those institutions by whose means they seek to order the gregariousness of our kind and to exploit the economic value of co-operation and combination. Rhythm, the comforting stability of a pattern of motions repeated, seems as desirable in social institutions as in the dances we invent. In some way, these social "dances" comfort us for our knowledge of death. Now the Incas were supremely and perhaps uniquely successful in creating a social and political state to a perfectly comprehensible and quite simple pattern, a vast, empire-wide dance figure in which every man, woman and child had a place and knew just what steps and motions to perform in order to maintain the pattern and rhythm of the whole. We have seen how and why this came about. In the loom of the cordillera man knows that he is small and ephemeral and must borrow significance from the gods and comfort from the creation of an order which pretends that things are "for ever" and not just for the time being.

But when the Spaniards burst into the Tahuantinsuyu they shattered this great pattern, they scattered the dancers and broke up the figure. Millions of men and women who had existed only, so to speak, as parts of a great pattern, suddenly found themselves individuals; they did not know how to be individuals, and the very nature of their land told them it was a futile thing to be in any case. The great dance had been their reality; they awoke into the nightmare of chaos. And they continue to live in it even now.

NOTES

CHAPTER ONE (*Pages 11–21*)

1. Prescott: "according to report." See Pizarro y Orellana, *Varones Ilustres*, p. 143.

CHAPTER TWO (*Pages 22–41*)

1. See Edward Hyams, *Soil and Civilization*.
2. Bushnell, in *Peru*, says:

> The process [*of technical and cultural progress*] began earlier in Middle America than it did in Peru, since agricultural peoples, settled in villages and making good pottery, were already established in Mexico by about 1500 B.C., and they grew maize, a plant which gives such good returns for the labour spent on it that there is much free time available for activities outside the production of food.

It would appear from this that the Mexicans had maize at least five hundred years before the Peruvians, since Peruvian farmers are supposed not to have been cultivating maize until after the Early Farmer period, which ended about 1000 B.C. Moreover:

3. Vavilov, in *The Origin, Variation, Immunity and Breeding of Cultivated Plants*, says:

> The use of the phytogeographic method has clearly shown that this [*Central America and southern Mexico*] is the primary center of maize and its most closely related wild species, teosinte. . . .
> Most of the plants of the irrigated region of Peru were imported from Central America or the eastern slopes of the cordilleras where one still finds growing wild in the forests such endemic species as the cocaine shrub. . . .

But:

4. Mangelsdorf and Reeves, in *The Origin of Indian Corn and Its Relatives*, say:

> It is also a fact that in Peru among the living forms, the stone and clay replicas, and the representations found on the pottery, a series of maize ears can be found illustrating many of the steps which we assume to have occurred since wild corn was first domesticated, while similar material found

265

in other regions illustrates only well-developed forms. It can be said, there-fore, that the archaeological evidence has favored slightly a South American origin of maize and at least has contradicted in no essential way the evidence from other sources which points to the Andean region.

The "evidence from other sources" referred to above is historical, but mainly genetical; it makes fascinating reading and is entirely convincing.

5. Vavilov (*op. cit.*) gives two different and unrelated centers of distribution of cotton as a cultigen:

> *Gossypium herbaceum was distributed from a Central Asiatic source; G. hirsutum (upland cotton) and G. purpurascens (Bourbon cotton) from a Central American one. Some evidence has been advanced for the presence of G. herbaceum genes in cultivars of American cottons; but the latter have a chromosome number of 52, the Asiatic cottons of 26, and even if the Asiatic genes are present in some American cottons, which is by no means certain, we cannot know when they were introduced.*

And since the different chromosome numbers entail a great difficulty in cross-ing the alien species, a difficulty only recently and partially overcome, it is probably simpler to believe that the cottons, like the Vites and some other plants, were introduced into both continents from a common Alasko-Siberian habitat in Tertiary times, and derive from a single proto-cotton ancestor common to the three species.

6. Some authorities hold that pyramids came later; that most of the sites con-sisted principally of dwellings and had few if any ceremonial buildings.

7. Quechua came to be so called because the first European to study it, the Spanish Dominican Santo Tomás, whose Quechua grammar was published in Spain in 1560, studied the language in the province of Quechua. J. Alden Mason prefers to call this language Inca-Quechua, and Arthur Helps, the biographer of Pizarro, prefers to call it Cuzcan. It seems to be a matter of taste rather than of learning.

8. Meillet and Cohen, *Les Langues du monde.*

9. Some authorities believe trepanning to have been religious, but they do not explain how or why. There is also an opinion that trepanned patients lived only for three months after the surgery.

CHAPTER THREE (*Pages 43–97*)

1. The *Comentarios reales* is an account of what the maternal uncle of Gar-cilaso, who was half Inca, told him about the origins of their tribe. But Cristóbal de Molina, priest of a hospital in Cuzco, writing in about 1570, says that the Indians believed there had been a universal deluge in which all per-ished but the proto-Inca and his sister, who survived by floating out the flood in a box. The Inca Ararat was Huanaco, near Tiahuanaco.

2. See R. Karsten, *A Totalitarian State of the Past.* Professor Karsten, though sound and thorough on the social system of the Incas, is possibly insufficiently critical of Garcilaso de la Vega.

3. Garcilaso puts this whole event back one generation; for him this national hero was Viracocha.

4. Louis Baudin, in *L'Empire socialiste des Inka,* says:

> *On voit combien il est difficile de qualifier l'état des Inka. Fort arriérés sur quelques points, très avancés sur d'autres, les Peruviens échappent à toute classification; ils ont à la fois des procédés techniques primitifs et d'autres très perfectionés; ils traitent les hommes comme du bétail, mais ils savent récompensier le mérite; ils font des tambours avec la peau des révoltés; mais ils laissent en fonction les chefs ennemis vaincus, après les avoir combler de présents; ils ignorent la roue, mais ils jouent des pièces de théâtre; ils ne savent pas écrire, mais ils dressent d'impeccables statistiques.*

5. Garcilaso says:

> It must be known that the Kings Incas from the first established it as a very stringent law and custom that the heir to the kingdom should marry his eldest sister, legitimate both on the side of the father and the mother, and she was his legitimate wife and was called Ccoya which is the same as queen or empress. The first-born of this brother and sister was the legitimate heir to the kingdom. . . . They had another ancient precedent . . . they believed in the time of their heathenry that the Moon was wife and sister of the Sun, from whom the Inca was descended. . . .

This chronicler, though much discredited, may be reliable in matters which do not affect the reputation of his ancestors and in this case he was not showing them in a good light by Spanish Christian standards. He is not supported by other chroniclers; and scientific history, for what it is worth, makes sister marriage a late institution.

6. Sarmiento de Gamboa, *Historia de los Incas.*

7. *Prehistoric Settlement Patterns in the Virú Valley, Peru,* Bulletin 155, Bureau of American Ethnology. Washington, D.C., Govt. Printing Office, 1953.

8. According to several authorities there were 158 days of rest or holidays in the Inca working year, which is considerably above the United States average.

9. If we allow for the inequality of the "thirds" into which the Inca gross national product was divided, we should suppose that the *puric* in the Tahuantinsuyu probably retained between 40 and 45 per cent of the product of his labor. In short, Inca taxation was onerous but not outrageous, and quite comparable with our own.

10. This organization provided historians with a means of estimating population. Philip Means put it between sixteen and thirty-two million. The lower figure is more probable, allowing five persons per family.

11. See Felipe Huamán Poma de Ayala, *Nueva corónica y buen gobierno.*

12. *Ibid.* Poma de Ayala was half-Inca. This work was found in the early 20th century in the Royal Library at Copenhagen, and published for the first time in 1927.

13. R. Karsten, *op. cit.*

14. Karsten writes:

> Every year at a certain date the provinces and villages were visited by royal inspectors, who summoned all persons of both sexes who were unengaged and free and asked them to line up in the market. Of the men most were, of course, quite young—according to Cobo, even youths under twenty-five— others were older, since even widowers could be married again. Men and women were arranged in rows opposite each other according to age, and each man had to select a wife among the women, chiefs and persons in more prominent positions having the right to begin. . . . It does not quite clearly appear among the sources whether the men really had the right to choose among the girls, or whether one of the girls to be married was simply given to him with whom he had to be content. . . . In many provinces a wedding ceremony took place consisting in the bridegroom putting on the right foot of the bride a sandal, which was made of wool if she was a virgin, of ichu grass if she was not.

15. This phenomenon is interesting, and it has been tentatively related to diet. It is well known that, in the case of earthworms for example, numbers increase where there is food for them, decrease where there is not enough. This is not a matter of migration to areas of plenty; numbers increase or decrease according to the food supply, in closed and inaccessible communities of earthworms. It is almost the same in human communities; in conditions of chronic famine, male births outnumber female births; in conditions of chronic plenty (which prevailed for more than six generations, and perhaps for ten, in the Tahuantinsuyu), "nature," perceiving that the population can be allowed to rise, provides potential mothers. This is putting it too anthropomorphically, no doubt; we might say, rather, that there is genetically inherent in us an organism chemically operated which provides for increase of the species at a greater rate in conditions of plenty.

16. For the benefit of the unmathematical reader: The arithmetical expression of the value π taken to three decimal places is 3.142. The value of each digit is expressed by its place. The digit in the first place to the right of the decimal point signifies the number of *tenths*, that in the second place the number of *hundredths*, that in the third place the number of *thousandths*; in the same progression, the digits to the left of the decimal point indicate the number of multiples of one, of ten, of one hundred, and so on. This "place value," and with it the concept of "zero," were invented three times in mankind's history—by the ancient Hindus, by the ancient Peruvians, and by the ancient Maya.

17. Markham, *The Incas of Peru*. It is notable in this connection that the main events of history as set down by various chroniclers working independently of each other from native sources, usually from *amautas* reading the *quipus*, are all substantially in agreement, but all differently "colored"—the color being, we believe, derived as much from the chronicler himself. See our analogue of musical interpretation.

18. Garcilaso de la Vega, in his *Comentarios reales*, tells us of an incident that took place at a court trial involving a very serious murder, in the province of

the Quechuas, after the Spanish conquest. The Spanish judge, before taking the deposition of a *curaca* who had been called as a witness, placed a cross before the man and told him to swear to God and the cross that he would speak the truth. The Indian replied that as he was not baptized he did not swear as the Christians swore. The judge then said that he must swear by his own gods, the sun, the moon and the Incas. The *curaca* answered, "We only use those names to worship them, and it is not lawful for me to swear by them." The judge inquired what evidence there would be of the truth of what the *curaca* said, if he would not take the oath. "My promise will suffice," said the *curaca*, "for I understand that I speak as it were before your king, seeing that you come to do justice in his name; for thus we felt in giving testimony before the officers of the Inca." The man finally did take the oath, by Earth. Having done so, he insisted on telling the *whole* truth, not the small fraction extracted from witnesses in an American or English court by forcing them to keep to a point chosen by the paid advocate. Although the judge declared that it would suffice if the witness answered the questions put to him, he persisted in saying that he would not be keeping his promise unless he related all he knew. That "all" included his knowledge of the accused's character and the characters of the victim's friends.

19. Bernabé Cobo, *Historia del nuevo mundo*.
20. Cristóbal de Molina, *An account of the fables and rites of the Incas*. Molina was priest of the parish of Our Lady of Healing of the Hospital for Natives in the city of Cuzco *circa* 1570.

CHAPTER FOUR (Pages 98–132)

1. "Aymara," for the Colla and Lupaca tongue, is an absurd misnomer. The Aymara were a small Quechua-speaking people. But it happened that the first European to study the Colla language did so in a Colla-speaking *mitmac* colony of Aymara people on an island in Lake Titicaca and his designating the language as "Aymara" was the result of his misunderstanding.
2. The word *palla* means "lady," but with an implication of noble blood, as in the English "my lady."
3. Nevertheless, a son—and possible claimant to the throne—Ninan Cuyuche, is attributed to her by some chroniclers.
4. Acosta says: "This Huayna Capac was adored by his people as God during his lifetime. This is affirmed by the old men."
5. Garcilaso de la Vega (*op. cit.*), quoting Blas Valera.
6. For a detailed description of these ceremonies and what followed them, see Cristóbal de Molina, *An account of the fables and rites of the Incas*.
7. Cabello de Balboa, *Historia del Perú*, says there were three campaigns.
8. From Salcamayhua, *An Account of the Antiquities of Peru*.
9. But this was not the normal custom. Royal mummies lived each in his own palace.
10. There is, in the story which follows, a chronological problem in fixing upon

the respective ages of Huáscar and Atahualpa. We have chosen the more probable date for Huáscar's birth; Sarmiento, however, believed that Huáscar was five years older than Atahualpa.

CHAPTER FIVE (Pages 133–150)

1. According to Señor de Madariaga, the influx of gold into Spain resulted in such inflation that prices rose 1,000 per cent.
2. Nothing in history is more ironic than this spectacle of the priest-king of a hideously cruel and bloody religion consistently behaving with Christian mildness and compliance in the face of bloody-minded bullying by a deeply pious exponent of Christianity—nor more discouraging for pacifists than the outcome of Moctezuma's Christian charity; he died for it, and his nation was destroyed and enslaved.
3. Prescott owed the verbatim quality of these exchanges to a manuscript history of the events by the Texcucan historian Ixtlilxochitl.
4. So frightful was the religion imposed by the Aztecs upon Mexico and even on the gentle and brilliant Maya, a religion of which, with its human sacrificial victims counted in tens of thousands, the mild and gentle Moctezuma was the great pillar, that it is difficult not to be glad that treachery, force and courage put a stop to rites so bloody that even sixteenth-century Spanish Catholicism looks very mild and gentle by comparison with them.

CHAPTER SIX (Pages 151–191)

1. The genus of the molle trees is *Schinus*, and three species were to be found in Inca gardens and planted woods: *S. dependens*, an evergreen shrub prettily covered in season with axillary racemes of yellow flowers, later with small purple fruit; *S. molle*, the Peruvian mastic, a tall evergreen tree with panicles of pale-yellow flowers, now much planted in California as a street tree, and bearing red fruit; and *S. terebinthyfolius*, a small evergreen tree with red fruit.

   Ornamental as well as useful in the Inca gardens were the several "peppers," or capsicums, with their green, yellow or red fruits. The tomato is an Andean native, and although we have it and its name from the Aztec gardens, it may have been first cultivated in Peru.

   Its relatives were Inca garden plants: *Solanum muricatum* provided the fruit called *cachun*, or, in Spanish, *pepino*; *Solanum quitoense*, the Spanish *naranjillo*, yielded a refreshing fruit drink; *Physalis ixocarpa* and *P. peruviana*, "Cape gooseberries," were much prized. That beautiful climber, *Tropaelium tuberosum*, may have been cultivated in gardens for its flowers, but it was more important as a farm crop for its tubers. (We use the distinction between farm and garden crops for the sake of clarity; but all the cultivation of the Tahuantinsuyu was essentially horticulture, not agriculture.) It is possible that the drug plants were grown in the pleasure gardens—not, of course, coca, but belladonna, mandragora and henbane. Likewise *Genipa americana* for its fruit, for the wine of that fruit, and for the dye. *Opuntia* cactus, prickly pear, was grown not for its fruit, although that is edible and is commonly marketed in southern Europe, but as fodder for the cochineal insect; *Jatropha* species and *Justicia pectoralis* were grown for aphrodisiacs; *Stenomessum varietatum* as a contraceptive; and, for their anesthetic properties, *Datura* and *Thevetia* species.

The several grains, of which maize, in enormous variety of size and color, was only one, were, of course, farm, not garden crops; and so were the many different kinds of potatoes, and the highland staple, quinoa; oca, the sweetish tuberous root of an oxalis; the sweet potato, *Convolvulus batata*, of which there were white, yellow and violet varieties. But the *sapallu*, gourds, were probably garden plants. The *cuchuchu* of the old Collasuyu, regarded as a great delicacy, seems, from the description, to have been an underground fungus, like truffle. Other fruit-garden shrubs were *Psidium guayava* (in Quechua, *savintu*; in Spanish, *guayava*); *Ussu*, described as a "sort of cherry," which we have not identified. The strawberry from which all our own large-fruited strawberries have been developed since 1800, *Fragaria chiloensis*, was found as a garden plant in the island of Chiloé, off the coast of what is now Chile; it may, therefore, have been an Inca garden plant. Some hints may be gathered by any curious gardener among our readers, as to the plants which the Inca gardeners had domesticated, by reference to an English translation of a book published in Seville in 1571, *Joyful Newes out of the New Found Worlde*, by Nicholas Monardes.

2. Archeologists do not agree that the hammock was a Peruvian invention but hold that it was of Caribbean origin. Here, as elsewhere, archeological findings are incompatible with traditions; and here as elsewhere we have preferred traditions, following Bushnell and Karsten, where the goods in question were perishable.

3. It should be noted at this point that by Prescott's account it was Huáscar who was long-suffering and Atahualpa who was aggressive. Prescott was following Garcilaso; he accepted the now untenable view that Huáscar was the elder brother and that his temper was generous and easy. In this part of his great history Prescott did not give nearly enough weight to Sarmiento; and he was more interested in the Spaniards than in the Incas.

4. Sarmiento calls him Huanca Auqui. The word *auqui* means "prince"; as a title it regularly precedes the name, and we have made it do so here. Sarmiento also makes Atoc commander in chief; but Atoc was dead.

5. Sarmiento de Gamboa, *op. cit.*

6. Other estimates are as high as thirty-two million and as low as eight million. The lowest estimates are the most modern, but we have decided to allow for that unconscious conviction that no system but a modern one, no civilization but a technological one, could support a large population, and for the unconscious wish on the part of the social historians to soften the unfavorable contrast between the prosperity of Peru under a "prehistoric" communist economy and a modern capitalist one. The population of Peru and Ecuador today is estimated to be about fifteen million.

7. This story has a curious sequel. After all the events yet to be described, and

when the empire was in Spanish hands, Golden Star went to Xauca to discover how matters stood. She was lucky in falling in with Hernando de Soto, one of the better Spaniards; he, having heard her story, sent for Quilacu, gave them both clothes, had them baptized under the names Hernando and Leonora, and helped them to marry as Christians. Quilacu, debilitated by wounds, died shortly thereafter. Later, Curi Coyllur became de Soto's mistress, and by him she had a daughter, Leonora de Soto, who married a lawyer named Carillo, of Cuzco. For all we know, descendants of the Sapa Inca Huáscar and his Golden Star still live in Peru; we hope they are flourishing.

8. In point of fact, some were put to death—the ringleaders of the Hurin faction below those of noblest ranks who were reserved for worse things. It should be made clear that not the whole enormous population of the city came out, but only the Inca *ayllus*. It is impossible to arrive at a number. These were, so to speak, the patricians, the full citizens, or what we might almost call the enfranchised, all of them holding administrative office of some sort. The vast majority of the Cuzcans were simply urbanized *purics*, artisans, servants, soldiers, and so forth.

9. Remember the tale of her being forced by Huáscar to go through a form of marriage ceremony with Huayna Capac's mummy.

10. This method of ensuring the throne was commonplace in the Arabian empire in the early Middle Ages, and in the Indo-Chinese kingdoms until recently. Late in the nineteenth century, King Thibaw of Ava (Upper Burma), another kingdom where sister-marriage was the custom in the royal house, the Alompra dynasty, had eighty men, women and children—all of them possible rivals for the throne—clubbed to death. When the Government of India sent a mild protest, Thibaw's Foreign Secretary replied that the massacre was "according to custom." And there is, of course, the case of King Herod and the Innocents, the latter all possible descendants of David.

How much credence are we to give to the story of Atahualpa's massacre of the legitimate royal family and—as Garcilaso tells it—of everyone, including servants and the servants of servants, in any way connected with them? There are two authorities for the massacre story: Sarmiento, writing in Peru and in touch with *amautas*, about thirty-five years after the event; and Garcilaso, writing from memory of his own youth in Peru, more than fifty years after the event. Garcilaso is so hard to swallow that at this point in his narrative even Prescott rejects him, pointing out that had his account been true, many Incas known to have survived could not have done so. Sarmiento's account is the more credible

11. Obscure.

12. Juan de Sámano, *Relación de los primeros descubrimientos de Francisco Pizarro y Diego de Almagro.*

CHAPTER SEVEN (Pages 193–226)

1. Gonzalo Fernandez de Oviedo y Valdés, *Historia general y natural de las Indias.*
2. Anonymous, *Relación del primer descubrimiento del Perú.*

3. *Ibid.*

4. There are two eyewitness accounts of this encounter: Hernando Pizarro's in his "Carta de Hernando Pizarro," preserved and published by the Licentiate Oviedo; and the other, *Relación del primer descubrimiento del Perú*, by an anonymous cavalryman, one of those who escorted Hernando. Hernando represents himself as talking to Atahualpa in a condescending, even hectoring manner, which is obviously untrue. Taking a hint from Prescott, we have followed the other and apparently less partial account.

5. Pedro Pizarro, *Relación del descubrimiento y conquista de los reinos del Perú.*

6. "El gobernador respondio: Di a tu, señor, que venga en hora buena como quisiere, que de la manera que viniere lo recibiré como amigo y hermano."

7. "Decildes a esos que vengan aca, que no pasaré de aqui hasta que me den cuenta y satisfagan y baguen lo que han hecho en la tierra." (Anonymous, *Relación del primer descubrimiento del Perú.*) But accounts of this scene vary in detail.

CHAPTER EIGHT (Pages 227–254)

1. John H. Rowe, "Sound Patterns in Three Inca Dialects," *International Journal of American Linguistics*, 1950, pp. 137-148.

2. Francisco de Xérez, *Verdadera relación de la conquista del Perú.* Hernando Pizarro, in his "Carta," says 35 feet long, 18 wide.

3. "Sabido esta por el gobernador, mostró, que le pesabo mucho: i dijo que erá mentira que no le havían muerto, que lo trujesen luego vivo; i sino, que el mandaría matar a Atabalipa." (Xérez, *op. cit.*)

4. This account is what we believe to have happened; but the authorities are much at variance. Here is the story, much more complex, as it is told by Pedro Pizarro and is confirmed by Urteaga, who probably used Pedro Pizarro as his authority:

Huáscar said, "Where does this dog Atahualpa get all the gold he is giving to the Christians? Doesn't he know it is mine? I will give it to them and then they will kill him." Chalcuchima heard him say this, and he sent the news to Atahualpa to know what he should do. When Atahualpa received this news he became very cunning. He asked the Marqués [F. Pizarro] to come and dine with him one day, as he often did; when he arrived he made out to be crying and very sad. The Marqués asked why this was. He refused to say why, but went on crying and being very sad; but at last the Marqués insisted on knowing the reason and he said, "I am like this because you must kill me." The Marqués assured him all was well and that he would not be killed. Then Atahualpa said, "Señor, you commanded me not to kill my brother Huáscar and that if I did you would kill me. But my officers have killed him without my knowledge, and now I know you will have to kill me." Then the Marqués, not understanding the trick, turned to him and said, "Are you sure he is dead?" Being told he was, the Marqués told the Indian to fear nothing as it had been done without the Inca's orders and he would not be killed or come to any harm. Then Atahualpa, discovering that nothing would happen to him after playing this trick, sent messengers to Chalcuchima to kill Huáscar, which was done either at Guambos or, as others say, at Guanan. When he had the news of it, Atahualpa ordered his two captains that Chalcuchima should post himself at Xauca with half the men, and that Quizquiz should go to Cuzco with the other half . . .

5. Miguel de Estete, *El descubrimiento y la conquista del Perú*, says that the main square could hold one hundred thousand people—obviously an exaggeration.

6. Mangelsdorf and Reeves, *The Origin of Indian Corn and Its Relatives*.

7. Full details of the division of the spoil are to be found in a document called *Acta de repartición del rescate*.

8. Xérez, *op. cit.*

9. Agustín de Zárate, *Historia del descubrimiento y conquista de la provincia del Perú*.

10. The theory, which is orthodox, that Pizarro was not responsible for the situation and was genuinely unwilling to kill Atahualpa will be found in Prescott.

BIBLIOGRAPHY

ACOSTA, JOSÉ DE, *The Natural and Moral History of the Indies* (1590), E. Grimston, tr.; C. R. Markham, ed. London, Hakluyt Soc., 1880.

ANONYMOUS, *Nouvelles certaines des Isles du Pérou*. 1534. ("On le vend à Lyon chez Frācoys Juste devāt Notre Dame de Lonfort.")

ANONYMOUS, *Relación del primer descubrimiento del Perú* (1563–64), T. Medina, ed. Lima, 1930.

ANONYMOUS, *Relazione della conquista del Peru con la descrizione de Cuzco, d'un segretario di Fran. Pizarro*. Venice, 1565.

AVILA, FRANCISCO DE, *De priscorum huaruchiriensium origine et institutis*. Madrid, Consejo Superior de Investigaciones Científicas, Instituto Gonzalo Fernandez de Oviedo, 1942.

———, *Relación acerca de los pueblos de indios de este arzobispado*. Lima, 1601.

BALLESTEROS GAIBROS, MANUEL, *Francisco Pizarro*. Madrid, Biblioteca Nueva, 1940.

BAUDIN, LOUIS, *L'Empire socialiste des Inka*. Paris, Institut d'Ethnologie, 1928.

BAUDIZZONE, LUIS M., *Poesía, música y danza Inca*. Buenos Aires, 1943.

BRION, MARCEL, *Bartolomé de las Casas*, Alicia Ortiz Oderigo, tr. Mexico, Editorial Divulgación, 1953.

BUSHNELL, G. H. S., *Peru*. London, Thames & Hudson, 1956.

CABELLO DE BALBOA, P. MIGUEL, *Historia del Perú* (1557–89?), H. H. Urteaga and C. A. Romero, eds. Lima, 1920.

CALANCHA, ANTONIO DE LA, *Corónica moralizada del orden de San Agustín en el Perú*. Barcelona, 1638.

CARRIÓN, BENJAMIN, *Atahualpa*. Mexico, Imprenta Mundial, 1934.

CIEZA DE LÉON, PEDRO DE, *Segunda parte de la chronica del Perú que trata del señorio de los Incas*, Biblioteca Hispano-Ultramarina, Vol. 5. Madrid, 1880.

CIPRIANI, L., "Su due 'quipus' del Museo Nazionale di Antropologia e Etnologia di Firenze." International Congress of Americanists, XXII, Part 1 (Rome, 1926).

COBO, P. BERNABÉ, *Historia del nuevo mundo* (1653). Seville, Jiménez de la Espada, 1890–95.

CORTES, HERNANDO, *Copia delle lettere alla Caesarea Maesta rescritte*, (1534). Book in British Museum (No. 1061.g. 47).

DOERING, H. UBBELHODE, *El Arte en el Imperio de las Incas*. Barcelona, Editorial Gustavo Gili, 1952.

DUPLESSIS, PIERRE, *Pizarro* (drama). London, 1785.

ESTETE, MIGUEL DE, *El descubrimiento y la conquista del Perú* (1534), C. R. Markham, tr. London, Hakluyt Soc., 1872.

FARFÁN, JOSÉ M. B., "Poesía folklórica Quechua," *Revista de Antropologia de la Universidad Nacional de Tucumán*, Vol. 2, No. 12 (1942).

GARCILASO DE LA VEGA, *The First Part of the Royal Commentaries of the Yncas*, C. R. Markham, ed. London, Hakluyt Soc., 1869–71.

GHEERBRANT, ALAIN, ed., *The Incas*. New York, Orion Press, 1962.

HELPS, ARTHUR, *The Spanish Conquest in America*. London and New York, J. Lane, 1900.

HERRERA Y TORDESILLAS, ANTONIO DE, *Historia general de las Indias*. Antwerp, 1728.

HOIJER, HARRY, and others, *Linguistic Structures of Native America*, Publications in Anthropology, No. 6. New York, Viking Fund, Inc., 1946.

HUMBOLDT, ALEXANDER VON, *Vues des cordillères et monuments des peuples indigènes d'Amérique*. Paris, 1810.

HYAMS, EDWARD, *Soil and Civilization*. London, Thames & Hudson, 1952.

KARSTEN, RAFAEL, "A Totalitarian State of the Past: The Civilization of the Inca Empire in Ancient Peru," *Proceedings of the Helsingfors Societas Scientiarum Fennica Humanarum Litterarum*, Vol. XVI, Part 1. Helsinki, 1949.

LARA, JESÚS, *La poesía Quechua*. Mexico, 1947.

LEHMANN, WALTER, and DOERING, HEINRICH UBBELHODE, eds., *The Art of Old Peru*. London, E. Benn, 1924.

LEVILLIER, ROBERTO, Los Incas. Seville, Escuela de Estudios Hispano-Americanos de Sevilla, 1956.

LÓPEZ DE GÓMARA, FRANCISCO, Hispania Victrix: Primera y segunda parte de la historia general de las Indias . . . hasta el año 1551. Zaragoza, 1552; and Madrid, Calpe, 1922.

MADARIAGA, SALVADOR DE, Rise of the Spanish American Empire. London, Hollis & Carter, 1947.

MANGELSDORF, P. C., and REEVES, R. G., The Origin of Indian Corn and Its Relatives, Bulletin 574, Texas Agricultural Experimental Station. College Station, 1939.

MARKHAM, CLEMENTS R., Contributions towards a Grammar and Dictionary of the Quichua, the Language of the Yncas of Peru. London, 1864.

———, The Incas of Peru, London, Smith, Elder and Co., 1910.

———, tr. and ed., The Narratives of the Rites and Laws of the Yncas. London, Hakluyt Soc., 1873.

MASON, J. ALDEN, The Ancient Civilizations of Peru. Harmondsworth, Middlesex, Penguin Books, 1957.

MEANS, PHILIP AINSWORTH, Ancient Civilizations of the Andes. New York, Scribner's, 1931.

———, Fall of the Inca Empire and Spanish Rule in Peru, 1530–1780. New York, Scribner's, 1932.

MEILLET, ANTOINE, and COHEN, MARCEL, Les Langues du monde. Paris, Société de Linguistique de Paris, 1952.

MENDIBURU, MANUEL DE, ed., Diccionario Histórico-Biográfico del Perú (2nd ed., 12 vols., with Appendix 4 vols.). Lima, Imprenta Enrique Palacios, 1931–34.

MOLINA, CRISTÓBAL DE (of Santiago, Chile), Relación de muchas cosas acaecidos en el Perú (1552). Lima, 1916.

MONARDES, NICOLAS, Ioyfull Newes out of the newe founde World (1577), John Frampton, tr. London, 1577.

MONTESINOS, F., Memorias antiguas historiales y politicas del Perú (1644). Madrid, Jiménez de la Espada, 1882.

MOODIE, ROY L., "Prehistoric Surgical Bandage from Peru," from Studies in Paleopathology in Annals of Medical History, XIV, Vol. 8, pp. 69–72. New York, 1926.

———, "Injuries to the Head among Pre-Columbian Peruvians," ibid., XXI, Vol. 9, pp. 277–307. New York, 1928.

———, "Surgery in Pre-Columbian Peru," ibid., XXII, new ser., Vol. I, pp. 698–728. New York, 1929.

MORÚA, MARTIN DE, *Historia del origen y genealogía real de los reyes Incas del Perú* (1590). Madrid, Instituto Santo Toribo, 1946.

NAHARRO, L., *Relación sumaria acerca de la conquista* (c. 1540), H. H. Urteaga, ed. Lima, 1917.

OVIEDO Y VALDÉS, GONZALO FERNANDO, *Historia general y natural de las Indias, Islas y Tierra-Firme del Mar Océano* (1533–57). Madrid, Academia de la Historia, 1851–55.

PIZARRO, HERNANDO, "Letter to the Royal Audience of Santo Domingo, Nov., 1533," *Reports on the Discovery of Peru*, Hakluyt Society Publications, No. 47, pp. 11–127. London, 1872.

PIZARRO, PEDRO, *Relación del descubrimiento y conquista de los reinos del Perú* (1571), H. H. Urteaga, ed. Lima, 1917.

PIZARRO Y ORELLANA, FERNANDO, *Varones ilustres del nuevo mundo.* Madrid, 1639.

POLO DE ONDEGARDO, JUAN, *Relación de los fundamentos acerca del notable daño que resulta de no guardar a los indios sus fueros* (1571). Collection of unedited documents, Archives of the Indies, Vol. XVII. Madrid, 1872.

POMA DE AYALA, FELIPE HUAMÁN, *Nueva corónica y buen gobierno* (1580–1620?). Paris, Institut d'Ethnologie, 1936.

PORRAS BARRENECHEA, RAÚL, ed., *Diego de Trujillo, Relación del descubrimiento del Reyno del Perú* (Ser. 7a, No. 4). Seville, Escuela de Estudios Hispano-Americanos, 1948.

PRESCOTT, WILLIAM H., *History of the Conquest of Peru, with a Preliminary View of the Civilization of the Incas.* London, 1847. (Many later editions.)

RADICATI DI PRIMEGLIO, CARLOS, *Introducción al estudio de los quipus.* Lima, Sociedad Peruana de Historia, 1951.

REYNIERS, FRANÇOIS, *Douze poèmes incaïques.* Lima, 1945.

ROWE, JOHN H., "Sound Patterns in Three Inca Dialects," *International Journal of American Linguistics*, 1950, pp. 137–48.

SALCAMAYHUA, J. DE SANTA CRUZ PACHACUTI-YAMQUI, *An Account of the Antiquities of Peru*, C. R. Markham, tr., in Markham's *Narratives of the Rites and Laws of the Incas.* London, Hakluyt Soc., 1873.

SÁMANO, JUAN, *Relación de los primeros descubrimientos de Francisco Pizarro y Diego de Almagro* (1526).

SARMIENTO DE GAMBOA, PEDRO, *Historia de los Incas* (1572), tr. and ed. by C. R. Markham, Hakluyt Society Publications, Series 2, No. 22. Cambridge, 1907.

SAUER, CARL O., "Cultivated Plants of Central and South America," *Handbook of South American Indians*, Vol. 3. Washington, D.C., Govt. Printing Office, 1950.

SITWELL, SACHEVERELL, *Golden Wall and Mirador*. London, Weidenfeld & Nicholson, 1961.

SPENGLER, OSWALD, *The Decline of the West*, C. F. Atkinson, tr. (2 vols.). New York, Knopf, 1926.

STEWARD, JULIAN HAYNES, ed., *Handbook of South American Indians*, Bulletin 143, Bureau of American Ethnology (7 vols.). Washington, D.C., Govt. Printing Office, 1946-59.

TOLEDO, FRANCISCO DE, *Informaciones que mandó levantar el Virrey Toledo sobre los Incas (c. 1600)*. Buenos Aires, 1940.

TOYNBEE, ARNOLD, *A Study of History* (10 vols.). London, Oxford University Press, 1934-54.

URTEAGA, HORACIO H., *Colección de libros y documentos referente a la historia del Perú*. Lima, Sanmarti y Cia., 1922.

———, *El fin de un imperio*. Lima, Gil, 1933.

VALERA, BLAS, *Relación de las costumbres antiguas de los naturales del Perú* (1585-89?). Madrid, 1879.

VAVILOV, NIKOLAI I., *The Origin, Variation, Immunity and Breeding of Cultivated Plants*. New York, Ronald Press, 1951.

Vocabulario castellano y keshua de Aneash, Forma parte del Políglota incaico. Lima, Tip. de Colegio de propaganda Fide del Perú, 1905.

WILLEY, GORDON RANDOLPH, *The Civilizations of Ancient America*. Chicago, University of Chicago Press, 1951.

———, *Prehistoric Settlement Patterns in the Virú Valley, Peru*, Bulletin 155, Bureau of American Ethnology. Washington, D.C., Govt. Printing Office, 1953.

WINSOR, JUSTIN, ed., *Narrative and Critical History of America* (8 vols.). London, Trübner and Co., and Cambridge, Mass., Sampson Low & Co., 1886-89.

XÉREZ, FRANCISCO DE, *Verdadera relación de la conquista del Perú y de la provincia del Cuzco* (1534). Madrid, 1891.

ZÁRATE, AGUSTÍN DE, *Historia del descubrimiento y conquista de la provincia del Perú* (1555). Biblioteca de Autores Españoles, Vol. 26. Madrid, 1853.

GLOSSARY

Acclahuasi. Convents for the training of Virgins of the Sun, girls dedicated to chastity and the service of the sun-god.

Amauta. A learned man; a teacher, mainly of religious and philosophic, and probably of scientific, subjects.

Apu. A military commander; freely, a general.

Apucama. A governmental council of four members, one from each province; it was responsible to the Sapa Inca, who presided at its sessions.

Aucca. Traitor; more generally, rebel or enemy.

Auqui. Prince; practically—within the framework of Inca customs—a young, unmarried heir to noble office.

Ayllu. Sib; an endogamous social group consisting of individuals descended from a common ancestor; originally a basic family unit, later somewhat arbitrarily constituted to provide an economic community of standard size.

Borla. A fillet, or headband, with a fringe; the crown of the Sapa Inca.

Camayoc. An administrative official at any of several levels. See *Chunca-camayoc; Huno-camayoc; Maranga-camayoc;* and *Pacha-camayoc.*

Capac-cocha. An annual festival, probably related to the autumnal equinox and instituted by Pachacuti; human sacrifice is said to have been practiced in connection with it.

Champi. A kind of club, probably for ceremonial use.

Chicha. A fermented liquor made from maize.

Chunca-camayoc. A nonhereditary headman or leader of ten *purics.*

Chuno. A food staple made from potatoes exposed alternately to frost and sun.

Cocha. Sea.

Cucuricuc. Literally, "he who sees all"; a civil administrator of a province, appointed by the Apucama.

-cuna. A suffix added to nouns to signify plural number.

Curaca. In effect, an honorary Inca; a member of a class recruited generally from the nobility or leadership of peoples conquered by the Incas.

Guarachicui. Literally, "a putting-on of the *guara*" (the garment worn by adult Incas); a puberty ceremony comparable to that of the Romans in connection with the assumption of the *toga virilis.*

Hamaca. A hammock; used as a litter for carrying persons of rank.

Hanan. Literally, "lower"; designating one of the two groups, primarily social but also quasi-political, to one of which every *ayllu* belonged.

Haravec. A poet; a teacher of literature, and probably of history, at the *Yacha-huasi.*

Hiwaya. A form of punishment consisting of the dropping of a heavy stone onto the back of a convicted lawbreaker from an elevation of three feet.

Huacca. A sacred object or place, venerated as the abode of the spirit of a minor divinity, as certain trees, rocks, lakes, or palaces; a shrine, a temple, or a cult object.

Huasca. A chain; especially the golden chain wrought in celebration of the birth of Huáscar, whose name is thus derived.

Huno-camayoc. An administrative officer with jurisdiction over ten thousand *purics* and their families.

Hurin. Literally, "upper"; designating one of the two groups, primarily social but also quasi-political, to one of which every *ayllu* belonged.

Incap Ranti. Viceroy; title given to Atahualpa as ruler of Quito under the sovereignty of Huáscar as Sapa Inca.

Itu. An expiatory fast.

Llactacamayoc. A domiciliary inspector who policed the work and the eating, dressing and washing practices of *puric* families.

Llama-michec. A herder of llamas.

Llanque. A kind of sandal.

Llauta. A multicolored scarf or shawl of vicuña wool, wound turbanlike about the head, worn by upper-class Incas.

Mama. Literally, "Mother"; appellation given to the *qoya.*

Mamamanchic. Literally, "Our Mother"; appellation given to the *qoya.*

Maranga-camayoc. An administrative officer with jurisdiction over one thousand *purics* and their families.

Michec. A herder, commonly of llamas, as *llama-michec.*

Mit'a. System of annual levy of *purics* for labor on public works or for military service.

Mitmac. A colonist; one of a community of "safe" subjects resettled among a subjugated people as an insurance against insurrection.

Orejones (Spanish). Literally, "big-eared ones"; descriptive applied to *curacas,* in reference to their distinctive practice of wearing ornaments inserted in the ear lobes, which thus became enlarged.

Pachacamac. Name (from *pacha,* "earth," and *camac,* "creator") of the principal deity; identified with *Viracocha* (*q.v.*) and sometimes used in combination with it.

Pacha-camayoc. An administrative officer with jurisdiction over one hundred *purics* and their families.

Palla. A lady of the court.

Pampa. A field or plain.

Puric. A male worker or peasant; a man of the lowest station; the common taxpayer.

Puti. A box or parcel.

Qoya. Literally, "Star"; title of the sister-wife of the Sapa Inca.

Quechua. Name of one of the tribes closely allied to and dominated by the Incas, and one of the first to be incorporated within the rising empire; also now used as the name of the official language of the Tahuantinsuyu.

Quipu. A contrivance consisting of variously colored cords on which knots were tied in significant patterns; used for the recording of quantitative values and as a mnemonic device for indicating the nature and sequence of important events. (See text, pages 77-85.)

Quipu-mayoc. A keeper, or reader, of the *quipu*.

Repartimiento (Spanish). A portion of territory granted by the Crown to a Conquistador, and the right to exploit the labor and wealth of the natives within that territory.

Runasimi. Literally, "man's mouth"; native designation of the official language of the Inca empire; now generally referred to as Quechua.

Sapa Inca. Literally, "Supreme" or "Unique Inca"; the ruler of the Incas.

Suyu. Province.

Taclla. A digging stick; a stout, pointed pole used for turning over the soil in preparation for planting.

Tahuantinsuyu. Literally, the "Kingdom of the Four Provinces"; the Inca empire.

Tambo (or *Tampu*). A resthouse, or storehouse, situated at any of numerous fixed points along the Peruvian roads.

Ticci Capac. Literally, "Lord of the World"; one of the titles of the Sapa Inca.

Tupu. A brooch, or pin.

Umu. A priest, or diviner.

Usuta. A kind of sandal.

Viracocha. Name (from *vira*, "foam" or "spirit," and *cocha*, "sea") of the principal deity; identified with *Pachacamac* (*q.v.*) and sometimes used in combination with it.

Yacha-huasi. Literally, "House of Teaching"; a school, the Peruvian equivalent of a university, for the higher education of Inca youth.

Yanacuna. A class of slaves.

INDEX

ABOUT THE AUTHORS

EDWARD HYAMS was born in London in 1910; he began to travel and to write shortly after leaving school. He has published eleven novels as well as a number of books on soil cultivation and other specialized topics; six of his books have been published in this country, including two novels, *The Unpossessed* and *Tillotson* (Simon and Schuster, 1960 and 1961), as well as *Soil and Civilization* and *The Wine Country of France*. His main concern today besides writing is the restoration of viticulture and vineyards in England. Mr. Hyams, who lives in Devonshire, has been a regular contributor to *The New Statesman* for the past twelve years and also writes a weekly page for the *Illustrated London News* as well as a monthly column in *The Financial Times*.

GEORGE ORDISH broadcasts and writes extensively in England on agricultural topics, in particular on raising productivity by pest control. His work for the United Nations in Latin America and his extensive knowledge of the pre-Columbian civilization led to his collaboration on this book. Mr. Ordish now lives in Hertfordshire with his wife and children.